A CORNELL BIRD LIBRARY GUIDE

Dedicated to feeder watchers and FeederWatchers and the birds we all celebrate.
—Margaret A. Barker and Jack Griggs

HarperCollins books may be purchased for educational, business, or sales promotional use. For information please write: Special Markets Department, HarperCollins Publishers Inc., 10 East 53rd Street, New York, NY 10022.

FIRST EDITION

Library of Congress Cataloging-in-Publication Data has been applied for.

ISBN 0-06273744-9

05 06 07 08   10 9 8 7 6 5

The FeederWatcher's Guide to
BIRD
FEEDING

by Margaret A. Barker and Jack Griggs

HarperResource
An Imprint of HarperCollinsPublishers

Acknowledgments

LAYOUT AND PRODUCTION BY
Jack Griggs

INTERIOR DESIGNER
Stuart L. Silberman

RESEARCH AND INTERVIEWS BY
Terrie I. Murray
Margaret A. Barker

ORNITHOLOGICAL EDITORS
Wesley M. Hochachka
Kenneth V. Rosenberg

PHOTO EDITOR
Shawneen E. Finnegan

PREPRESS BY
U.S. Color
John E. Griggs

COVER DESIGNER
Robin Bilardello

COVER PHOTOGRAPH BY
Richard Day/Daybreak Imagery

COPY EDITOR
Virginia Croft

PROOFREADER
Sally Bennett

ILLUSTRATORS
Larry McQueen: 66–71
Hans Peeters: 72

PHOTOGRAPHERS
Names of photographers are followed by the page number
on which their work appears. L = left, C = center, R = right,
T = top, B = bottom.

Tony Beck: 6T, 7, 111BL
Cliff Beittel: 117BR, 122 (lower center)
Jeffrey E. Belth: 12, 28, 29L, 29R, 30T, 64
Steve Bentsen: 75, 93TL, 118B, 128C
William P. Bergen: 19, 78R, 107B
Boyd Conservation Field Center: 22
Rose Bray: 41T
Bradley A. Brockman: 41BL, 41BR, 42T, 42B, 43
J. Calder: 61B
Bonnie Campion: 63
Jeanette Carson: 14
Connecticut Post: 31R
Jim Corbett: 62
Rob Curtis/The Early Birder: 80B, 85R, 97T, 104BR,
    114TR, 129C
Mike Danzenbaker: 102B, 124B
Richard Day/Daybreak Imagery: Front Cover, 16R, 65,
    74TL, 79BL, 84T, 86BL, 88B, 90R, 121T
Vern Dayhoff: 30B
John Dennis: 38
Don DesJardin: 112C, 117BL
Hans S. Dommasch: 49T, 49B
John Droske: 13
Don Dunsmore: 6B
Dutchess Day School: 18B
Cristina Eisenberg: 44TL, 44TR, 45T, 45B, 46T, 76B, 94T,
    119B, 126B
Shawneen E. Finnegan, 127C

James R. Gallagher/Sea and Sage Audubon: 74BC, 93TR,
    98T, 100T, 108T, 112T, 112B, 119T, 122B, 125B, 127B,
    128T, 132T
Sylvia R. Gallagher/Sea and Sage Audubon: 95
Marilyn C. Hardy: 53B, 54
Ron Hellstern: 47, 48
Nancy W. Henke: 27
Michael Jaques: 34R, 35
Kevin T. Karlson: 86BR, 92R, 97BL, 104TL 116T, 116B,
    122T, 125T, 130BL, 130T
Roger Lawson: 32
Tony Leukering: 86T, 120BL
Diane A. Lutman: 24
Bruce Mactavish: 9, 124T, 127T
Steve and Dave Maslowski: 8, 16L, 17, 18T, 20, 21L, 23,
    59, 76T, 79BC, 79BR, 88T, 94B, 96BR, 103L, 103R,
    104BL, 106B, 108BR, 109T, 111T, 115, 120BR, 122
    (upper center), 124C, 126C, 128B, 129BL, 131BR, 132C
Laura Elaine Moore: 114L
Betty Moroz: 57
National Sunflower Assoc: 11L, 11R
Blair Nikula: 53T
Orri: 44B
Julia Pahountis-Opacic: 39L, 39R, 40L, 40R
Bryan Pearson: 46B
Marie Read: 74TR, 77, 81, 82B, 85L, 93B, 98B, 102T
Ron Saldino: 55L, 55R, 56L, 56R
Larry Sansone: 26, 74BL, 101, 107T, 113B, 114C, 120T,
    123C, 129T, 130BR
Russ Schipper: 50T, 50B
Carol Seiler: 58B
John Shaw: 31L
Brian E. Small: 74BR, 87, 90L, 100BR, 104TR, 105, 110L,
    121BR, 129BR
Hugh P. Smith, Jr: 21R, 78L, 79T, 83, 85C, 89, 106T, 108BL,
    109B, 110R, 119C, 121BL, 123T, 123B, 126T, 131BL
Roger L. Stevens, Jr: 36TL, 36TR, 36B, 37
Annette Stewart: 132T
William Toothacker: 60
Mark Rogers and Steve Tracy: 51, 52
Dale Turner: 25
Tom Vezo: 15, 78C, 80TL, 80TR, 84B, 91B, 96T, 96BL, 99,
    100BL, 111BR, 113T, 117T, 117C, 118T, 121C
Mary Catherine Wheeler: 114B
Bob Winckler: 33L. 33R, 34L
Scott Wright: 58T, 61T, 82T, 91T, 92L, 97BR

SPECIAL THANKS TO
John W. Fitzpatrick
    Louis Agassiz Fuertes Director
    Cornell Lab of Ornithology
Laura M. Kammermeier
    Project Leader, Project FeederWatch
Anne Marie Johnson
    Project Assistant, Project FeederWatch
Megan Newman
    Editorial Director, HarperResource
Linda Cunningham
Patricia Leasure

VERY SPECIAL THANKS TO
All the FeederWatchers who generously shared their
experiences and knowledge to make this book possible.

The FeederWatcher's suggestions made herein are not
necessarily the recommendations of Project FeederWatch,
the Cornell Lab of Ornithology, or the partner organizations
of Project FeederWatch.

The FeederWatcher's Guide to Bird Feeding

CONTENTS

The Flight of FeederWatch: Bird Feeding Can Be Science

It wasn't long ago that bird feeding meant feeding game birds in winter or throwing table scraps out back. But since the late 1900s, there has been what Minnesota biologist and noted wildlife author Carrol Henderson calls a "bird-feeding revolution." FeederWatchers have been in the forefront.

From November to April, thousands of Feeder-Watchers share their sightings of feeder birds with scientists at the Cornell Lab of Ornithology (CLO) and its partners. On selected days, they identify and make standardized counts of their feeder visitors, watching for as little or as long as they wish. By counting and reporting according to a simple scientific protocol, they contribute to a greater understanding of feeder bird populations and the changes they undergo. At the same time, FeederWatchers learn more about birds and the way science works.

Project FeederWatch began in the winter of 1976–77 as the Ontario Bird Feeder Survey, conducted by the Long Point Bird Observatory (now Bird Studies Canada). In the first year, 333 "kitchen-window researchers" took part and proved that a feeder survey could document seasonal changes in abundance at feeders, as well as food and habitat preferences.

After 10 years, the Canadian survey joined with CLO so that bird populations could be monitored continent-wide. It was renamed Project Feeder-Watch, and in the winter of 1987–88, over 4,000 fledgling FeederWatchers from across North America signed up.

One of those original FeederWatchers was Dave Riffle from Homerville, Ohio: "I joined FeederWatch to learn more about my local birds; I had just started watching them seriously. I also liked the idea that ornithologists would use my backyard 'watches' to help learn more about birds in general."

All backyard birders are welcome to become FeederWatchers. To join, contact the Cornell Lab of Ornithology in the United States or Bird Studies Canada in Canada. New Feeder-Watchers receive a research kit with full instructions.

Cornell Lab of Ornithology
Project FeederWatch/WBG
159 Sapsucker Woods Rd.
Ithaca, NY 14850
1-800-843-2473 (BIRD)
http://birds.cornell.edu

Bird Studies Canada
Project FeederWatch/WBG
P.O. Box 160
Port Rowan, Ontario
N0E 1M0
1-888-448-2473 (BIRD)
http://www.bsc-eoc.org/
pfw.html

Dr. Erica Dunn began Project FeederWatch when she was with the Long Point Bird Observatory, "simply to find out which birds were feeding at what feeders."

Working together, FeederWatchers and scientists have detected cycles in the movements of winter finches like redpolls and pine siskins, declines in house sparrow populations and expansions of eastern house finches westward and Carolina wrens northward, and the invasion of Eurasian collared-doves. Ornithologists "mine" FeederWatch data and publish the results in scientific journals like the *Proceedings of the National Academy of Sciences.*

CLO director John Fitzpatrick says, "Keeping this sort of network going, 'an army of FeederWatchers,' is a big part of what Project FeederWatch is about." For example, FeederWatchers were in place, ready to first detect and then monitor the spread of house finch eye disease when it erupted in the mid-1990s. "Being able to respond quickly like this is powerful."

Near its 10-year mark, Project FeederWatch evolved again, gaining the National Audubon Society and the Canadian Nature Federation as partners. CLO and Audubon developed an interactive online bird database that many FeederWatchers use to submit their counts. Because of its power to organize and display data, Fitzpatrick says, "This takes FeederWatch to a higher level. We can now analyze and understand bird populations like never before."

Veteran FeederWatcher and National Audubon Society board member Pat Heidenreich says, "I like knowing that my FeederWatching is a strong conservation tool. I want to help ensure that the common birds we enjoy at our feeders today don't become the endangered or even the extinct birds of North America's future." Heidenreich adds, "FeederWatch is something useful to do during our long Iowa winters — and it's fun!"

Don Dunsmore of Maryland keeps his FeederWatch records on computer and submits them over the Internet. His feeders hang outside his home office window.

Attracting and
FEEDING

BIRDS

Although often quarrel-some, the voracious evening grosbeaks are eagerly welcomed by FeederWatchers.

About Landscaping, Cover, and Homegrown Winter Foods

"Landscaping is the key to winter feeding success," says Richie Brill of Massachusetts. His backyard bushes offer birds "safety from enemies, shelter from cold wind, and a place for them to wait for nearby water and feeder food."

Jackie Gribble in Columbus, Ohio, says her hawthorn "is the place my birds head first when danger threatens. Can they possibly understand the added protection they get from those barbs?"

FeederWatchers who provide **natural cover** of dense vegetation like vines, thickets, and hedgerows are doing their birds a favor. The best defense a small songbird has against a hungry hawk is to hide. Hedgerow tangles of plants, small trees, and vines are favorite bird shelters.

In his 1995 book, *The Bird Garden,* Cornell Lab of Ornithology research fellow Stephen Kress encourages the use of native plants that are well adapted to local weather, soil, insects, and diseases. He urges backyard gardeners to consider "our native serviceberries, dogwoods, viburnums, and the other native bird-attracting plants."

In West Bloomfield, Michigan, Susan Freeman got a "suburban bird pack" through an agricultural extension office. "This one had native plants with berries and trees. It's a wonderful thing! We got 100 evergreens for ten bucks, something like that. They were just little twigs, but it's a start." Another FeederWatcher got native plants inexpensively from her conservation district.

Examples of natural cover are described in "How We Rearranged Our Yards" (starting p. 28).

Many FeederWatchers create a **brush pile** near their feeders for cover. "It doesn't have to be huge, just something the birds can pop into when danger threatens or there's severe weather," says Alice Topping of Franklin Grove, Illinois.

Vicki Sebela of Wheaton, Illinois, says her brush pile is a busy place. "Cardinals love it. They use it for cover, and it looks like they use it for foraging. It's neat to watch them in there." Katherine Smith of Glen Allen, Virginia, says, "We have a family of towhees, bobwhites, and brown thrashers that call our two brush piles home each year. Many birds dive in during rough weather."

Christmas trees are instant portable brush piles, and plenty of FeederWatchers use them. Carol Takacs in Madison, Ohio, always puts her used tree, along with her neighbor's, on either side of her main feeder area. "The birds use them for shelter, especially when it is windy and snowy, which it frequently is here on the Lake Erie shore." Trees can be anchored in garbage cans filled with dirt or sand, or several can be tied together near birdfeeders or lashed onto birdfeeder poles. Vicki Hedrick of Carlinville, Illinois, throws seed into her old Christmas tree every time she fills her nearby feeders.

Brush piles can happen by accident. Janet Maynard in Hershey, Pennsylvania, trimmed her maple trees and meant to cut up two piles of limbs for firewood. "Before we got around to do it, wrens and chipmunks were already in the brush." But most successful brush piles are planned.

Richie Brill advises, "Maintain some space in the internal parts of the pile for animals to move around in." To do this, start with several parallel logs a foot

Goldfinches in winter garb happily use tube feeders placed near the protective cover of thick conifers.

or so apart. Crisscross another set of logs on top of the first group. Limbs and branches are heaped on top until there is a dome about 3 feet high. Make the brush pile thickest on the side facing prevailing winds. Carrie Smith of Grove, Oklahoma, notes that "brush piles lose height as they age and settle." Some FeederWatchers swear by adding rosebush clippings or brambles to their brush piles to "help discourage cats, foxes, and raccoons." Don't add grass clippings. Put them in a compost pile.

Alice Topping suggests finding some small branches that still have leaves attached. "Use those to 'cap' the top of the brush pile and make it drier down inside. Insert the branches with stick end down. Keep adding them until you have created a 'roof' to catch the winter snow." Katherine Smith tops hers off with evergreen boughs.

Brush piles should not be placed too close to a house, as they can draw "undesirables." Jane Blumenthal in Falls Church, Virginia, had to dismantle her brush pile because it became home to a large "r-a-t. This exceeded my tolerance level." In remote areas, brush piles can be dangerous, attracting the interest of mountain lions and other large predators.

Snags are dead trees. They are an essential part of any good forest-area habitat, and they can be a lively and central component of a bird-feeding site. A New Jersey FeederWatcher says, "We leave the dead trees alone, and we have a lot of them. That's why we've got downies and hairies and a family of red-bellies." Jeanne Eberle of Libertytown, Maryland, says she leaves dead trees for the birds "if they are not a hazard to humans or lying in the way of cars."

Richie Brill planted a 9-foot-tall snag at his feeding site. "I sunk it about 2 feet deep. It is a wonderful source of insects and acts as a perch too. I hang feeders on it. I suspect my white-breasted nuthatches store food in the tiny weathered cracks."

Ecologist Scott Shalaway, author of *Building a Backyard Bird Habitat* and longtime FeederWatcher, has some snag-planting tips. "Choose snags with stout limbs on which you can hang feeders. Plant them in a hole several feet deep and 8 inches wider than the trunk diameter. Brace the snag and fill the hole with concrete. A birdbath can be placed under the snag's limbs, or vines can be planted at the base. The birds will love it."

Several FeederWatchers like adding a rotting log or two to their feeder sites. "Roll these over occasionally to expose fresh crops of bugs and worms. Flickers, nuthatches, downies, and chickadees will dismantle them," reports an Oregon FeederWatcher.

An Ohio FeederWatcher hauls two or three soft, decaying hardwood logs, like red maple, basswood, or cottonwood, to his winter feeder site each fall. He props them up in the low crotches of the crab apple tree, "which is the focal point of our feeding area. The woodpeckers and other birds probe around, and

A pine grosbeak enjoys a winter meal of bright red mountain ash berries.

the chips and wood dust fly all winter long!"

Birds are expert at finding **natural foods** in winter. One of the easiest ways to provide for birds is to do nothing and let at least part of a yard grow wild. Birds feast on the seed-packed weeds through fall and winter. Helen Peterson of Hattiesburg, Mississippi, says she leaves a small section of land bordering her carport "completely wild with weeds for the birds." Favorite bird weeds that can probably be counted on to sprout up include crabgrass, dandelion, dock, foxtail grasses, goldenrod, jewelweed, lamb's quarters, mullein, and ragweed.

Don McMordie of Coos Bay, Oregon, has one of the best success stories. He fought weeds on the south side of his house for years. But the birds liked them, so one day he started watering and feeding them. "They prospered. The birds were happy. The weeds' deep roots broke up the ground. They put nutrients back into the soil. I kept raking

Native Fruits That Hang on During the Hard (Wintry) Times

- *Crab Apples: There are more than 80 different cultivars. For finches, crossbills, and grosbeaks, choose ones with small fruits that persist through winter.*

- *Dogwoods: Red berries of the flowering dogwood tree are often stripped clean by late fall. White berries of the red osier and gray dogwoods are also popular.*

- *Hawthorns: These trees and shrubs produce round red berries high in vitamin C.*

- *Hollies: Berries of American holly, winterberry, and yaupon are bird favorites.*

- *Junipers: Waxy blue juniper cones, or "berries," attract waxwings, among others.*

- *Mountain ash: Bright red fall fruits make the American mountain ash a special favorite of robins and waxwings.*

- *Sumac: Hairy red fruits of staghorn sumac attract dozens of different bird species. Other sumac species are bird lures too.*

- *Viburnums: American highbush cranberry's brilliant red fruits last through the entire winter. Some viburnum shrub varieties produce blue or purple fruits.*

and throwing grass seed there. In about a year and a half, I had thick, green grass."

FeederWatchers also grow things like flowers and vegetables and then deliberately let them go to seed. Flowers that they grow and "let go" include daisies, asters, marigolds, zinnias, coneflowers, and black-eyed Susans. Let a few lettuce plants and other vegetables and herbs grow into stalks. Birds will relish the seeds well into fall. Melissa Kimak grows late-ripening melons and pumpkins just for the birds in her Pennsylvania home garden.

Janna Howell in Chemung, New York, says that after Halloween, she and her family cut the pumpkins in half and fill them with cracked corn and sunflower seed. "Jays and chickadees especially like this. They get their 'regular' seed, plus the pumpkin seeds and the pumpkin itself. We just keep filling up the pumpkin halves until they disappear around the holidays."

Winter berries are an important food source for birds. One Wyoming FeederWatcher who "birdscaped" her yard planted evergreen junipers especially "for their winter berries." Judy Fall in River Ridge, Louisiana, has had great luck with wax myrtle, also known as southern bayberry. "The birds love it for cover and food."

Some FeederWatchers bring berries to the birds by tying berry-laden holly cuttings to their feeders or decorating them with branches of wild staghorn sumac. Berry wreaths made out of winterberries and garlands of different hollies can be both bird and human holiday treats.

About Seeds:
The Choices Wild Birds Make

"One big mistake I made as a beginning birdwatcher was to put out junk seed, you know, some of the stuff they sell at the grocery store?" A lot of FeederWatchers voice such a sentiment. They soon learn what seeds their birds eat and what is scattered to rot. Discovering birds' **seed preferences** is part of the fun of feeding them.

Some observations are universal. "My goldfinches go nuts over niger" or "A house finch will eat anything!" But FeederWatchers who experiment discover their birds have interesting preferences. Dick Meyers of Princeton, New Jersey, filled one side of a hanging tray feeder with black-oil sunflower seed and the other side with safflower seed. "Mourning doves usually sat on top of the safflower and ate the black-oilers. Black-capped chickadees would take whatever was closest to where they landed. House finches straddled the middle and ate first from one side, then the other, just as a person would alternate between two vegetables on a plate."

The most famous formal study, *The Relative Attractiveness of Different Foods at Wild Bird Feeders,* was conducted by Dr. Aelred D. Geis in

1980. At the top of his list: black-oil sunflower, which at the time hadn't been in use very long. White proso millet was found to be the most popular food among the sparrows and juncos. Milo, along with wheat, oats, and cracked corn, was significantly below sunflower and white millet. At the bottom of his list were flax, canary, and rape seeds.

In the mid-1990s, the Cornell Lab of Ornithology conducted a continent-wide seed preference test on birds' choices at ground level among black-oil sunflower, white proso millet, and red milo. Results showed that tree-feeding species like chickadees, titmice, and evening grosbeaks most often flew to the sunflower seeds. Most of the ground-dwellers, especially the native sparrows, indicated millet was their "beaks down" favorite. Only three species, all in the Southwest, showed a preference for red milo.

FeederWatchers who compare the results of their own seed tests find that among the universal truths are many baffling inconsistencies. Marlton, New Jersey, FeederWatcher Ilene Schneider might have the clearest insight on birds' food choices. "Sometimes they remind me of toddlers that love only one kind of food for a couple of weeks and then refuse to eat it again."

"It may be weeks or months before a bird will try something new," says veteran FeederWatcher Bonnie Campion. "Be very patient. Offer new foods in familiar feeders. Birds are suspicious of new feeders."

It is no accident that **black-oil sunflower seed** ranked highest on the two formal seed preference studies cited. USDA research geneticist Jerry Miller, who specializes in the sunflower, says the black-oilers are good food, full of essential fatty and amino acids, as well as vitamins and minerals. If you feed only a single seed, FeederWatchers agree near unanimously that more species come in larger numbers for black-oilers than for anything else. Chickadees, titmice, cardinals, jays, nuthatches, and finches of all kinds are some of the birds that enjoy them.

Black-oilers are native to North America in a roundabout way. Spanish explorers took sunflowers from here to Europe around 1500. After hundreds of years of plant breeding, mostly in Russia, the black-oil variety was reintroduced to the U.S. and Canada back in the 1960s for oil production. It came to be used as a wild bird food during the 1970s, when there was a shortage of striped sunflower seeds.

Striped sunflower seed returned to North America with Russian Mennonite immigrants in the 1880s. In the 1940s, the large gray-striped seeds started being used by bird-feeding "hobbyists." Black-striped sunflower seeds are now used in birdseed, either whole or hulled. These are cast-offs, seeds too small to be sold for human consumption. Smaller seedeating birds prefer the thinner-shelled black-oilers, but heavy-billed birds like cardinals and jays are quite happy with the striped varieties.

Do sunflower hulls have an herbicidal effect on plants, as rumored? FeederWatchers who compost them say no. Sunflower specialist Jerry Miller of the USDA's Northern Crops Science Laboratory says there is no scientific evidence to support this common belief. "However, hull buildup under feeders can block light and smother plant life."

The bright gold sunflower on the left could be producing either the striped or the black-oil sunflower seeds on the right. Ruth Isaak of the National Sunflower Association says, "At this stage, you can't tell if it is an oil or confection (striped) sunflower."

Hulled sunflower seeds — "hearts" or "meaties," as they are sometimes called — were originally from striped sunflower seeds only, but black-oil sunflower seeds are now available hulled. Hulled seeds mold easily and must be kept dry.

Cracked or broken bits of shelled sunflower hearts are sold as sunflower chips. The finest size — about the size of coffee grounds — is small enough to use in a thistle feeder. "Goldfinches love it," says an Iowa FeederWatcher. "It's cheaper than niger seed, and there are no messy hulls." It works in Texas too. "The goldfinches who spend the winter here are little piggies and don't care what they eat."

It doesn't work for everybody. Terrie Murray in the rainy Northwest says that her "fine sunflower seed got wet and moldy a lot faster than straight thistle — and that's the same reason I feed black-oil sunflower WITH shells in the winter." In Burlington, Iowa, Ron Piper gets weather protection by placing his fine sunflower seed feeder under a large squirrel baffle. "The birds love that umbrella in bad weather."

FeederWatchers often mix the sunflower fines with niger seed or buy them mixed in a "finch mix."

Millet is a grass seed, one of the world's oldest cultivated foods. In many countries today, it is a staple used to make flour or a breakfast porridge. Much of what is grown in North America is destined for the caged and wild bird seed markets. It is a common ingredient in birdseed mixes, and for good reason. It is a favorite food of ground-feeders like native sparrows and doves.

The seeds are shiny, round, and creamy white or reddish brown. Birds may show a preference for the white millet.

Millet sprays, the seed head and stem of the plant often found in pet stores for caged birds, are becoming popular wild bird fare. Alice Topping reports success offering them. "I tied millet sprays to bushes for the juncos. After three days, they went for them." A Virginia FeederWatcher says "cardinals and white-throated sparrows really go for them."

One Massachusetts FeederWatcher "hung them in various places, and not a single one has been touched." Another discovered that "hanging sprays do not go over well. Ones on the ground do. I cannot keep enough of them on hand."

The thistle seed listed on a bag of birdseed is not thistle seed. What is called thistle seed is actually **niger seed.** The confusion has deterred many people, like Gaye Weisner of Staten Island, New York, from trying this seed at all. "I avoided 'thistle seed' for years, thinking I'd have big purple thistle weeds sprouting up all over my little yard. Then I found out this black seed has nothing to do with thistle, and because it's imported, it's heat-treated and won't sprout." True thistle seed has never been marketed as a wild bird seed.

Niger seed is imported primarily from Ethiopia, India, Myanmar (formerly Burma), and Nepal. In those countries, it is pressed for cooking oil. In North America, it lives up to its hype as a finch magnet. Redpolls, siskins, and goldfinches flock to it.

The Name Game: Niger/Thistle/Nyjer

Guizotia abyssinica is the scientific name of the plant in question; niger *is the agricultural name. It is much smaller than a sunflower but has a blossom that is just as yellow. When niger started to be marketed as wild bird seed in the 1970s, it was called "thistle" primarily to take advantage of the affinity that goldfinches have for both seeds. The marketing name backfired a bit as people hesitated buying "thistle" seed, fearing that fallen seeds would germinate and produce thistle plants. Led by the Wild Bird Feeding Institute, a consortium of many wild bird feeding companies, the industry is beginning to use the name* nyjer. *The new spelling of* niger *eliminates mispronunciation of the word. At this writing,* thistle *and* niger *are the commonly used terms, and we use both in this book.*

Four cardinals and a blue jay catch a meal at a fly-through feeder during a winter snow. To keep squirrely neighbors away, the *sciurus* kind, FeederWatchers often feed safflower seed. Most squirrels don't like it; cardinals do.

Since 1996, the USDA has required imported niger seed to be heat-treated to 250 degrees for 15 minutes at ports of entry. At the ETO Sterilization facility in Linden, New Jersey, ETO's Karen Burns says the process devitalizes any weed seeds, such as dodder. It also means niger seeds won't develop moths or germinate under your feeders.

A cautionary note — FeederWatchers report that if it gets wet, niger spoils quickly. It seems to have a limited shelf life as well.

Some birds seriously dislike **safflower seed,** and that's the point of using it; it has a bitter taste. "Starlings don't like it — only the younger ones try it — and house sparrows don't go near it," says an Illinois FeederWatcher who uses safflower almost exclusively. "We get cardinals, up to seven at a time, along with house finches, chickadees, and a few doves." Other birds that ignore the white, oil-rich seeds are grackles and blackbirds.

A few FeederWatchers say none of their birds like safflower seeds. One says birds didn't eat them when she served them alone, but when she mixed them with other seeds, they were a hit.

Some northerners, like Stan Merrill of St. Paul, Minnesota, feed the cheaper black-oilers in winter and switch to safflower in spring to deter the hordes of grackles and blackbirds when they arrive. "Cardinals, house finches, and all my regulars adapted to safflower just fine."

Safflower seeds are used around the world for cooking oil, as dye, and as medicine. The bright orange flower is often found in dried flower arrangements. It is widely grown in the American West and has been used for bird-feeding since about 1990. Industry insiders expect its use to increase steadily.

The many birds that eat safflower may not all prefer it to black-oil sunflower seed, but some FeederWatchers who conducted an informal preference study concluded that most of their birds ate whichever was in their favorite feeder.

Don McMordie found that his ground-feeding thrushes in Oregon had a liking for the safflower seed that spilled from his feeder. "Instead of two or three thrushes doing hit and run, I got up to seven varied thrushes at a time skipping around on the grass, hunting for safflower seed. I even saw robins come under the feeders after seed instead of flying around with worms dangling from their beaks."

"Evening grosbeaks love safflower," says Gayle Keeney of Plains, Montana. "They park on the tube feeder and ruminate. A true cow of a bird."

Safflower is also fed where squirrels are a problem. One FeederWatcher reports, "It's probably their least preferred food, but when squirrels are hungry or it's all that there is, they can do a good job on it." Reese Otts of Charleston, West Virginia, says his squirrels don't like safflower. "I saw one at the feeder a couple of days ago, but his heart wasn't in it."

How to offer **peanuts** — in or out of their waffly shells? A FeederWatcher in Virginia has reason to offer unshelled peanuts. "We had problems with squirrels and blue jays burying the shelled peanuts."

Store in a Cool, Dry Place

These words on the back of most bags of seed are important to follow. Seeds mold when they get wet, and moldy seeds are dangerous (see p. 64). If seeds get warm, miller's moths (the same ones that like your pantry grains) are likely to hatch from eggs deposited on them. The eggs can be killed by either high heat or freezing cold, but the best method is to buy good seed, store it in a tight container, and use it quickly. FeederWatchers often look for retailers that offer quantity discounts and supply seed for pickup as needed. One important note you won't find on a seed bag is "Store in a metal container." Rodents will gnaw through anything less.

But Janet Busky of West Virginia finds the hoarding habits of jays entertaining. "A jay flew into the woods with each of the peanuts I put out. It disappeared for about an hour and then returned, trumpeting to get my attention. So I put out more. It hoarded all of those too."

Roasted shelled peanuts served in wire-mesh feeders have been popular at European "bird tables" for many years and have been gaining in popularity in North America. Shelly Ducharme in Auburn, Alabama, offers shelled peanuts in a wire-mesh feeder with success. "The small birds love them — the titmice, chickadees, Carolina wrens, and the brown-headed nuthatches."

Other FeederWatchers, like John Isles of Plymouth, Michigan, have given up using whole shelled peanuts. "My birds mostly ignored them in favor of the black-oilers, thistle seed, and suet cakes that are also on the menu here. About the only interest in peanuts was from the squirrels."

There are health questions for both birds and squirrels about raw peanuts if they are fed continuously. Roasted peanuts are recognized as safe.

Other, more pricey nuts are occasionally fed as treats as well. Pecans are a bird favorite. A Vermont FeederWatcher buys mixed nuts in the shell after the holidays, when they are on sale. "Of course, the squirrels get what they can. It sure is fun to watch a squirrel with a Brazil nut," she says.

Red milo is a variety of sorghum, and the two names are used interchangeably in lists of birdseed ingredients. It is a round, soft-fleshed seed that is fed most often to livestock and poultry. Its color can range from white to yellow to tan to red. In mixed birdseed, it usually is red. The redder the seed, the more tannin is in it. While many bird-watchers consider it a "trash" seed, nutritionally it is very close to corn, and some birds in the West and Southwest may actually prefer it to corn.

Corn is a common ingredient in many bulk seed mixes. It can be offered to birds as cracked corn (in coarse, medium, or fine grades), shelled corn, and corn on the cob. Ground into meal, it is often mixed with suet or peanut butter. Because corn is a favorite food of house sparrows and squirrels, many FeederWatchers avoid it. Others add it to their ground-feeding mix or serve it specifically for game bird visitors like pheasants, turkeys, and quail.

Specially grown or treated seeds are coming on the market. Organically grown birdseed is distributed by Wild Wings Organic Bird Food. Wagner Bros. Feed packages birdseed that is vitamin-enriched and tinted with berry colors that some birds may find visually appealing.

FeederWatchers often make their own **seed mixes.** Even people who feed only sunflower seeds might prepare a mixture of chips, hearts, and whole seeds in the shell to satisfy the widest variety of birds. Homemade seed mixes can be formulated to attract birds selectively and to ensure that ingredients are consumed at a similar rate.

Commercial mixes are endless. Every retailer and distributor finds it easy to create house blends. Wild Birds Unlimited, for example, uses formulas based upon regional considerations. Others create mixes for every conceivable circumstance and price. There are mixes designed to appeal to a wide variety of species, and others designed to be species selective. Blends designed for woodpeckers are a popular selective mix, but FeederWatchers report that 'dees, titmice, nuthatches, starlings, and blue jays are as likely to find and enjoy them as woodpeckers.

A California FeederWatcher buys "big bags of a parrot food mix that has peanuts and big sunflower seeds and other special things in it. I set it out as a treat on the platform feeder."

Seed mixes can be bound together and sold in bricks, bells, or a variety of other shapes, including whimsical edible birdhouses. Many of these products are budget items and contain low-quality seeds, but quality seed cakes are widely available. The binder is an animal glue that, in rain, will slowly melt. For that reason, FeederWatchers often hang items like seed cakes under protective coverings.

About Birdfeeders for Seeds: From Fancy to Do-It-Yourself Simple

FeederWatchers, who admittedly are not typical "feeder watchers," use an average of seven or eight feeders per site by one survey, and many yards have a dozen or more. Almost everyone has the same experience: more birds come when the number

During the winter 1995–96 FeederWatch season, records show that the average Feeder-Watcher used 300 pounds of birdseed and 20 pounds of suet- and fat-based puddings.

John Droske of Elk Mound, Wisconsin, used a big wooden spool as the base for a giant plywood fly-through feeder that has been dubbed "the backyard airport." "It works great!" says Droske. "Juncos, chickadees, titmice, cardinals, and goldfinches are regular diners."

and variety of feeders are increased and their location is varied. But too many feeders are difficult to maintain, and feeding can become costly. As one FeederWatcher exclaimed, "Maybe I can convince all my kids to give me birdseed for Christmas."

The variety of feeders available for purchase is astounding. At the high end, the Birdsfly Company makes a copper Estate Bird Feeder with mount that weighs over 100 pounds, holds 30 pounds of seed, stands a lordly 8½ feet high, and is counterweighted for easy lowering and refilling. It is the birdfeeder equivalent of a Rolls-Royce, and it lists for more than $1,000. None of the FeederWatchers interviewed owned one.

Very few FeederWatchers own the poorly constructed "budget item" feeders available at the other extreme of the market, either. Denise Hughes in Caldwell, Idaho, says when she first started feeding birds, she put out some cheap, flimsy feeders, and to her amazement, "the squirrels ate them!"

Ilene Schneider cautions, "Some of the feeders that look nice and decorative are really folk art, not feeders. Squirrels chew them up." Wooden feeders that are stapled together soon fall apart. Quality wooden feeders are assembled with screws and are usually made from kiln-dried clear cedar or white pine from ⅝ to 1 inch thick.

Most FeederWatchers learn these lessons the hard way and eventually construct quality feeders or buy ones made by local craftsmen or specialists in the birdfeeder business. Good feeders typically come with guarantees that last several years to a lifetime.

Quality construction and price aren't the only feeder concerns. "They have to be easy for me to fill," says Victoria Wegner of Somonauk, Illinois. "Otherwise, I won't use them." Terrie Murray adds, "I choose a feeder carefully, based on how easy it is going to be to get debris cleaned out of the crevices."

Nearly all FeederWatchers have one or more **platform feeders,** flat surfaces as simple as a piece of plywood on a post, which welcome all kinds of birds — plus squirrels and anything else that can reach them. They can be placed on or near the ground or well above it. One FeederWatcher in California puts out a birdseed mix along with peanuts and fruit in a pie pan on the ground. Others scatter seed on platforms like rocks or tree stumps.

Platforms with a roof are often called fly-through feeders (shown, pp. 12, 13). Wisconsin Feeder-Watcher Phyllis Boldig says her "best feeder" is a fly-through feeder she made using a cake pan lid for a roof and a flat piece of wood as a base. "Birds seem to like the openness."

One problem with platform feeders is that plenty of bird food gets kicked to the ground. That's OK with Katherine Smith. "My 'ground crew' of thrashers, towhees, and doves eat all the spills that enthusiastic feeders throw from the platform."

Adding raised edges to a platform feeder transforms it into a feeder tray and helps to counter food-flinging, but trays create their own problem. The edges that keep seeds from falling to the ground also retain seed hulls, debris, and water. Trays need drainage holes and regular cleaning. Kris McNew in California came up with an easy feeder tray solution. "I made a tray feeder out of an old window screen," he says. "Water and most debris fall right through."

Katherine Wolfthal of Weston, Massachusetts, purchased a screen platform that has a hole in the middle for mounting on a pole. She placed it about 1 foot below a pole-mounted tube feeder. "It catches seeds that the smaller birds throw down. Jays, cardinals, doves, and juncos eat on the platform, and the squirrels and other ground feeders get whatever falls from there."

Tray feeders can be hung. A popular hanging model, the Droll Yankees X-1 Seed Saver (shown, p. 30), is protected by a dome to keep seed dry and prevent squirrels from raiding. While not designed specifically for it, this feeder has found extensive use among FeederWatchers as a mealworm feeder. It turns out that the dome can easily be adjusted to deter mockingbirds, which will dominate a mealworm feeder if allowed to do so.

"I can lower the dome enough that the pushy mockers can't get to the tray," explains Edie Lotz of Milford, Ohio. Bluebirds need a chance to get accustomed to the lowered dome, so for the first few days, Edie left the dome high when she put out mealworms and kept the mockers away herself. Now the dome does the job, "and we are all happy again."

A New Jersey FeederWatcher cautions, "I had to cover the drainage holes with tape — the mealworms were escaping. It's pretty funny to see mealworms dangling out of the bottom of the feeder."

A wire cage over a table feeder fails to keep out a hungry squirrel. Or maybe it's a squirrel *trap*. The mesh is wide enough to let him squeeze in, but once he fills his tummy…. Cages like this do keep out grackles, starlings, and other large birds.

Food placed on platforms and in trays doesn't last long; birds gobble it up or kick it off fast. By placing the seed in a container with a bottom opening just above the platform, a hopper is created from which seed can flow. Roofs of **hopper feeders** typically are hinged or removable to allow easy refilling. The hanging feeder shown on p. 7 is a classic wooden hopper with clear sides for viewing the seed.

Some hoppers have large wooden or screen feeding trays that the birds can walk on; others have small trays or only a rail on which birds perch to reach a narrow hopper opening. Hoppers with large trays serve more birds and attract more species but can be dominated by larger birds. A Massachusetts FeederWatcher notes that cardinals will sometimes alight on the rail of her hopper feeder, "but they are clearly less comfortable than on a larger, flatter surface."

Hopper feeders aren't always rectangular. They can be many-sided or tubular, resembling a gazebo, lantern, or silo, and may be called by those names. Conant Custom Brass makes a handsome series of clear silo hopper feeders in their Heirloom series. The roof and platform are solid copper.

A popular round hopper design is the Sky Cafe by Arundale, a hanging feeder made entirely of clear polycarbonate. The hopper and feeding platform are protected by a large, steeply sloped hood designed to foil squirrels. The idea of a large dome above a feeder to protect it from squirrels is incorporated in a number of feeder designs, including Droll Yankees' Big Top. The domes are also available separately.

Schrodt Designs makes some particularly elegant hoppers of wood and etched glass in their Lantern series (shown, p. 29). Wooden parts are fashioned from redwood mill scrap.

One of the significant innovations in hopper feeders has been the "squirrel-proof" models created by Heritage Farms, such as The Absolute and The Birder's Choice (similar model shown, p. 38). Birds must sit on a rail to reach the seed tray. The rail has a counterweight that can be adjusted so that a squirrel's weight (or that of a jay or a blackbird) will cause a shield to lower in front of the tray.

It works for Lois Goelz of Long Island, New York. "Squirrels have not gotten into it in four years, in spite of the fact that they do try. They are just too heavy; the shield closes and they cannot get the seed." Lois says she felt so bad for the squirrels "that I put seed out for them on a table under my hanging feeder. I'm a sap."

One FeederWatcher reported a problem with "clueless doves. They'll sit on the rail forever, keeping the other birds away and apparently thinking that the shield will open for them at any moment."

The Absolute might not be the feeder you would want to use as a background for a picture of your

A fearless tufted titmouse arrives for a "handout" from its exclusive feeder.

favorite cardinal, but the John Deere green painted-metal construction does keep squirrels from gnawing their way into the hopper. There are some squirrel engineers, however, that have managed to defeat these formidable feeders.

Heidi Kushlan of Paxtang, Pennsylvania, says her squirrels have learned not to stand on the rail. "They hang from the roof by their hind legs! At first, they could only hang a few seconds before falling. Now they can hold on long enough to clean me out."

Vicki Sebela's raccoons have learned the same technique. "They lie across the top and reach down so they're not stepping on the part that closes. Still, the food lasts a fairly long time."

A North Dakota FeederWatcher tells the story of a locked-out red-winged blackbird that would perch on the rail and "periodically jump in the air, grab a sunflower seed out of the tray when it opened, and then sit on the rail to eat it. I decided any bird that clever deserves to be allowed to eat."

Tube feeders are a third traditional feeder type found in almost every FeederWatcher's yard. "Finch feeders," they are sometimes called, as finches are what they typically attract. House sparrows and some larger birds can manage the small perches and feeder ports, but because it isn't easy to do, they seldom try if there are alternatives.

How One Birdfeeder Was "Born"

"New ideas from customers and inventors come to Duncraft regularly," says Sharon Dunn, co-owner of Duncraft. One inventor sent Duncraft a novel platform feeder constructed with a chicken-wire screen on top of the seed. It was meant to be squirrel-proof. They tried it; it worked! Birds, both large and small, could feast; squirrels could not. "We asked a designer to translate the inventor's wood-and-wire prototype into a plastic design that would be unchewable by squirrels and simple to manufacture and distribute." After three years of designing, testing, and developing, Duncraft introduced the patented Squirrel-Blocker Platform in 1999. "In its first year on the market, it became our top-selling item."

Goldfinches take seed from a large-ported Vari-Craft tube feeder. The cage minimizes pilferage by squirrels and large birds. The reservoir holds 3 gallons of seed.

A flock of goldfinches eat niger at a small-ported Droll Yankees tube feeder. This armored model is meant to withstand the most determined squirrels.

There are two styles of tube feeders. One is designed with small feeding ports for the tiny niger seeds; the other has larger ports for such seeds as black-oil sunflower, safflower, or mixed birdseed.

Not all "tube" feeders are cylinders. There are tube feeders with three, four, or more sides. It is the idea of feeding ports built into the elongated seed container that makes a feeder a tube feeder, whatever its cross section looks like.

The Droll Yankees A6 Tube Feeder that started it all (shown, p. 29) is still a top seller. "It is such a high-quality product," says Scott Edwards, owner of a Wild Bird Center in Aston, Pennsylvania. "The UV-treated polycarbonate is so durable that squirrels do not enjoy chewing on it. They can, but it is tough stuff. Droll Yankees feeders have a lifetime guarantee, and when I sell them, they hardly ever come back."

Numerous interesting and useful variations have evolved in tube feeders. Perky Pet, in an inspired moment, developed and patented the Upside-Down Thistle Feeder (shown, p. 79). Perches are placed above the feeding ports so that seed can be accessed only by finches that can feed upside down, a design that excludes house finches.

Two or three tubes are sometimes ganged together, as in the Opus TopFlight Triple Tube Feeder. With a total of 12 ports, it can feed more birds than a single tube, and it also has the option of being filled with a different seed type in each tube — a perfect feeder for performing comparative seed tests. A dome is included for squirrel and weather protection.

Most tube feeders are made of transparent plastics, but Vari-Craft makes particularly attractive tube feeders of white PVC (shown above and p. 8). Ports are made of Lexan, a hard plastic. A squirrel-proof model — meaning only that squirrels can't destroy it — is available with stainless-steel ports.

The end caps and ports of tube feeders are often made of metal, such as die-cast aluminum, brass, copper, and stainless steel, to deter squirrels. Droll Yankees goes all out and makes an Armored Thistle Tube Feeder (shown above) that has stainless-steel bands girdling the cylinder and protecting the feeder ports from squirrels.

High-Tech Accessories

Computers, video cameras, sound systems, and TV hookups can all enhance the bird-feeding experience. Many FeederWatchers use computers to maintain their bird lists and run CDs on bird identification or bird songs. An increasing number report their data to Cornell over the Internet. Some of the more technically savvy hook up video cameras and microphones (see p. 39). Baby monitors, placed outdoors in weather-protected areas, bring birds' musical chatter indoors. Nature Vision sells a Bird-Vu feeding station that includes a tray feeder, camera, mike, and wireless transmitter. A receiver is supplied that attaches to a TV for monitoring. It has proven to be a hit at nursing homes.

Most tube feeders can be fitted with round trays underneath that catch spillage from birds like finches, which are notoriously messy eaters. The tray serves double duty as a small platform feeder for such birds as cardinals and doves, which benefit from the flung seed.

Tube feeders are sometimes placed inside a wire-mesh cage for protection from squirrels. Cages also keep large birds like grackles from perching on a tray and reaching up to the feeder ports. In many cases, the cages are a fixed part of the feeder, but they are also available separately.

Stan Merrill tried a cage and discovered that "the diameter was too small. Grackles could reach through the 1½-inch squares and feed. A perfect setup for them." Large-diameter cages, such as Duncraft's Selective Haven, work best.

If the new developments in the old standbys — platforms, hoppers, and tube feeders — don't answer your seed-feeding needs, check out some of these other innovative seed-feeder designs.

Wire-mesh feeders, perfect for holding shelled peanuts, are becoming increasingly popular. "Blue jays, woodpeckers, and chickadees go crazy over mine," says a Texas FeederWatcher. Birds cling to the mesh and pick seeds out one at a time, almost as if pulling seeds from the head of a flower. Squirrels can pick seeds too, but one seed at a time is painfully slow for most squirrels.

A very simple feeder of this type can be made of hardware cloth. Although often called peanut feeders, wire-mesh feeders work equally well dispensing black-oil sunflower seeds and most other larger seeds. Small, round millet grains pour through the openings, however.

Wild Bird Center stores offer a distinctive Mobi Mesh feeder that is made from expanded steel rather than wire mesh. It is so resistant to gnawing squirrels that it comes with a lifetime guarantee. There are two mesh sizes available to accommodate different size seeds.

Wild Birds Unlimited has several wire-mesh feeders in their catalog. One is a fine-mesh model called a Finch Feeder (shown, p. 42), designed for dispensing niger seed. "It comes apart easily for cleaning," says a Massachusetts FeederWatcher.

Most commercial wire-mesh feeders are tubular, but some are shaped like hoppers and may be attached to a platform where birds can perch to feed, rather than having to cling to the mesh.

Mesh bags, often called **thistle socks,** are also available for dispensing niger seed. "I've never had so many goldfinches feeding at the same time" is a typical FeederWatcher experience with these feeders. "They hang all over the socks." Refillable socks made of fabric and disposable ones made of plastic are both available. Squirrels or rain can quickly ruin thistle socks, so hang them in a protected place.

There are **woodpecker-selective feeders** for seeds. One is made by Wild Birds Unlimited and quite appropriately called The Woodpecker Feeder. The seeds are behind a panel of 1½-inch-thick wood. A woodie's long bill can reach though a hole drilled in the panel and get the seeds.

Globe or bubble feeders, such as Duncraft's Cling-a-Wing and Satellite feeders, are designed for birds capable of clinging, such as chickadees, titmice, nuthatches, siskins, and goldfinches. Inside the transparent sphere is a hopper that funnels seed into a shallow layer on the bottom. Holes on the lower half of the sphere provide ports for the birds to reach the seed layer. The Cling-a-Wing has four ports; the Satellite feeds a single small bird at a time.

Peter Witt of Bridgewater, New Jersey, showers high praise on these feeders: "We've eliminated all feeders with perches because of the grackles and starlings. Now we use mostly the globe feeders and others like it. Only the small birds we want to attract can grab hold of these."

Globe feeders are designed to be hung, and because of their transparency, they are often an attractive choice for suspending outside an office window against a background of blue sky.

Sara Anderson of Arlington, Virginia, has a Satellite feeder outside her kitchen window. "I raise and lower it with a pulley and heavy cord. This way, I get to see the birds close up."

For an even closer encounter with birds — perfect for kids and indoor cats — there are **window feeders** that attach with suction cups. Typically made of clear plastic, models by Aspects, Duncraft, and K-Feeder Enterprises are among those widely available.

An elaborate and particularly attractive suction cup design is the Meta Magic Window Feeder by Birdsfly. It includes several feeding ports and a gold-tone one-way mirror that keeps birds from being disturbed by movements inside the room. Reflective film can be purchased at some hardware

Nectar feeders are provided for Anna's hummingbirds by more than half the FeederWatchers in the California and North Pacific regions (see Region Map, p. 73). Since most Feeder-Watchers experience hummers as summer visitors, the birds and their feeders are explored in a succeeding volume of The Cornell Bird Library devoted to summer bird-feeding.

A male cardinal sits on the single perch of a Duncraft Classic feeder. It is not floating in space as it might appear but is held to a window by suction cups.

and bird specialty stores for use on windows with other suction cup feeders.

A Massachusetts FeederWatcher has successfully used suction cup feeders for years. "I have a seed feeder and a suet cage wired to a suction cup cannibalized from a defunct window feeder."

Trays can also be placed on windowsills or seed spread on the sill itself. "Windowsill feeders work like alarm clocks, since the birds appear at dawn and begin pecking," advises a Texas FeederWatcher.

If bringing birds to a window is not close enough, how about bringing them right into the room? That's what can be done with the Songview or the Deluxe In-House Window Feeder by The Birding Company. First marketed in 1996, they are designed to fit into a window opening much as an air conditioner does, but mounted backwards so that the box hangs inside the room rather than outside.

A one-way mirror allows the feeding activity to be observed while keeping the birds from being disturbed. "It's like having the birds in an aquarium, or is it 'aviarium'? I can get within inches of them," says Katherine Wolfthal. She fills her feeder with suet and a variety of seeds. In summer, hummingbird feeders can be placed inside.

The feeders need to be placed in a sunny spot for the one-way mirror to work. Katherine discovered that her jays and white-breasted nutties would, at first, attack their reflections, but flocking birds, which are used to each other, didn't seem to mind.

The feeder can be cleaned and food replaced from inside the house, a big plus in cold weather. Most feeders of this design allow the outside window to be closed at night for security. Be sure to seal the unit carefully to prevent insect problems.

And if squirrels have totally frustrated you, there are **battery-driven feeders** to consider. Wild

Suction cups depend upon an airtight seal to maintain suction and hold a feeder in place. When the weather is cold, they become more rigid, and the seal can break more easily. Apply them when they are clean, warm, and flexible. A very thin film of oil will improve the seal. It can be applied by rubbing a finger on the oily part of your nose or chin and then on the suction cups. The window must be clean, dry, and free of scratches.

This Wild Bill's Electric Feeder has a tray and a dozen feeding ports for birds. Squirrels attempting to feed complete an electric circuit and get a mild shock.

Bill's Electric Feeders use a 9-volt battery to zap the squirrels. The Flipper, made by Droll Yankees, has a battery-powered motor that spins the perch and flips squirrels off.

The jolt given by a Wild Bill's Electric Feeder is small and does no real harm. Birds don't receive any shock. (The Wild Bill people deny the rumor that squirrels have been seen hooking up ground wires to their birdfeeders.)

A Virginia FeederWatcher, Bill Teetz, has been using an electrified feeder for about five years. "The squirrels have learned not to mess with this feeder. They often study it but don't often try to feed from it." Others complain that batteries stop working in cold weather, and not everyone is comfortable with shocking squirrels.

Droll Yankees' Flipper is not yet available at this writing but promises to be a significant innovation in the continuing battle with squirrels. It is a tube feeder with four ports, all at the bottom of the tube and facing different directions. To feed, birds sit on a ring extending from the bottom. When a squirrel sits on the ring, its weight causes a motor to engage that starts the ring spinning and sends the squirrel flying.

Droll Yankees claims squirrels won't be able to outwit the Flipper. They offer a lifetime guarantee. One FeederWatcher is not so sure. "Better feeders, smarter squirrels. It's an evolutionary process!"

There are differing opinions about **feeder placement.** Many people have feeders clustered in

Students at Dutchess Day School in Millbrook, New York, get a close-up view of birds in their classroom in-window feeder. But the birds can't see *them!*

view of a dining room window, where they provide hours of entertainment. But they won't bring in the numbers or variety of birds that can be attracted with feeders of different types mounted at different levels and at different places around a yard.

Even birds that will feed most anywhere have feeding preferences. Birds that are very selective about their feeding habitat will rarely approach a feeder that doesn't meet their requirements. Brown creepers need big tree trunks; towhees and many sparrows stay low and keep near brushy cover; chickadees and titmice seldom touch the ground.

Cats and hawks influence feeder placement, and so do all the various feeder raiders, such as squirrels and raccoons. Mice and other rodents can be a problem if seed is available on the ground or near it. These issues are discussed in the chapter "How We Cope With" (starting p. 57).

Feeder placement should also accommodate severe weather conditions. Birds don't like freezing winds, hard rain, and driven snow any more than we do. During prolonged storms, they'll use feeders placed in protected areas but will abandon feeders set in areas exposed to the storm just when they need them most.

A Corinth, Mississippi, FeederWatcher houses his feeders in a shelter made of PVC pipe and corrugated roofing. "Holds up against the high winds we get, but the best thing is squirrels don't bother the feeders in there. It's the only thing that works."

In Kamloops, British Columbia, a FeederWatcher places her feeders inside an A-frame shelter. Birds can fly in, perch, and feed during a storm.

About Suet and Peanut Butter In All Their Variations

Suet brings in woodpeckers, nuthatches, and numerous other insect-eating birds. Starlings too, unfortunately, but they can be controlled by the way suet is offered (p. 22). FeederWatchers report plenty of birds, like brown creepers, that may never go to a suet feeder directly but are drawn to suet crumbs that fall beneath it. In Mississippi, one FeederWatcher counted brown thrashers, towhees, and wood thrushes among the ground-feeding suet opportunists at his site.

"It's not necessary to make suet," says Bob Coppernoll of rural central Illinois. He gets his suet from the local meat market. **Raw suet** is the fat surrounding kidneys in the loins of animals like cows and sheep. It is the purest, hardest piece of fat on an animal and has a waxy look to it. "If you get the whole chunk from around the kidney of a cow, it will weigh about 15 to 20 pounds." All Bob does is slice it to fit his suet feeders, which are onion and potato sacks. He freezes what he doesn't use. "Just put the slabs in your feeders without other fuss, such as melting the suet or putting in seeds."

A pine warbler contemplates a block of suet. Pine warblers are one of the few warblers to overwinter in the U.S. Most migrate to southern pine forests in winter, but some remain in cold country and often become regulars at suet feeders.

In the wild, birds can get suet and other animal fat from carcasses. Author and FeederWatcher Myrna Pearsman of Sylvan Lake, Alberta, once watched what happened to the carcass of a black mule deer that had died on nearby ice. "After the coyotes, the ravens came. Next to visit were the bald eagles, gray jays, and then the chickadees. At one point, the deer carcass looked like a great big birdfeeder."

Susan Campbell in Whispering Pines, North Carolina, serves only venison suet in one of her feeders. "My husband hunts, and so we have a ready supply of venison. I have commercial suet cakes too, but my birds go for the venison suet first." A New York FeederWatcher/hunter found that venison suet attracted pileated woodpeckers. "They come to beef suet and suet cakes, but they seem to like the venison better. I also hang a large chunk of fatty rib section around a tree trunk. Once they discovered that, they were regulars."

Raw suet can be rendered and formed into cakes or other shapes. Rendered suet will keep fresh longer than raw suet, but in winter, the differences

Suet, Suet Cakes, and Suet-less Suet

For most people, suet is a hard fat purchased from a butcher. (It is known as tallow when used in candle or soap making.) For backyard birders, cakes of rendered suet with various additions are also known simply as suet. By extension, homemade fatty mixtures that have no actual suet in them, such as lard or peanut butter mixtures, are sometimes referred to as suet because they are used like suet and attract the same birds. Gorp and pudding are common FeederWatcher names for mixes that aren't suet-based.

What the Birds Have Taught Us

aren't often of practical importance. The main reason for making **homemade suet cakes** is to add other ingredients, such as nuts, grains, seeds, fruit, grape jelly, and eggshells. Some FeederWatchers like to mold rendered suet into balls, bells, or egg shapes with a loop of string and use them to ornament a tree.

Suet is preferred over other animal fat for making cakes "because it is easiest to work with, has less impurities, and forms harder cakes," says Karen Alstott, co-owner of C&S Products, the leading manufacturer of suet cakes.

To render suet, chop or grind it and then melt it over medium heat. Strain it through cheesecloth to remove impurities and pour into pie pans, tin foil baking cups, or pine cones, or when it cools, roll it into balls. The process is easy, but the smell of suet being rendered is another matter. "Yuck! I wasn't completely revolted, but it wasn't easy on my nose," exclaimed one FeederWatcher. It doesn't help that most directions call for rendering suet twice before molding. There is no magic number of renderings. Each rendering and filtering removes more impurities and makes a "power bar" for the birds that holds together better.

A Pennsylvania FeederWatcher adds about 3 cups of seeds, nuts, and raisins to each cup of rendered suet. In nearby New York, Corrina Frigon uses more flexible proportions: "Get the amount of suet you want to work with, render it down, and then start putting things in." The things she puts in include oats, cornmeal, peanut butter, raisins, and cherries. She likes the color that cherry juice gives the mix.

The logic of adding seeds to rendered suet is debatable. Many bug-eating birds that come to suet don't eat seeds; they just peck around them to get the suet. Birds that do eat seeds find the ones in suet covered with grease and difficult to hull.

A male downy woodpecker clings to a suet feeder. The tail-brace extension is designed to make it easy for woodpeckers to perch and eat their fill.

Most FeederWatchers find it more convenient to substitute another fat for suet when they want to make mixtures or puddings. Plenty of high-fat foods are appealing to birds, including lard, bacon drippings, peanut butter, and vegetable shortening.

If FeederWatchers want suet cakes, they generally buy them. And buy them they do. The sales of **commercial suet cakes** increase every year, and Karen Alstott feels it will be a long time before they stop growing. Go to any wild bird supply store or look through any wild bird catalog and you are sure to find an array of different suet products, from 12-ounce cakes to 3-pound bricks and more. Some grocery stores carry them too.

Pine Tree Farms in Interlaken, New York, for example, produces its own brand of beef kidney suet cakes — 14 different kinds — in addition to making suet products for other wild bird supply companies. Flavors range from a standard peanut butter suet cake to an orange-papaya suet dough to an exotic concoction that combines dried crickets and mealworms.

The orange-papaya suet dough is a "summer suet" or "no-melt suet." Summer suets contain enough flour or meal to bind them together and keep them from melting. Because rendered suet has few impurities, it does not go rancid on a hot day. Raw suet can go rancid, which means it can rot and stink and shouldn't be offered in hot weather.

Several FeederWatchers recommend using small suet cakes so they can be changed often. Deena Richmond of Los Osos, on Morro Bay in California, says her trick is to hang one small suet cage in each of her four birch trees with a different kind of suet in each feeder. That way, birds have a choice. She says she's tried almost all of Wild Birds Unlimited's suet cakes. Nut 'n Raisin is most popular with her birds. She feeds Bug Bites during the rainy season and a calcium-fortified cake in spring.

The virtues of raw suet versus commercially produced suet mixes versus homemade bird puddings are often debated. "I can hang out store-bought suet cakes, and they'll last a couple of weeks. I hang out my homemade cakes, and they're gone in a day or two," says a Wisconsin FeederWatcher.

An Alabama FeederWatcher has noticed some preferences among her feeder birds. "My mockers love pure suet and my homemade gorp, as do the brown thrashers. They will eat it year-round if it is there." She says she hasn't seen cardinals go after suet, "but they definitely eat the peanut butter mix I make, as do the yellow-rumped and pine warblers in winter."

One Minnesota FeederWatcher says, "When I offer both raw suet and puddings, downies and hairies go to the raw stuff every time. Nuthatches and chickadees don't seem so particular." On the other hand, a North Carolina FeederWatcher makes

A brown creeper gets a tasty mouthful of sticky peanut butter pudding from a hardware-cloth cage.

A red-breasted nuthatch, used to picking seeds from pine cones, finds one filled with peanut butter gorp.

gorp and serves it in small pieces on her platform feeder. "This works better than suet. Downies and red-bellies are regulars. Daily visits from a Carolina wren are a nice surprise."

Squirrels in most FeederWatchers' yards leave raw suet alone. "Neither the red nor gray squirrels found it appealing — not even the chipmunks," says Priscilla Trudell of New Hampshire. "Of course, the raccoons thought it was wondrous, and the bears came for miles for it."

Carol Takacs says the squirrels ignore her raw suet, "but if I put out gorp, they are all over it." It is the corn, peanuts, and other seeds in gorp and commercial suet cakes that attract most squirrels.

At his Bethesda, Maryland, home, FeederWatcher Ben Lin had no takers for either raw suet or commercial suet cakes. So before throwing everything out, he melted the uneaten suet and suet cakes together and added cornmeal, cracked corn, some mixed seed, and what turned out to be a key previously missing ingredient — peanut butter. "The recycled cakes were eaten within a week!"

Peanut butter is a high-fat, high-protein food that birds love. It is a favorite FeederWatch food, and one of the most popular ways to serve it is slathered plain on hanging pine cones. Some people are a little wary of offering it plain, however. Urban legend has it that birds can choke to death on the stuff. There is no evidence to support the fear, but those with doubts can mix it with a little cornmeal. One FeederWatcher says because of the stickiness and saltiness of peanut butter, she makes sure fresh water is always nearby.

Carrie Smith takes a spatula and smears peanut butter right into the bark of a backyard tree. "Then I sprinkle it with mixed birdseed. That 'feeder' is a hard one to keep filled." A Virginia FeederWatcher says if you paint peanut butter on just one side of the tree, the brown creepers stay put for a while to eat. "They don't go around to the tree's back side every time I want to get a good look at them!"

A Colorado FeederWatcher adds 3 pounds of assorted seeds and 1^1/$_2$ pounds of cornmeal to a 2^1/$_2$-pound jar of chunky peanut butter before spreading it about. In spring, he adds 12 ounces of finely crushed sterilized eggshells to the mix for extra calcium during egg laying.

Gaye Weisner feeds peanut oil. "I buy pure peanut butter for the house. When the oil rises to the top, I drain it off and save it in the fridge, where it turns solid. In the winter, I spread the lard-like oil on whole-grain bread and offer it to the birds in a suet-style basket."

Peanut butter is used in most recipes for gorp or puddings. Catherine Fagan of Carlisle, Ohio, makes a mixture of one part peanut butter, one part vegetable shortening, and three parts cornmeal or whole-grain flour. She smears it on a "peanut butter paddle." "This is a board with heavy wire mesh on both sides. After I smear it on, I press mixed seeds and raisins into it. Kinda messy, but the birds love it!"

Many FeederWatchers have their own pudding variation. Geoff Elliot of Lansing, West Virginia, makes a fruit pudding of rendered suet, peanut butter, cornmeal, and frozen fruit, such as grocery store blueberries and raspberries. He spreads the mixture directly onto tree trunks and branches. "I just smear it with a sandwich spreading knife. Yellow-bellied sapsuckers and chickadees like it."

For a mixture that can be cut into squares and used like suet cakes, try Victoria Wegner's peanut butter/lard mix. Melt and cream together 2 cups each lard and chunky peanut butter. Add 2 cups flour, 1/2 cup sugar, and 4 cups each oatmeal and cornmeal. Press into a 9-by-13-inch pan. Cool and cut into squares. "Chickadees, titmice, and all the woodpeckers love this," says Victoria.

Ron Piper has a similar lard and peanut butter mix that he uses to keep a gorp log replenished. He buys lard in 8-pound tubs at a discount. In the microwave, he melts 4 cups of lard and 1 cup of peanut butter. He then stirs in oatmeal and corn-meal until it starts to thicken. As a final step, he adds mixed birdseed. He stores the mix in the refrigerator, and "whenever I need some, I just nuke it 'til soft and load up the log feeder."

A female pileated woodpecker picks suet from a suet log. Most suet logs are hung from a chain. This one is pole-mounted; it has an open can on the bottom as a cylindrical baffle to deter hungry raiders.

Shelly Ducharme likes to set out gorp all year and uses a formula "that has no animal grease to rot." To one part each peanut butter, vegetable shortening, and whole-wheat flour, she adds three parts corn-meal and handfuls of seeds, raisins, and peanuts.

About Feeders for Suet: Sacks, Logs, Cones, and Cages

Suet feeders are not nearly as complex as some seed feeders. They can be as simple as a mesh sack — the kind often used for onions and potatoes. Toss a chunk of raw suet in an empty mesh sack and hang it on a tree trunk or from a branch or pole.

Hardware cloth can be fashioned easily into a suet cage (shown, p. 102). The birds won't mind the appearance, and if you do, there are countless more attractive wire suet cages available inexpensively. Many are designed specifically to hold commercial suet cakes and birdseed cakes.

A popular way of presenting suet and puddings for birds is in homemade suet logs. Ron Piper took a small log approximately 4 inches in diameter and 15 inches long, "and I drilled about 12 holes in it. The holes are about 1 inch diameter and 1 1/2 inches deep. I placed a hook in one end and hung it from a small chain."

Perches aren't necessary and if used will attract grackles and starlings. Woodpeckers and small clinging birds can get a grip on the rough wood. Stuffed with suet or puddings, these logs are regularly visited by woodpeckers. Standing dead snags can be drilled and filled like giant suet logs.

If meant to attract woodpeckers, a suet feeder is likely to be found most quickly if it is attached initially to a tree trunk. Once the woodies have found it, the feeder can be moved to other spots and the birds will follow.

Suet cages are sometimes combined with seed feeders. Heath Manufacturing makes a beautiful redwood hopper feeder with suet cages at either end, the Classic Suet 'n Seed Feeder (shown, p. 65). The style is widespread; Woodlink makes a similar model with a copper roof.

Starlings and many of the larger birds enjoy suet as much as woodpeckers, and they can make off with large amounts quickly. To defeat them, FeederWatchers cage the suet so that it can be reached only from the bottom. For example, a plywood box with a hardware-cloth bottom works well. Similar but more durable commercial feeders are also available. Woodpeckers, nuthatches, chickadees, and titmice easily cling upside down to feed; starlings can't. At least, most of them can't.

A Virginia FeederWatcher relates a typical experience with starlings at a bottom-access suet feeder. "At first, one starling could get one foot on for a short time and had some success but had to keep its wings flapping furiously." Soon tiring, the starling fell to the ground, but others imitated it. "Now, after a week, at least three out of a dozen have mastered hanging on without continuous flapping while they feast on peanut butter gorp."

Another woodpecker-selective suet feeder is Avian Aquatics' Suet-Sandwich. An ingenious design, it exploits the fact that woodpeckers, and only woodpeckers, have tongues that can probe several inches into a tunnel to gather wood-boring insects. A layer of suet is sandwiched between two layers of simulated bark (shown, p. 39). To feed, the woodie perches on the narrow edge of the sandwich and cleans out the suet with its long tongue. Homemade puddings also work well in the Suet-Sandwich.

About Other Foods:
Some Different Goodies Birds Go For

"Raisins are by far the most popular **fruit** in winter here in my urban backyard," says Pamela Parson of Harrisburg, Pennsylvania. "Cardinals, jays, robins, and catbirds go for them." Bluebirds love them too. If the raisins (or currants) are extremely hard, they should be softened for a few minutes in a little hot water. Pamela also puts out other dried fruit, such as mangoes, pineapples, blueberries, "whatever I have on hand. It always gets eaten."

Cut-up fresh fruit may have some takers but is more often served in spring and summer. And then, as Helen Peterson warns, "it just attracts too many insects." Squirrels will eat it as well.

Whole fresh grapes and persimmons are proven winners with birds. Keith Payne in Charleston, South Carolina, has been putting out grapes for four years. "In winter, thrashers, mockers, and robins fight over them. This spring, birds were taking grapes to their young. Some of the young even started following the adults to the grapes to be fed." Persimmons draw the same crew of fruit-eaters when they get ripe and mushy.

Birds don't care if fruit is fresh or has been frozen, so some FeederWatchers harvest grapes, blueberries, or persimmons and store them in a freezer. They can be thawed when needed and served at specific times of the day when birds learn to expect them.

All the wild berries that birds like (p. 9) can be harvested in fall, stored, and set out for the birds regularly throughout the winter. Ron Kingston of the North American Bluebird Society says he feeds dogwood berries, currants, and freeze-dried blueberries. "The red dogwood berries attract bluebirds, and then they find the other fruits. By using the fruits, I can attract bluebirds and don't have to use mealworms." If Ron runs out of dogwood berries, he buys them from The Home for Bluebirds in Bailey, North Carolina, the only supplier at this writing. Jack Finch, the owner, has an "orchard"

An eastern bluebird at a tray of raisins and suet bits. Insect- and fruit-eaters like bluebirds, robins, and mockingbirds won't come to feeders for seeds but can be attracted with some delicious berries, fruits, and insects.

of dogwoods that have been carefully selected for late fall fruiting.

Many FeederWatchers offer **insects** in the broad sense; that is, they follow Marli Lintner's advice to "leave the spiderwebs under your eaves. Kinglets will come and eat the spiders during winter." Wrens and other bug-eating birds will also search eaves and decks.

Mealworms were the first insects offered commercially as food for backyard birds, and that didn't really begin until Grubco started marketing them in 1996. Before then, mealworms had been sold as reptile and fish food and as a food for bluebirds during nesting, and were used by wildlife rehabilitators. Now other live insects are being marketed for birds.

When Shelly Ducharme first set out mealworms, she discovered "the mockers and thrashers love them, and the yellow-rumped warblers have now discovered them. I am hoping that the wrens and titmice will soon find them."

Shelly ordered her mealworms by mail. Several companies now sell them. They can be kept in a dormant stage by placing them in a refrigerator. Feeding mealworms means either buying them monthly or growing your own. It takes about a month for the larvae to pupate and another month for them to turn into mature beetles. Keep in mind you can create quite a colony: one female can lay up to 275 eggs. At Grubco facilities in Fairfield, Ohio, president Dale Cochran says that "25 to 30 million worms are growing here at any given time."

The mealworm you buy is the yellow mealworm, or Tenebrio molitar, the larva of the darkling beetle. This is the same insect that can infest the grain or cereal products in your pantry. For birds, mealworms offer 63% moisture, 19% protein, and 14% fat.

Nutrition studies show that birds require much the same vitamins and minerals that we do. Lack of calcium can be a severe problem, especially for game birds, which lay many eggs. In Missouri, it was found that a single soil type, rich in limestone (calcium carbonate), supports 70 percent of the state's wild turkeys.

Ed Sheidlower in Honeoye Falls, New York, is one of many FeederWatchers who feed bluebirds in winter. From his platform feeder, he offers them Garden Alive's Bird Grub, which is dried caterpillars. "Blue jays found them first. A number of different species, including bluebirds, love them." Vicki Hedrick agrees. "I feed dried grubs. Titmice love them. Chickadees love them."

Bird Grub is dry and easy to handle, keeps for months in storage, and has a higher nutritional value than live mealworms. The fact that the grubs can't go crawling about has some appeal, but they are relatively expensive and can't be "farmed" like mealworms.

Some suet cakes include dried insects, such as crickets and mealworms. They are expensive but popular treats.

A number of FeederWatchers say they want birds to eat the grubs, larvae, and overwintering pupae in their yards. Bonnie Campion in Princeton, Texas, says she doesn't feed insects to her birds because "I want the bluebirds, woodpeckers, and mockingbirds to eat the pecan shuck worms and tent caterpillars that infest my pecan trees. In return, they get free baths and suet."

Table scraps and baked goods are not usually a regular part of the menu offered by Feeder-Watchers, but when the refrigerator gets cleaned out, birds often find some unusual items at their "table." Crows and other corvids put table scraps high on their list of delicacies, right up there with roadkill. And yes, some FeederWatchers do collect roadkill and place it in their yard. An anonymous Florida FeederWatcher worries, "Cornell probably thinks I'm strange for reporting the turkey vultures that came to the roadkill I set out for them."

A New England FeederWatcher has a small family of crows that she feeds "table scraps, leftover cat food, and things nobody in the house wants. When the weather is really bad, I buy dog food especially for them. They swoop in, snarf it all down, and leave."

An Ontario FeederWatcher, D. J. Bowie, "found" his family of crows accidentally. "I occasionally give my dog a large bone to chew on that I get at the butcher's. The bone does not come inside at night. One morning five crows were pecking away at one, and now they come looking for them."

Mary Schwartz in Brewster, New York, confirms that crows love bone marrow. "I try to buy bones that are about 4 inches long. After my dog, Nellie, has gnawed off the meat, the crows get the marrow."

Jim Kittinger of Indiana set out the turkey carcass from a holiday feast. Other FeederWatchers had told him that crows and vultures would find it. "Around noon, I spotted a hawk perched low on a tree branch right above the carcass. After sitting there for some time, he dropped down and began

A gazebo feeder filled with eggshells hangs from the Lutmans' sycamore tree in Kansas City, Missouri. Intended as a calcium boost during nesting season, it attracts blue jays year-round.

to feed. This morning he took a piece of the turkey and flew up to a nearby tree, where he passed it off to his mate."

FeederWatchers occasionally offer treats of homemade bird cookies or purchased bakery items, including white bread and pizza crust. Although it is lacking in nutrition, many birds regard white bread with the passion that a kid feels for soda pop.

"Yesterday I put out some leftover white bread and a couple of slices of two-day-old turkey," relates Katherine Wolfthal. "I was astonished to see that the crows preferred the white bread to the turkey. Even stranger was that the titmice deserted feeders chock full of seed to fly off with a piece of bread half their own size!"

Be careful that any scraps set out are not spoiled or moldy. Bad food can cause disease.

Salt licks aren't just for deer, squirrels, and rabbits. Birds like them too. In Crawford, Colorado, Jane Cartwright says, "All the birds love the salt and mineral blocks I have out for my other wildlife. In fact, the birds eat more than any other creature does."

Few FeederWatchers provide salt other than that in peanut butter. Birds regulate salt, excreting any excess. It seems that some individuals may develop a taste for salt, and flocks of finches, like crossbills and grosbeaks, are often seen eating rock salt on roadsides.

Seedeating birds require **grit,** such as small quartz pebbles or pieces of sand, which they use in their gizzards to "chew" their food. It can be mixed with seed or provided in a separate container. Birds will actually come to a separate dish for it. They are sometimes seen getting grit from the sides of roads.

Victoria Wegner says, "I offer coarse sand — the kind used in construction work, not in sandboxes —

on the ground in an open area to give birds a supply of grit and a place to do some winter sand bathing. When it snows, I just kick off the snow and expose the grit. Some days there are as many birds at the 'grit and bath station' as there are at my feeders."

Commercial grit often contains crushed oyster shells and can be a two-for-one, providing a digestive aid as well as a **calcium** boost. Calcium is an essential element in all birds' diets. Their natural sources are calcium-rich soils, snail shells, and eggshells. Many FeederWatchers provide crushed oyster shells or eggshells during the spring nesting season, when females need extra calcium to produce strong eggs. Some continue having customers for calcium throughout the winter and feed it regularly.

Karen Von Bargen of Scotts Valley, California, feeds oyster shells. "Band-tailed pigeons fight over this. Chestnut-backed chickadees go for it, as do acorn woodpeckers, scrub-jays, and Steller's jays. Somehow they found it here on my condo deck."

Participants in a Cornell Lab of Ornithology study on calcium discovered that jays and crows were by far the most frequent of the 67 species observed eating shells. A Minnesota participant said that in his backyard blue jays were "practically gulping them."

A FeederWatcher in Union, New Jersey, says he sometimes shares his breakfast with the crows. "The crows like the egg whites I scramble for my breakfast. To what I serve them, I add the eggshell halves. Crows aren't too fussy."

Mary Wenberg of the USDA cautions that eggshells, like the eggs they contain and the chickens that they come from, must be heated to at least 160 degrees to kill food-borne pathogens such as salmonella. Boiling the eggshells or heating them briefly in the oven or microwave does the trick.

Many FeederWatchers crush the sterilized shells with rolling pins. Others offer bigger pieces.

Sara Anderson notes that when she has more than one eggshell at a time, it is usually because she is baking something. "So when I take out the last tray of cookies or the pie, I put the eggshells in. The oven is already hot, so the extra 10 minutes I leave it on to bake and sterilize the shells doesn't use that much more energy."

About Water
For Drinking and Bathing

Ain't nothin' says lovin' to birds like open water in the dead of a bitter cold winter. Most FeederWatchers offer water for birds and firmly believe that many of the species they count would not be there if not for the water. In the words of one FeederWatcher, "I have had better luck attracting birds with my bird-bath than with anything else I've tried." And water is an avian attraction that is a true benefit to birds, especially in very cold or dry weather when water is hard to find.

Birds sometimes travel long distances to seek out natural water sources they can use for drinking and bathing. FeederWatchers have reported savvy birds drinking from places like rooftop gutters and flying up to house eaves to catch icicle drips. Snow and ice crystals are drinking-water options, but not great ones. And even though it might be cold, birds bathe to keep feathers clean for good insulation.

Birds seem to relish a good bath in winter. Most will dunk their heads first and then start beating their wings and splashing around. "The house finches will get in there so thick they can hardly move without swatting each other in the beak," notes a Washington state FeederWatcher.

It looks like play, and it probably does feel good, but those movements are knocking off dirt and ectoparasites like feather mites. While the outside feathers get wet, the down feathers beneath stay dry and keep the birds' bodies warm. Feather preening usually follows bathing.

When birds preen, they are distributing their natural oils over the feathers, so having the feathers wet helps them first strip off the old dirty oils before coating them with clean new oils. Bonnie Campion has it figured out. "I think it works the same way you would clean your hardwood floor — first wash off the dirt and then rewax."

Water can be offered in **simple containers** like a terra-cotta flowerpot saucer, an old broiler pan, or the choice of one Alabama FeederWatcher — a black plastic plant tray. "I have it on a slight slope so there is both a deeper and a shallower part, from a couple of inches to about half an inch."

Many people use an upside-down trash can lid. A little inelegant, but it does the trick. Tilt it slightly, keep the deepest water level less than 3 inches, and put in a brick or stone "island" on which birds can perch and waterlogged insects can dry themselves out. See who finds you first.

If the lid is slick, birds may slip and have difficulty bathing. Sand or pebbles on the bottom will

A bathing frenzy develops as birds find the shallow water in a broiler pan to be exactly to their liking.

A California towhee tests the water in a ground-level bath.

give them a solid footing but need to be replaced or cleaned each week when the bath is cleaned.

Gaye Weisner has discovered the ultimate easy way to provide water. She recycles things like plastic mushroom trays and take-out Chinese food containers by turning them into birdbaths. "I do not have the time or inclination to keep a commercial birdbath well cleaned. But every day I can put out a clean new container of fresh water." She sorts out the dark containers "to use in winter because they'll absorb extra heat from the sun."

But most people offer water in attractive **commercially made birdbaths** of concrete, ceramic, or durable, easy-to-clean plastic. Instead of a brick or stone in the center, you might see a sculpted frog or turtle — or stone squirrel — which looks nice in a garden or on a deck when it is full of drinking or bathing birds.

Large pedestal birdbaths are available at lawn and garden stores. Wild bird stores carry them and other designs as well. There are numerous birdbaths made for decks and for pole mounting in yards. Many birds, however, seem to be more comfortable bathing near the ground. "Very seldom in nature is water provided for birds on a pedestal," observes Roger Taylor, owner of a Wild Bird Center in Kalamazoo, Michigan.

"I find that thrashers, towhees, and little guys like 'dees and titmice like to bathe in a terra-cotta plant saucer on the ground instead of the big birdbath," says one Texas FeederWatcher.

Robin Ballard in St. Johns, Michigan, has a pedestal birdbath in the center of her yard, but she says "by far the most popular bath is the smallish Avian Aquatics ground bath, with the fake rock and a pump to keep the water moving. I have to turn it off when we are away because the birds splash so much water out it can't pump. Even the cardinal bathes in the ground bath."

Ground birdbaths have less heat loss in winter than those on pedestals or poles because the ground is often much warmer than the air.

Avian Aquatics makes a line of molded-plastic ground-level birdbaths and numerous other water features for birds, even recirculating creeks. One of their designs is molded from a large granite boulder. Bill Fintel, who founded Avian Aquatics in 1990, recommends that birdbath materials have a rough finish so birds don't slip and slide. Check edges for places birds can perch and drink.

Birdbaths can be works of art. The 12-inch-diameter Misty Birdbath by Schrodt Designs is a beauty made of spun copper and turned wood. It includes a small fountain or mister in the center.

So how do FeederWatchers keep the water in their birdbaths from freezing? One Massachusetts FeederWatcher admits, "I've cracked a few baths over the years making bad judgments on nighttime temps." Others put out water in shallow containers each morning and hope the birds get their drinks and baths before it freezes. Many use specially designed **electric de-icers.**

There are several all-weather heating elements with safety features that are made especially for outdoor birdbaths. They automatically turn on just above freezing and cycle off when the water temperature reaches 40 to 45° F. These can be purchased separately and added to a birdbath, but many commercial birdbaths have heating elements included. A FeederWatcher in chilly Alaska says his works even at 40 below zero (F).

Birds generally have enough sense not to bathe in water when temperatures are dangerously below freezing. A Nebraska FeederWatcher describes a starling that probably knew better but decided to bathe when the temperature was –20° F. "As he left the birdbath, a gust of wind blew him against a small metal pole. His wet feathers stuck fast to the pole, and he died there."

Farm supply stores and many wild bird stores sell an inexpensive model made by Farm Innovators that is used by many FeederWatchers. The C-50 is a 150-watt heater designed specifically for birdbaths. "I've used one for three years without problems," says a Wyoming FeederWatcher. All the major wild bird stores and catalog companies sell various brands of water heaters too. Some of them are designed to turn off if they are not covered with water.

De-icers should be plugged into ground fault circuit interrupter (GFCI) outlets, which have been the required outdoor outlets for homes built since about 1985. If any moisture drips into the outlet, the circuit shuts down. Wind-driven winter snow finds its way into any kind of crevice, and so that protection is needed. Make sure you use proper outdoor extension cords.

Other FeederWatchers swear by the Happy Bird Corporation's line of **Solar Sippers.** Made of a tough plastic, these portable water stations (shown, p. 41) are designed to keep water from freezing down to about 20° F by absorbing the warmth of the winter sun. Do they work?

Janet Maynard says it depends on how bitter cold the weather gets. "The Solar Sipper works great if you bring it in at night, when there's no solar power, and then take it back out in the morning. Otherwise, if it gets down in the teens or lower at night, you are going to have ice." Vicki Sebela says the chickadees love hers. "They went right to the top and stuck their heads in. I like it because it is small and easy to maintain."

Water is certainly compelling to birds, and the sound of **dripping water** is downright enchanting. Drip, drop, drip, drop. In bird-speak, that must translate as drink, bathe, drink, bathe. Mesmerized, they come. A Massachusetts FeederWatcher who has a birdbath with a dripper and one without observes that *"all* birds prefer the dripper." If they can, some birds will catch the drops as they fall.

The FeederWatcher no-frills dripper is a plastic gallon jug full of water and with its cap on. Make a pinprick on the side about an inch from the bottom and another in the cap. Hang it over your birdbath. If the water doesn't drip fast enough, prick the side again. A Michigan FeederWatcher managed her pinholes so that "a gallon of water would last just about the entire day, until I returned home from work." On the other hand, she says, "I spend far too much time trying to get my new store-bought dripper to drip properly."

Commercial drippers are available that can sit in your present birdbath. Newer birdbath models often have a dripper included or offered as an option. Some models are recirculating and powered by a pump. The pumps can easily get clogged from debris, so the filter must be cleaned often. Upside: the birdbath is kept clean and debris-free.

Most drippers are meant to be attached to a faucet and come with a valve and 50 feet or so of tubing. They are the easiest to maintain. Solar-powered pumps are employed in some of the latest designs, including a floating solar-powered fountain. When the sun shines, you have the magic sound of sprinkling water.

Fine mists of water also attract birds, but misters are used primarily on warm days rather than winter days. They are as readily available as drippers, and some units are combination dripper/misters. One FeederWatcher reports her chickadees like the mister so much they ask her to turn it on. "They will *zee* at me until I put on the fine spray and aim it upward into a tree so they can all shower. It's a kick!"

Most drippers and misters don't work in freezing weather, but some recirculating systems have heating elements capable of keeping water liquid at temperatures as low as 0° F. Birds invariably concentrate at these sources when other water is frozen.

Amid misters, recirculating pumps, and solar-powered fountains, Avian Aquatics has reinvented the gallon jug dripper in the form of a flowerpot. Their Floral Dripper is a set of 12-inch-diameter flowerpots. The shallower one rests inside the deeper one and will hold your choice of plants. The bottom pot conceals about a gallon of water and has a valve controlling the drip rate.

Besides bathing in water, birds keep clean by ruffling and shaking themselves in dust, sand, snow, rain, and sunlight.

A flock of thirsty robins at Nancy Henke's birdbath in Lakewood, Colorado. "It was 10 degrees that morning, so drinking water was at a premium," says Nancy. "A flock of close to 50 robins waited in my chokecherry for their turn to drink."

Sandy Belth
Rolling Hills of Southern Indiana

Sandy Belth's 2-acre partially wooded yard in a rural neighborhood is an ongoing experiment, shaped year by year primarily by what she learns from her feeder birds.

"After you feed birds for a while, you start figuring out what they like and don't like. They let you know. I'm always changing things around, trying out new feeders, new foods, new plants."

Sandy is certain that the backyard feature that has been "the single best thing we've done to improve our feeding station" is the addition of running water. Initially, however, the water improvement was not for the birds.

A short creek ends in a shallow pond built from a commercial kit. The water is recirculated by pump and is an ideal depth for birds.

One summer day, Sandy started digging a butterfly puddle for her yard, a small, shallow spot where butterflies could get needed moisture and minerals. She cleared out some dirt in her herb garden, lined the depression with a trash bag, and filled it with pea gravel and water.

But she had dug out too much. The water was too deep for butterflies.

Dirty from digging and disappointed that she had a lot more work to do to correct her mistake, Sandy went inside the house. "While washing my hands, I looked out the bathroom window at the puddle, and there were birds already bathing in it." The puddle was perfect for them. She watched them splash around in her mistake and quickly redubbed it a birdbath. "We had so many birds that summer. We couldn't believe what a difference this little puddle made."

Because raccoons kept punching holes in the trash bag lining when they drank during the night, she replaced it with a commercial pond liner. But soon the bird-attracting success of the tiny puddle bath led to bigger ideas. For Christmas, Sandy's husband, Jeff, gave her an Avian Aquatics Bird-Creek Bird Pond kit. That spring, as soon as the ground had thawed, they dug a 6-foot-diameter hole for a pond and removed a 10-foot-long, 2-foot-wide section of sod to create a creek. Eventually the creek was extended to 16 feet long. Heaters keep the water open and running during the winter.

The sound of running water seems to hold particular appeal for birds. In winter, when other water sources are frozen solid, Sandy says, "It is incredible how many different kinds of birds visit the creek and pond. We've counted 84 species, including all six of our woodpeckers, over two dozen warblers, and both Cooper's and sharp-shinned hawks. I've even seen a big pileated woodpecker take a bath and then vigorously shake itself off. Quite a sight."

Sandy noticed birds often perching above the creek on overhanging lilac branches. Birds like to sit on a safe, dry branch before venturing in and getting wet, she concluded. So she lined the whole length of the creek with dead branches.

The creek branch perches were immediately popular with Sandy's avian guests and led to a similar idea for her feeder site. At the very top of one of her feeder posts, she drilled a hole into which she fit a 5-foot-tall sassafras sapling, branches and all.

"Birds can wait for a spot to open up at the feeders while perched on the sapling branches above. I often look out and see the feeders full and as many as a half-dozen goldfinches and house finches sitting on the sassafras."

The extra perch idea has been incorporated into several of her wooden bird feeders. She drills a

A lantern feeder from Schrodt Designs, with limbs added for perches, hangs directly outside the Belths' observation window.

couple of holes in the feeder and then fastens twigs to it with wire. "It's an easy way to enhance feeders and provide a more natural perch." Replacing old perches is as easy as picking twigs off the ground.

Near the feeder posts, Sandy has created a small thicket or brush pile of twigs and branches. Sparrows and juncos use it for shelter between short trips to the feeders. On windy days, when birds want to stay under cover, Sandy places seed on the ground under the brush.

Her two 10-foot-tall wooden feeder posts (see photo at right) also create a natural effect, acting like feeder trees. Stationary metal bracket arms are bolted near the top of each 4-by-4 post. Hung from each of the arms is a feeder: a Droll Yankees A-6-3 sunflower tube feeder, a Wild Birds Unlimited large mesh peanut feeder, a Wild Birds Unlimited small mesh thistle feeder, and a Birdstuff Color Dome sunflower feeder. Hanging from the side of the support post itself is a suet cage. The diversity of feeders attracts a diversity of birds.

To keep squirrels and raccoons from the smorgasbord, the Belths have attached a Wild Birds Unlimited squirrel baffle specially designed to slide over a 4-by-4 post. "The baffle has been a tremendous improvement for our feeder site."

Not all of Sandy's feeder stations are elaborate. Some are simply old tree stumps where she broadcasts seed like red and white millet and cracked corn for ground-feeding birds.

A feeder post attracts a flock of American goldfinches to the feeders hanging from its arms. The sapling at the top of the post provides perches.

A popular but very simple feeder is her mealworm feeder. She uses a Droll Yankees X-1 Seed Saver because it has a clear tub that allows her to see the worms and a plastic dome to keep them dry. The mealworms are put out sparingly as a treat. When Sandy does put them out, tufted titmice, Carolina chickadees, and Carolina wrens are drawn to them like a magnet.

Sandy says she believes her feeder bird populations wouldn't be as sizable as they are were it not for something else she and her husband have done or, rather, not done. They've stopped mowing some of their yard.

The area where they live is a karst region, characterized by limestone bedrock with sinkholes and

Although designed for seeds, the Belths' Droll Yankees X-1 Seed Saver serves as a mealworm feeder for a happy tufted titmouse.

caves. Both front and back yards have sinkholes. These areas, kept mowed by the previous owner, have been allowed to revert to thickets. They are now full of berry-producing plants that birds love, like spicebush and raspberries. A new addition she has planted, a high-bush cranberry, has also proven a bird favorite.

The yard is lined with 30-year-old pines and is also home to hardwoods — mature black walnut, shagbark hickory, red oak, and tulip poplar. Poison ivy grows well too, with several large vines on the pines and oaks. Sandy doesn't view the poison ivy as something to get rid of. Instead, she leaves it alone; its white berries are favorites of mocking-birds, woodpeckers, and migrating fall warblers.

An environmental educator, Sandy says her entire yard and her feeder site reflect the philoso-phy she has developed while learning about nature and teaching others about the natural world. "I like to encourage people to allow a certain area of their yard to just grow wild. That's what we have done. It feels like we are sharing our space with nature rather than shutting nature out."

Vern Dayhoff
Rocky Mountain Foothills at 7,150 Feet

When Vern Dayhoff moved to his Rocky Mountain foothills home in view of Pikes Peak in the late 1960s, about the only thing growing in his 5-acre yard was scrub oak and prairie short grass. With the exception of a couple of seasonal bluebirds, the only birds he ever saw were scrub-jays and American crows. So he started planting. "As a high school biology teacher, I wanted to learn firsthand about native trees. Plus I wanted to plant some-thing for the birds here. I began with evergreens."

After putting in just a couple of dozen saplings, he saw a brand-new species — a Steller's jay.

Over 30 years later, his backyard consists of a ponderosa pine forest with scattered groups of evergreens, including Colorado blue spruce, Rocky

Mountain juniper, piñon pine, Douglas fir, and white fir, along with a wide variety of native and exotic fruit trees. It is also full of birds, over 120 species of which Vern has seen over the years.

The evergreens provide rotating seed crops for birds like red crossbills and serve as windbreaks, all-important cover, and homes for insects. Fruit trees like Canadian cherry offer fuel stops for birds like American robins. But it is Vern's FeederWatch site that is "bird central."

In the middle of a protective wide circle of brush and local granite and dolomite rocks, he's placed an 8-foot-tall dead pine tree. Covered with drilled-out holes full of beef suet and hung with a variety of commercial and homemade feeders, the tree is the focal point of his feeding site. He says pine cone feeders are some of the birds' favorites. "These are just the big ponderosa pine cones. I slather the scales with a peanut-butter, seed, and cornmeal mix, hang up the cones on the dead pine's limbs, and watch the birds go to them."

Over the years, to help shier birds like nuthatch-es make their way from the ponderosa pine forest to the feeder hub, Vern has built a pine pathway, or "flyway," as he calls it.

"About every 20 feet or so from the forest to the feeders, I planted a ponderosa pine. So now there's a 75-yard-long tree trail leading to the feeders." He

A pine snag at the center of the Dayhoff feeding circle offers suet in cages and stuffed in holes drilled in the wood.

Vern Dayhoff adds ears of whole corn on the cob to a side tray on his tray feeder. "The jays will eat four of them a day during the winter," Vern says. "My squirrels ignore them and eat the sunflower seed."

says typically, birds like black-capped and mountain chickadees, downy and hairy woodpeckers, and red-breasted, white-breasted, and pygmy nuthatches fly up and down the tree trail route, back and forth, from forest to feeders.

Three other points of bird activity include a 4-foot-long tray feeder, a slab of plywood set out under a big Douglas fir at the edge of his feeding site, and a heated birdbath.

Vern built the main section of his tray feeder with three separate compartments, "so I could see for myself which birds like what seeds." He fills one section with black-oil sunflower seed, another with cracked corn, and a third with a 50/50 mix of thistle seed and finely ground eggshells — a favorite of pine siskins. The feeder rests on a post about 5 feet off the ground. At night, local mule deer and other mammals find the leftover sunflower seeds irresistible.

His ground-feeding birds like things simple. A sheet of plywood spread with white millet, cracked corn, and black-oil sunflower seed and placed under the Douglas fir gives the usual dark-eyed junco crowd both cover and food. This is also a favorite site for flocking species like the jays, house and Cassin's finches, and red-winged blackbirds.

But it's the heated plastic birdbath where he finds the most diverse gatherings of local birds.

"It's great to look out my den window and see mountain and black-capped chickadees, American goldfinches, and pine siskins all sitting together around the rim of the birdbath."

Vern says he's seen his regular jay population undergo the most dramatic changes. "Since those first couple of winters, the scrub-jays and Steller's jays have tripled in numbers. We have a newcomer too, a bird I used to just see back east — the blue jay." He says he often sees half a dozen or so of these westward-expanding birds at his feeders.

Overall, time spent planting trees and shrubs and creating and maintaining his bird-feeding site have been worth it. "As a trained teacher, I can tell you that the personal experiences I've had with birds are more valuable than any book learning I ever had."

Roger Lawson, Lead Program Specialist
Kellogg Environmental Center, Connecticut

Hundreds of New Englanders can FeederWatch at one site in Connecticut. The state-owned Kellogg Environmental Center in Derby, Connecticut, is a hub of both feeder bird and FeederWatch activity.

Located near the convergence of the Naugatuck and Housatonic rivers, the 400-acre property was a working dairy farm less than 50 years ago. While surrounding farmland has been turned into subdivisions, most of the land immediately adjacent to the Kellogg Environmental Center is being maintained as open space. Instead of milk and butter, the old farm site now produces Connecticut-based environmental education.

Program specialist Roger Lawson says one of the center's goals is to involve the public directly with a wildlife environmental monitoring program. "Project

Roger Lawson, lead program specialist, describes Project FeederWatch procedures to volunteers at the Kellogg Environmental Center.

FeederWatch is perfect for us. It ties folks into local birds and the scientific process. Volunteers park themselves in tall padded stools in our bird observatory, really our old solar demonstration room, which has a bank of both east- and south-facing windows. They sit back, a hot cup of tea or coffee in hand, and commence to FeederWatching."

The center's feeder site has been kept as simple and unassuming as possible so it can serve as a model that anyone can copy. "Most of our feeders are the homemade variety. Any commercial feeders we have are easy for others to purchase."

One of the feeders is a hopper feeder consisting of a sunflower or safflower seed reservoir with a roof and platform. The hopper is made with 1/4-inch wire-mesh hardware cloth. Birds perch on the platform and pull out the seeds. That's what the squirrels do too. "This feeder isn't squirrel-proof, but it makes the squirrels work harder than usual. They have to pick out the seeds one by one." Replacing sunflower seeds with safflower seeds, not a favorite of the furry ones, also helps keep squirrel activity down.

In addition to several Plexiglas sunflower tube feeders hung at varying heights around the site, there are two homemade tray and suet feeders constructed by maintenance staff from plans found in a birding magazine.

One tray feeder, popular with squirrels, sits on a post near the ground; the other rests atop a 5-foot-tall wooden post girded with flashing to keep the squirrels out. The floors of these double-framed tray feeders are the same hardware cloth used in the hopper feeder, topped with a layer of window screen. All manner of seeds can be scattered there. Tray cleaning is easy and natural: wind, rain, and sunlight.

The suet feeders are made by screwing short scraps of lumber together into a frame and fastening it to a piece of plywood. Hardware cloth is stapled over the wooden frame, and the feeder is mounted on a post. "All of these homemade feeders are simple, functional, long-lasting, and relatively easy for people to make. They are also getting the ultimate bird-squirrel testing in our garden so everyone can see how they hold up."

Fruit-bearing plants near the feeder site and a year-round birdbath add to the site's avian allure.

Nature Center FeederWatch

Project FeederWatch is on the programs of nature centers and sanctuaries across the United States and Canada, including the Aullwood Audubon Center and Farm in Dayton, Ohio. "It serves many audiences, which is perfect for us," says Tom Hissong, education coordinator. "At Aullwood, visiting school groups count birds with senior volunteers. It's great to see the excitement of watching birds transcend all ages." At the Martha Lafite Thompson Nature Sanctuary in Liberty, Missouri, naturalist Rebecca Hill-Larsen admits that FeederWatching has become a sport for staff. "It's fun to see how many new birds we can count during our lunch break."

A suet feeder made of scrap lumber. The piece at the top is attached by only a single screw at one end. It swings open for easy refilling.

The popularity of Project FeederWatch at the Kellogg Environmental Center has added a word to Roger's job description: consultant. "I'm now being asked by nature centers around the state about ways they can incorporate FeederWatching into their education programs. It's exciting to help FeederWatch and bird awareness grow here in New England."

Bob and Anne Winckler
Matanuska-Susitna Valley: The Anchorage 'Burbs

When Bob Winckler and his wife, Anne, first started watching and feeding birds, Bob was working for the U.S. Navy at Adak, in the middle of Alaska's stormy Aleutian Islands. They saw a very limited number of regular feeder customers: snow buntings, gray-crowned rosy finches, and ravens.

To counter the effects of wind-driven rain, the feeder they used in the Aleutians worked like a weather vane, the forward section of the vane pointed into the wind, protecting the open back end, where birds could find dry seed.

When they moved to the Alaskan mainland and their Mat-Su Valley home close to the Cook Inlet, the Wincklers spent time planning their new feeder site in hopes of attracting many bird species. They now have a system that works well both for them and for the birds, although Bob characterizes it as a "work in progress."

The site covers an area of several hundred feet in an open space between the southeast side of their house and a strip of mature black spruce, birch, and alder woods that the birds use for cover. Several brush piles provide additional safety retreats.

There are about a dozen different feeders and a white plastic all-weather birdbath with an imbedded heating element "mostly used for drinking." The entire site can be seen from the dining room window.

Feeder highlights include a multi-perch pole-mounted tube feeder full of niger seed that satisfies the redpolls and siskins. Bob fills a double-sided pole-mounted hopper feeder with black-oil sunflower seeds and puts peanuts in a tree-hung cylindrical wire-mesh feeder. Both of these feeders attract a variety of birds.

At two elevated covered platform feeders, the Wincklers offer a mixture of sunflower chips, peanut chips, and "red and white millet when the pine siskins are in town." A dining room window's suction cup feeder has three removable compartments; two are filled with sunflower chips; the other, with peanut chips. "Gray jays are too big for this feeder, but everybody else visits."

At first, Bob fed suet only from a hanging double-sided feeder, but gray jays became a problem. "They were hauling off huge chunks of expensive commercially made suet, the kind mixed with peanut butter, another mixed with insects — good stuff I had to go into Anchorage to get. We couldn't keep the feeder stocked for the other birds."

So a new suet feeder was added to the collection, one that is open only at the bottom, designed to attract small agile birds. First visitor? "A gray jay, hanging upside down and eating just as nice as you please."

Now with more cage-type suet feeders and seed feeders deployed, there is plenty of food for all of the Wincklers' regular feeder birds. Common redpolls get the "most frequent fly-in" award; Bob once counted more than 80 of them at his feeders at one time.

In addition to the redpolls and gray jays, the Wincklers see black-capped and boreal chickadees, hoary redpolls, pine siskins, pine grosbeaks, red-breasted nuthatches, black-billed magpies, downy woodpeckers, hairy woodpeckers, dark-eyed juncos, and at least once a day — a merlin!

In late November 1998, with plenty of snow already on the ground in south-central Alaska, Bob and his wife, Anne, saw a black-capped chickadee under one of their suet feeders carrying a small twig. Nesting materials in November? Something wasn't quite right about that picture. "My wife and I looked at the bird again. The twig wasn't a twig at all. It was the bird's beak!"

Curious and slightly disturbed by what they saw — a grossly long and decurved upper mandible crossing over the shorter, straighter, but also deformed lower mandible — the Wincklers began a daily watch of this bird's eating and social behaviors. They nicknamed the chickadee "Cyrano."

Over the next several months, they watched Cyrano struggle to eat and succeed using a specific feeding strategy. With its elongated beak, cracking open black-oil sunflower seed wasn't a food option for the chickadee, but fallen suet crumbs worked just fine.

Cyrano figured out that downies and hairies are messy eaters and drop plenty of peanut-butter suet crumbs. When a woodpecker visited the suet feeder, Cyrano immediately would fly to the suet crumbs and grasp a piece in one of his feet. He would then stick out a wing, bracing it against the hard snow. Next he would lower his head between his feet, rotate it sideways, and scoot his mouth opening up to the suet piece. This went on repeatedly.

Despite the feeding hardships, Cyrano fed successfully even during a week of −40° F temperatures. The resourceful bird also discovered how to keep warm, sometimes perching near a heating vent on the Wincklers' rooftop. The last time they saw Cyrano was just after the late-winter arrival of a northern shrike. "Maybe there's no connection here," says Bob. "But after what Cyrano survived, I'll always be suspicious."

A red squirrel feeds at "The Squirrel Lunch Box" made by Woodlink. It has a hinged top and clear plastic front that allows the squirrels to see the food. Inside are black-oil sunflower seeds, whole corn kernels, and peanuts in the shell. Sometimes the squirrels go completely inside the box. "It's a tight fit," says Bob, "but that doesn't seem to bother them."

"Cyrano" was the first of six chickadees with deformed beaks that visited the Wincklers' feeders. None of the others had deformities as severe as Cyrano's.

Moose, foxes, snowshoe hares, and lynx compete with the birds and squirrels for feeder food. And when bears leave their dens in spring, Bob has to take all the feeders down until fall.

At one time, the Wincklers had a problem with birds hitting their windows, but an inconspicuous clear plastic spiderweb window decal (the Warning Web by Droll Yankees) with a highly visible vertical zigzag center has worked wonders. "On windows where we have the web, we've had no bird hits," not even from birds being chased by merlins.

What about those once-a-day merlin visits? "At least one checks out the feeding area every day. They always come in low and fast, about 8 feet off the ground, the sun at their backs, making them hard for the little birds to see. They remind me of the jet-powered motorcycle riders zooming through the sequoia forests in one of the *Star Wars* films." Bob estimates the merlins' success rate at catching feeder birds to be only about 10 percent. "The good tree cover and brush piles save the feeder birds."

The trees offer shelter from snowstorms too. "Really, the birds up here stick out the cold weather in pretty good shape, just as we do," says Bob.

Beak Deformity Investigation

Based on the reports and photographs of Bob Winkler and others, the United States Geological Survey's (USGS) Alaska Biological Science Center launched an investigation into the cause of the beak malformations. Since late 1998, hundreds of birds with bill deformities have been documented, mostly chickadees in south-central Alaska. USGS biologist Colleen Handel says discovering the exact cause of the bill deformities could take a while. Since nearly all of the reports of malformations have come from people watching bird feeders in residential areas, as part of the USGS study, feeders have also been set up in parks and remote areas where people do not live. "This should help tell us if the geographic clusters that we have recorded so far are real or not," says Colleen.

Joyce and Michael Jaques
Farmland North of Lake Ontario

Not only are Joyce and Michael Jaques original FeederWatchers, joining the program during the 1987–88 season, but they are also former participants in the predecessor to Project FeederWatch, the Ontario Bird Feeder Survey. "We have been feeding birds a long time — for 17 years at our home here — on our own and with the projects. Our feeders get counted for the annual Christmas Bird Count too," says Michael.

Just north of Lake Ontario on Mississippi Lake, a 10-mile stretch of ice from December to April, winters can seem endless. But when watching birds from their bungalow's big picture window, the Jaques say time passes quickly. Over years of watching, they've been able to do more than admire the different birds that visit. They've been able to note, and document, bird population changes.

The colorful and "squabbly" evening grosbeaks, for example, don't visit in great numbers as they used to. Pine siskins aren't as abundant in the Jaques' yard either. "Even as recently as the late 1980s, pine siskins used to stay the winter. Now they show up only in November and March." But some birds are being seen more often.

Michael says, "When we started counting for FeederWatch, it was rare to see a mourning dove. Now we have 20 or more consistently at the feeders. Northern cardinals, too, used to be unheard of. Within the last five years, we have been getting a few sightings each year."

The common redpoll ranked as the most abundant visitor to the Jaques' feeders during the winter of 2000, with up to 125 at a time making their feeder rounds. But Michael says they seem to be totally absent in alternate years. "We can look back

Joyce Jaques scans the line of feeders that extends from her window to the maple tree at the far left.

at our personal records, which I have logged into a computer program, and we can see this on-off pattern. This goes right along with the Canadian/U.S. FeederWatch findings for the entire Northeast."

Joyce says looking out their picture window is like viewing a big feeder bird painting. Two feeders are quite close to the house — one is a cylindrical hanging feeder of wire mesh that has a cage of metal bars built around it. "There's nearly always a small bird here gobbling down the 'oilers.' We leave it up year-round because the grackles can't get at the seeds."

Other hanging feeders include a cylindrical wire-mesh feeder peanut container, always popular with the chickadees, and a simple tube feeder filled with sunflower seeds for redpolls and goldfinches.

The Jaques suspend all of these from wire strung from the eaves of the house to a 20-year-old maple. What about hungry squirrels? "We added a squirrel foiler here that works pretty well. On both ends of the wire we've attached plastic funnels. Squirrels try to grip the funnels and spin off before they can get to the feeders—usually. There is always the odd squirrel genius who manages to reach the treasure."

From the tree itself hangs a clear plastic tube feeder that contains niger seed. Very small holes make it a finch-only feeder. "The redpolls and goldfinches stop by here for treats, but it's the pine siskins who relish the niger seed. They go crazy over it."

The tree is also where they hang two suet feeders, ever popular with the downy and hairy woodpecker crowd. Both of these feeders are hung on the tree on straightened-out metal clothes hangers. "This is another squirrel foiler we came up with. The hanger's length makes it hard, but of course not impossible, for squirrels to reach the suet."

To help keep feeder food costs down, Michael decided to get his suet directly from a local country butcher. "At the start of winter, the butcher supplied us with a 2- to 3-foot-long hunk of suet. It lasted us through the FeederWatch season. That was just one trip and didn't cost much in the first place."

A homemade tray feeder near the house consists of a big piece of plywood with protective side rims and a roof. It offers black-oil sunflower seed. This is the feeder that draws in the most redpolls. It also gets black-capped chickadees, white-breasted nuthatches, house finches, and the occasional blue jay and evening grosbeak.

One bird-feeding tip the Jaques advise others to do is keep feeder sightings on computer, using one of several commercial software programs available to do this. In addition to the documented redpoll movements in their yard, they've been able to track interesting movements of some other species too.

"One day in November, we'll be sitting here looking out the window and notice that the tree

A tray feeder with a humorous design for humans and seeds for the redpolls hangs from the Jaques' tree.

sparrows have arrived from breeding grounds up north. They stay a couple of days and then most disappear, probably to feed a little south of us. Sometimes a couple will stay the whole winter. Our records show that in early spring, the flocks are here again on their northbound flight.

"Fall and winter can often seem long here in southeastern Ontario. Birds brighten our days."

Linda De Rosa
A Small Mountainside in East-Central Maine

The harsh winter weather of Springfield, Maine, doesn't deter hardy FeederWatchers such as Linda De Rosa. She spends about an hour each morning cleaning and filling her feeders, even during a blizzard. "I'm out first thing in the morning, about 5:30 a.m. All 18 feeders get cleaned of crud and filled with food. If we have a winter storm, I'll go out several times during the day and sweep off the new snow."

The temperatures can get down to minus 20 (F) in January and February, with a wind chill that makes it even colder. Even so, there is always open water for birds and other wildlife at the De Rosas'.

Several years ago, while drilling for a well, the De Rosas hit an aquifer, and water gushed out. Using a system of pipes, they redirected the flow to where they wanted it, creating three small ponds near the FeederWatch site. Constantly moving water in the main pool means the ponds don't freeze.

The ponds were the only thing that didn't freeze during the huge northeastern ice storm in the winter of 1998. Linda says they had to feed the birds twice as much then. "They showed up in the hundreds. We had our regular birds and then all these others."

Linda De Rosa fills the two clusters of feeders that are outside her kitchen window. The numerous tree limbs "planted" at the base of the dead trees provide perches for birds approaching the feeders. When the birds sense danger, they flee to the evergreens nearby.

Ice buildup on the feeders was a big problem then, as it is during the smaller, more frequent ice and snow storms of a regular winter. Linda figured out a way to clean the feeders of ice during her morning rounds by using a razor-blade scraper.

"Each morning, I'll chisel out the frozen bird food with the scraper and fling it on the ground. Ground-feeding birds, like mourning doves and juncos, along with my free-range domestic chickens will feed on the frozen 'seed-sicles.' Anything left over, the red squirrels pick up."

About once a week, Linda removes each feeder for a thorough cleaning, replacing it with a clean and dry double. Having replacement feeders is an efficient way to keep things clean "especially in the middle of winter."

Most of the feeding action takes place right around the De Rosa home, a fenced-in 3-acre spot in the middle of 65 acres that adjoin an expansive Indian reservation. Linda maintains four feeding sites; the two sites that she can see at one time from her kitchen window are what she uses for her FeederWatch counts.

There she has an array of feeders, ranging from various tube and platform feeders to suet cages. Common redpolls are a frequent winter feeder sight. American goldfinches have at times descended in flocks of 80 or more. Evening grosbeaks are regulars. Linda says that what her birds like best isn't what she has read that they like best.

"Everybody says black-oil sunflower is the best all-round seed. But my birds clearly like the striped sunflower best. They'll ignore the black-oil and go for the striped when given a choice." But because striped sunflower seed has become more expensive in recent years, Linda has switched to a combination of black-oil sunflower and hulled sunflower

chips, or "meaties," seeds and seed bits that are too small to be sold for human consumption and so get used in bird food.

But Linda says the real bird attractant in her yard is suet. "I go through more than 50 pounds of beef kidney suet a winter. I order it in bulk." Linda swears by the beef suet, as opposed to commercially made suet cakes. "I find that after a while, if they haven't been eaten right away, the suet cakes will disintegrate from the constant rain and snow." Linda's suet visitors can include half a dozen red-breasted nuthatches at once and about as many hairy woodpeckers.

Linda says her feeders draw in birds from the surrounding cedar swamp and birch and hemlock forests. Her yard itself is full of white pines and, most important, dead white pines and birches. "These are a mecca for all sorts of birds. Just the other day, on a dead tree right near the house, I watched a brown creeper searching the bark for food. In a way, old dead trees are sort of big, natural bird feeders."

Redpolls barely wait until the platform feeder is filled with mixed seeds before stuffing themselves.

A hungry jay prepares to make its entrance to Linda's food bonanza. The numerous feeders ensure that jays don't drive away the smaller birds.

She hasn't planted anything special for the birds yet. "There's plenty here, probably plenty the birds have planted." Linda has very little formal lawn; she is content to let flowers and weeds die off and go to seed. Because of the wildlife benefits, Linda's yard has earned certification as a National Wildlife Federation backyard habitat.

Linda admits she's become a bit obsessed about her birds. She explains that she moved to the forests of Maine after living in a condominium community in Connecticut where condo rules disallowed bird-feeding. "I was so happy to get to feed birds. I started with a couple of feeders and sunflower seed. Then, as more birds came, I bought more and more feeders and then tried different feeders and different seeds. I've actually tried to cut back on my feeding a little lately."

What inspires her to make the hour-long feeder rounds each morning at the height of winter? "You really reap the bennies. I just love watching birds."

John V. Dennis
A Suburb on Maryland's Eastern Shore

After many years of feeding birds and Feeder-Watching, author and bird biologist John Dennis says he's boiled down his own backyard feeding site to a couple of good workhorse feeders, a few types of seed, suet, and a ground-level birdbath.

There's more to it than that, of course, including nearly 50 years of learning how to feed birds, most of which have been spent at his ancestral home located on the Eastern Shore of Maryland.

John got his bird-feeding start serving as director of the Massachusetts Audubon Society's Moose Hill bird sanctuary near Sharon, Massachusetts. "In the late 1940s, bird-feeding was just catching on as a popular hobby. People would come by to watch birds at our many feeders. Then they asked for advice on the best ways to feed their birds at home."

"I wanted to give out the best bird-feeding information available," John says, "but after doing some research, I realized no one had written a comprehensive book on feeding birds. I decided to do it." In 1975, Alfred A. Knopf published his *Complete Guide to Bird Feeding,* which has subsequently been reprinted several times. He has also followed the success of that benchmark book with regional feeding guides.

John says he collected his bird-feeding tips from personal experiences at the sanctuary's feeding site, from his own backyard, from enthusiastic bird-feeding people in the Sharon area who would stop by to share their expertise, and especially from Droll Yankees founder and bird feeder inventor Peter Kilham. "Among the things I learned during many memorable visits with Peter over the years is that birds don't care what the feeders look like. They just want to get to the food."

Considering birds' special needs for cold-weather shelter, John purposely located the main feeding site at his Maryland home on the south side of his house so that the house serves to block cold winds from the north. Various plantings or "living shelters" like red cedars also help to deflect wind, providing protective cover while producing fruits and berries for the birds.

This is where he has placed a mostly squirrel-proof counterweighted hopper-type feeder (which consists of a balance bar rim that closes off the food supply as soon as a "heavyweight" bird or mammal sits on it), as well as a domed Droll Yankees garden feeder secured on top of a stationary pole. In both of these feeders, he serves only black-oil sunflower seed. A suet feeder hangs on a flowering dogwood tree, which at all times is "well-patronized by various woodpeckers and Carolina wrens."

A pedestal-less birdbath sits on the ground: "Birds can get to it more easily." Birds find quick escape from danger in the cover of a nearby tangle of honeysuckle, located at least 5 feet from the feeding site to prevent surprise attacks from cats. In ground feeders or old-fashioned bird tables and directly onto the ground, John spreads a seed mix of millet, sorghum, canary seed, and finely cracked corn. This is where the juncos, white-throated sparrows, and cardinals congregate.

At one time, cats and squirrels were hard for John to outwit in his residential backyard. He relied

Bird-feeding pioneer and FeederWatcher John V. Dennis fills his "squirrel-proof" hopper feeder.

on the same strategies he recommends in his books, including placing feeders on poles just far enough from cover that cats can't hide in ambush and squirrels can't jump to the feeders. The poles are baffled so that they can't be climbed.

There were numerous squirrel and predator remedies John heard about and researched for his books, including a variety of squirrel shields and other squirrel-foiling contraptions. He now feels he

has found the best method yet — his Jack Russell terrier. "Jackie chases all the non-birds away. She never really catches anything, but I know she's having a great deal of fun."

John says he's learned from the birds that it is best to spread out his feeders. "This prevents over-crowding and lends itself to luring a greater variety of birds." His own feeders are placed at different levels to help attract birds that feed naturally at different heights. Most are at his south-side feeding station, relatively close to the house for easy viewing. But he deliberately placed a thistle feeder on the north side of his house, away from the main feeding site and human activity. Once John saw a white-and-yellow canary chowing on the niger seed.

As far as food goes, "It's hard to beat black-oil sunflower." John rates it best for being a high-fat, high-protein food with more edible kernel than the striped sunflower seed. In fact, John's bird-feeding books helped popularize the use of black-oil sunflower and niger seeds as wild bird food. He says if you have to get by feeding birds on just two foods, stick with the black-oil sunflower seed and either plain suet or commercially made suet cakes.

Despite his reputation for promoting bird-feeding, John says, "Natural growth and natural food can't be emphasized enough." Overall, he has planted his one-acre suburban yard as a food and shelter habitat for birds and butterflies, with shrubs, bushes, flowers, and trees — living and dead — taking up more space than grassy lawn.

"Feeding birds is so entertaining. You learn so much from them seeing them up close. Sometimes, when there's a shortage of insects and other natural foods, our feeding might even help them." He says what he's really learned over his many years of feeding birds and investigating ways to feed them is that ultimately it is the rekindled awareness of the natural world that is most important.

The introduction to *A Complete Guide to Bird Feeding* seems to best sum up John's take on the whole bird-feeding hobby. "To many, the joy of feeding birds is that it takes so little skill and equipment. Without much more than daily offerings of food and a feeder or two we can set up a contact with birds that is rewarding both to them and to us."

Julia Pahountis-Opacic
Mature Suburb Near Pittsburgh, Pennsylvania

Julia Pahountis-Opacic can view her FeederWatch site from any one of four windows — three of the windows are in her house; the fourth is on her computer screen.

"I've gone a little high-tech, I guess. I wanted to watch at least some of my neighborhood feeder birds while I'm working on the computer."

So Julia and a friend affixed a small digital video camera to a back porch railing, aimed it at the

Additional Bird-Feeding Pioneers

1930s: Peter Kilham founds Droll Yankees, develops tubular hanging feeder.

1940s: Gilbert Dunn designs windowsill feeders, founds Duncraft in 1952.

1950s: Bill Engler, Sr., of Kaytee Co. teams with Simon Wagner of Wagner Brothers Feed Corp. to package and market "birdseed" to grocery stores.

1958: Mitch Erickson, founder of Perky Pet Co., creates first commercial hummingbird feeder.

1970s: Leon Gainesboro, founder of Opus, Inc., develops and introduces stick-on window feeders.

1972: Don Hyde, founder of Hyde Bird Feeder Co., creates thistle (niger) feeder.

1981: Jim Carpenter founds Wild Birds Unlimited. Wild Bird Centers follows in 1985, and Wild Bird Marketplace in 1990.

1985: C&S Products Co. starts manufacturing suet cakes.

A digital video camera focuses on a suet feeder and peanut feeder at the edge of Julia's patio.

peanut and suet feeders, and using a long cable, connected it to her computer. "I keep tabs on an active part of my FeederWatch site just by looking at an adjustable window on a portion of my computer screen. I see the downies and my favorite Carolina wrens at the suet and the nuthatches and maybe some surprise visitors at the peanut feeder, all moving about and feeding in the background while I'm typing away."

Not only does modern technology let Julia visually telecommute to her feeder site, but a Wing Song microphone system lets her eavesdrop on her feeder birds, bringing their calls and feeding sounds inside her house.

She attached a microphone to the porch awning in the middle of her main feeding area. "I can hear everything — munching, cracking, soft chip notes, even wing flutters. I can almost tell the sounds of red-breasted nuthatches pecking at the peanuts. When they say their *ank, ank!* there's no mistaking who's there. Those tiny birds are loud!" Julia says the microphone has opened a whole new world of feeder birding for her. "Often I'll hear sounds I didn't know the birds made. Goldfinches might be my favorite bird to listen to up close. Their little cheeps and seeps are incessant and so variable. It's like they're constantly talking to each other."

Julia says the microphones have also revealed birds that are in her yard but don't usually come to her feeders, including warblers and kinglets and a variety of sparrows and eastern towhees.

The rest of Julia's feeder site relies on nonelectronic bird-feeding tools. A gorp log and a suet sandwich feeder hang from a red pine. A peanut feeder hangs from the horizontal support pole of her porch awning. Five other feeders hang from metal poles planted just off her arrow-shaped slate patio.

The pole to the left of the arrow's point has a disposable thistle sock; the pole on the right supports suet and peanut feeders and, except when the grackles and starlings are in town, also includes a platform feeder. "This is a setup I've been working on since I started feeding birds here in 1989. I'm happy with it. I can see all of these feeders at once from my kitchen and computer room windows."

Julia fills her tube feeders with black-oil sunflower seed, nothing else. "I bought the grocery-store mix for a long time, before I knew much about feeding birds. The birds would throw out half of the seed. It was so frustrating." Julia says she could see the birds were eating mostly the black-oil sunflower seed, picking it out and tossing the rest. Then she discovered hardware and bird specialty stores selling bags of just black-oil sunflower seed. "I haven't bought mixed seed since."

She now buys only hulled black-oil sunflower seeds. "The shells made a mess. I'd have to carefully clean the slate patio surface and get in between cracks in the stone slabs. After a while, I said to myself, 'I'm not doing this.' So I pay more for the hulled seeds, but it's worth it."

A homemade gorp log with perches attached hangs from Julia's pine tree next to an Avian Aquatics Wood Bark Suet Sandwich feeder. Both are filled with her special lard, peanut butter, and pecan bird pudding (gorp). "It's a bit of a luxury to add the pecans, I realize. But the birds here really go for them." However, in early spring when the starlings and grackles return in their huge flocks, Julia takes the gorp log down and replaces it with an upside-down suet feeder. "Starlings and grackles can't get into it or the sandwich feeder to eat those expensive pecans."

A yellow-shafted (northern) flicker clings to the side of a sandwich feeder. A thick layer of gorp fills the two imitation wood-bark sides of the feeder. A woodpecker can reach all the gorp with its long tongue; starlings and grackles can't.

On one baffled pole, Julia hangs a Droll Yankees New Generation Peanut Feeder (filled with hulled sunflower seed); a platform feeder by local bird feeder craftsman Bill Craig; and a Vari-Craft Suet Feeder.

In another corner of her yard, Julia has a "fancy heated Duncraft birdbath. It was a generous gift," where the likes of titmice, sparrows, chickadees, nuthatches, and goldfinches find precious water in winter. The heating element is embedded in the large basin; all but the cord is out of sight. "Finding heated water when everything else is frozen must be such a relief for the birds. Adding water has made my entire yard more bird-friendly."

She says she hasn't done any special bird planting on her one-acre suburban yard. "I let the birds do the planting and they do a pretty good job." The property is full of all kinds of berry bushes, including mulberries that robins and starlings seem to relish in summer. There are yews and mature pines, various evergreens, some red maples, three silver maples, and "one huge copper beech." But it's the crab apple trees that "all the birds go crazy over. Towhees and robins stake out the big apple tree, going for the rotting fruit in mid-September."

Record-keeping is another satisfying aspect to watching birds for Julia. She says FeederWatching has been great because it "validated all these yard records I was already keeping. Scientists can really use my feeder bird counts." She enjoys comparing her records with those of others in bird computer news groups in the Northeast. Her personal yard records show an increase in woodpeckers: downies, hairies, red-bellieds, and flickers. "The suet disappears a lot faster now than it used to."

Her records show that her first-ever Carolina wren appeared at her suet feeders in August 1997. Soon after, while out watering the porch plants, Julia watered a pair of wrens. "They were roosting in the potted plant. To avoid that happening again, I created a special roosting site for them."

At a garage sale, she found a basket made of coconut husks that seemed just right. She filled it with sphagnum moss and silk greenery and hung it from her porch ceiling. "The wrens moved right in and have been there ever since."

Julia became curious about how they make it through western Pennsylvania winter nights. To find out how warm the roost gets, she attached a small camouflaged temperature probe inside the basket, connected it to a long cable, and started taking systematic readings.

What she discovered is that the birds give off a lot of heat. "When it is at or just below freezing, 30 to 35 degrees (F), the bird basket can get up to 65 to 70 degrees." One night the outside temperature registered 43 degrees; inside the basket, Julia recorded 80.9 degrees. She says she's calculated that the basket temperature stabilizes at 37.2 degrees higher than the outside temperature.

Julia says this experiment has whetted her interest in the winter roosting strategies of birds and she wants to learn more. "It's really fun to look out and see the Carolina wrens on the suet during the day, knowing they've had a cozy night before in the little coconut basket on my porch. These are birds I can track individually, and that's really satisfying."

A Carolina wren, one of a pair that roosts on Julia Pahountis-Opacic's porch, investigates a railing.

Rose Bray
Rural Arkansas "Hills and Hollers"

Rose Bray has lived in the hilly country of north-western Arkansas ever since marrying her husband, Reldon. Along with chickens and cattle, they have raised three boys there together. The hills are pastureland; the hollows, or "hollers," as they are called locally, are filled with cedars and deciduous trees and brush. There are two hollows near Rose's house. "That's where the birds roost in the evening," she says. "I can watch them settle in for the night."

Rose has been feeding birds for six years. Her motivation for starting was unusual, but her progress has been something that every experienced backyard birder will recognize. For those just beginning to attract birds, Rose is a crystal ball providing glimpses of a bird-feeding future.

"My husband's mother passed away about six years ago," Rose explains. "She loved birds, especially cardinals and wrens, and she fed them. I wanted to pass the tradition down to my grandchildren so they would enjoy birds and learn about them." Rose asked her husband to build one feeder for her.

The hopper feeder he built was placed in the backyard where Rose could watch it through the dining room window. "I filled it with a seed mixture that I got from a discount retailer, and I got birds!" And she enjoyed them. She also enjoyed her youngest granddaughter's excitement when she'd call out, "Nanny, there's three redbirds out there!"

After a time, Rose thought why not watch birds in the front yard? She bought her first thistle feeder, placed it in the front of the house, and watched the finches flock to it. Then she bought her first thistle sock. "The finches went crazy over that, so I bought a second one." And then, one after another, came a second hopper feeder, a platform feeder, and a suet feeder. "I had a little something for everybody," Rose recalls.

The whole process was an experiment. Try something, see how it works. Rose experiments with pudding mixtures and seeds, as well as feeders. "Make your backyard your own little science lab," she advises. "Have fun!" When she fed the different seeds in her mix separately, she found that some went uneaten. "The birds completely ignored a feeder filled with safflower seeds. I couldn't get any birds to eat it except in mixes." Grass seed was another experiment. "I had read that birds like grass seed, but when I put it out, they didn't eat it. I did get a nice patch of grass under the feeder, however."

Rose's latest yard addition for the birds is water in winter. She doesn't have an outside electrical outlet to power a heater that would keep the birdbath water from freezing. "And I have a dog that would chew the cord and electrocute himself if I did have one," she says. The answer was a Solar Sipper. It is a device made of black plastic that absorbs the sun's

A Solar Sipper by Happy Bird keeps water unfrozen for birds to drink at temperatures down to 20° F.

rays and keeps the water in it from freezing during the day at the temperatures she gets in Arkansas. It has a small hole on top that the birds drink from. "It didn't take them long to figure it out," says Rose. "They discovered it in about a day. They can't take a bath in it, but they do get a drink."

When one of Rose's dogwood trees fell down and had to be replaced, it started her thinking about planting for the birds. Interesting habitat experiments seem soon to follow. "I'm thinking about planting one or two more evergreens, something pretty, to give the birds more cover. And some berry-producing shrubs around the house would be nice, and..."

Brad Brockman
Desert Scrub in Tucson, Arizona

In the desert Southwest, there is one sure-fire bird attractant: water. Two Wild Birds Unlimited recirculating waterfall birdbaths under a palo verde tree are

Two southwestern specialties, a cactus wren and a male pyrrhuloxia, each find a Wild Birds Unlimited wire mesh feeder in Brad Brockman's yard to their liking.

the focal point of Brad Brockman's yard in the Catalina Mountain foothills.

Brad says some of his usual feeder birds have fallen into a bit of a routine. Typically, a few of them will first stop at a birdbath and then head to any one of three feeders close by. "I can look out at any time and see birds splashing around and tipping their heads back drinking. Unlike the feeders, where there is periodic scuffling over food, the baths are where all kinds of different species will just hang out together." Even the mockingbirds will bathe and drink with others in relative peace.

At his birdbaths, Brad sees many birds that are particular to this part of the arid Southwest — lesser goldfinches, pyrrhuloxias, cactus wrens, Gila woodpeckers, curve-billed thrashers, and Gambel's quail. Costa's and Anna's hummingbirds are year-round regulars.

As the owner of a Wild Birds Unlimited store, Brad tries out all sorts of feeders and feeder foods he sells or plans to sell. Consequently, his yard is full of nearly every commercial feeder type and thus a wide array of bird visitors.

There are some opportunistic relationships that have formed at his feeders. Brad says he's noticed some of the quail that visit his yard carefully watch for birds to arrive at his hanging feeders. As soon as a bird starts feeding, the quail scurry underneath the feeder to catch anything that falls.

Brad stops ground-feeding in spring. "It encouraged the doves and pigeons. Not that they aren't beautiful birds; it's just that in the large numbers I was getting, they become aggressive and create a nuisance." His mixed-seed feeders are surrounded

Lesser goldfinches share a Wild Birds Unlimited Copper Top Finch Feeder with house finches.

with wire guards. Smaller feeder birds gain access to the free food; the doves cannot. He also makes sure his seed blends contain no milo, millet, or cracked corn. "When I offered seed mixes with those foods, plenty of birds would just fling it to the ground as they tried to get to the sunflower seeds and chips." The flung-out discards were welcomed by the doves. "You have to understand birds' needs and preferences to try to control them. My strategy has worked pretty well the past couple of years."

Southwestern bird-feeding peculiarities include some pesky mammals. One is the peccary, or javelina, a small, dark gray, pig-like creature that Brad says can cause "almost as much destruction as a black bear." They roam in fearless herds, mostly at night but sometimes during the day, running over plants, feeders, anything in their way. They especially like peanuts and suet. Brad purposely keeps feeders elevated so food is out of their reach. "Otherwise, they would visit daily." One main reason his birdbaths are concrete is because javelinas can't easily destroy them.

Brad says what gives him the most satisfaction in his job is introducing someone to birds for the first time. "You can see people go through stages. They'll come into the store so excited about their feeder birds. Next time I see them, we'll talk about

A Cooper's hawk at one of Brad Brockman's recirculating birdbaths with a dripper. "Upon arrival, hawks tend to get the baths all to themselves," says Brad.

A female cardinal contemplates the next peanut to be taken. Arizona cardinals are larger than the races in the East.

the way birds live, their food, water, shelter, breeding, habitat needs. After a while, people go beyond the bird feeder and start caring about the whole environmental picture."

Feeding Birds in Small Spaces
Urban Areas Continent-Wide

Instead of bemoaning their lack of yard space, some urban FeederWatchers figure out creative ways to watch and feed their local birds. More often than not, they are rewarded for their efforts.

In busy suburban Santa Rosa, California, just 400 yards from a major interstate highway, Gail Roper bird-watches on her second-floor balcony, to which she has added some natural touches. "Alongside my feeders, I have strewn dead branches to resemble a wooded habitat." Vines even grow on some of the wood. The balcony habitat is completed with shelves and benches of living plants, including primroses, grapevine, and bougainvillea.

How well does this work? Gail's "yard list" is one any northern Californian would be proud of, including scrub-jays and Steller's jays, spotted and California towhees, and lesser and American goldfinches. Anna's hummingbirds are regulars.

Not only does she record golden-crowned, fox, and song sparrows, but she gets one unusual sparrow visitor to the West Coast. During the winter of 1999–2000, "my white-throated sparrow returned again. Fourth winter in a row!"

Gail offers three tube feeders filled with black-oil sunflower seed, one thistle sock, and a peanut feeder. "I scatter millet and cracked corn on the balcony itself for the sparrows, juncos, and towhees. One of the most fun birds to watch is the sparrows, which will skulk about in the brush pile and then

pop out onto the deck to eat. They are a constant delight."

There are plenty of unique challenges to balcony feeding — keeping seeds from falling to the patio below, for example. Gail has laid out 2-by-4s around the balcony edges, "which works."

Another second-floor balcony feeder, Dianne Taggart of Yaphank, Long Island, New York, covers her balcony floor with outdoor carpet and uses shell-less sunflower seeds to keep litter from dropping to her neighbors underneath. Even so, some seed bits do fall. She says every now and then, "to keep the peace," she'll go downstairs and sweep up her neighbor's patio.

Using hull-free sunflower seeds is an almost universal tip from FeederWatchers who live in small places. It is the seed that Karen Konoicki has switched to at her New York City fire escape site, which she calls her "little nature reserve." In addition to the house finches, mourning doves, and house sparrows that are regulars, Karen says her tube feeder has lured a couple of black-capped chickadees, a few tufted titmice, and some surprise visitors on a FeederWatch count day — a northern flicker and a white-throated sparrow.

Julia Hartman of Tuscaloosa, Alabama, has a little different situation. She feeds from the third floor of a University of Alabama office building. Plenty of birds have visited her Duncraft suction-cup window feeder in the seven years she has quietly been feeding birds, including "several generations of red-bellied woodpeckers."

Her office window feeding tip? "I put up reflecting film on the inside of the window so the birds don't get scared by the movements of my typing and telephone talking. It's not very aesthetically pleasing, but it works."

Jeanette Carson FeederWatches on her small plot at an RV campground in east-central Texas. "I get a good variety of birds," she says, "in spite of all the cats, dogs, vehicles, people, rules, and regulations."

Her best tips? "I keep my feeders as far apart as

A Condominium Without Birds ?

Residents in my condominium complex were notified that bird-feeding would no longer be allowed on the premises. Here's how I approached the board.

- *Thick bird-feeding information packets were prepared for each board member.*
- *Each was given a federal report that lists bird-watching as the second most popular recreational activity in the U.S.*
- *I showed that bird-feeding adds to the quality of condominium living.*
- *Negative questions were countered with straightforward answers.*
- *I volunteered to help draw up bird-feeding regulations, assist any resident with questions, and write birdfeeding articles for our condominium newsletter.*
- *I made my presentation in a friendly way.*

Result? The association rescinded the order. Success!

Jackie Gribble, Dublin, Ohio

A black-capped chickadee (above and opposite) samples the black-oil sunflower seeds from a tube feeder at the edge of Cristina Eisenberg's meadow. After enjoying the seeds, the little chickadees will fly across the meadow to feeders of suet and puddings. "They seem to love to make a circuit from feeder to feeder, over and over, and are very playful about it," says Cristina.

possible and at as many different heights as possible on the one tree at my site." Because "rules forbid planting anything in the ground," she has filled about 20 big, colorful, rope-handled, plastic storage tubs with a variety of bird-friendly plants. She has also trellised vines such as jasmine and different varieties of honeysuckle in tubs right next to each other. Jeanette says, "It has created a sort of vine wall. Works great. It is always full of sparrows and cardinals. I've even found some nests in there."

For a long time, Jeanette was confused why "the birds just ignored the big white concrete and terracotta birdbaths I got for them. Couldn't have cared less." One day, she discovered why. She saw birds bathing and drinking from a puddle created by the

A single tube feeder hangs in Karen Konicki's New York City "backyard."

constant drip of water from her RV's air-conditioning unit. "So I put a flowerpot dish on the ground there, and they splash around in that. They drink from my neighbor's air conditioner drips, too. We think it must be the movement and sound of running water that they really like."

Sometimes small-space bird-feeding doesn't work. Judith Togher of Long Island, New York, recalls her New York City efforts. "It is difficult there. For one thing, you get mostly pigeons. Some apartment leases or local ordinances forbid feeding birds. The second thing is, the neighbors complain. They don't appreciate the spring song of a house finch."

Karen Konicki's New York City fire escape feeder played a role in a little house finch courtship that included plenty of spring song. One day she watched a male fly to the tube feeder and grab a sunflower seed. He flew back to the railing, landed next to a female, and carefully set the seed down in front of himself. Then "he sang and sang and sang." The female fluttered a bit as if begging and then snatched the seed. "The moment she took the seed," remembers Karen, "the two flew off together. This was the sort of natural experience I had been yearning for."

Gail Roper muses that she's glad to live in a small northern California urban apartment because it affords her one of the ultimate bird-watching experiences — birding in bed. "Often I lie in bed and watch the birds come in with the dawn. What an incredible way to start the day."

Cristina Eisenberg
Northwest Montana Wilderness

Steve and Cristina Eisenberg's property sits on the slope of a Rocky Mountain peak, next to a chunk of the 54 million acres that President Clinton designat-

ed as roadless wilderness in 2000. Around 1970, an oval-shaped acre was cleared on what is now the Eisenberg property, and a log cabin constructed at the western end. Until then, as Cristina explains, "It was just land." Most of it still is.

The clearing has grown into a meadow lush with wildflowers and berry bushes in summer. Willows grow by the small stream that meanders down the slope. "Birds and four-footed animals alike are attracted to the meadow because there is food, water, and sunlight," Cristina says.

In winter, however, the meadow lies under several feet of snow, and only the tops of sapling spruces, firs, maples, and a few other trees and shrubs dot the windblown snowscape. The only natural foods available are the dried remnants of last summer's berries clinging to the bare branches of several bushes. These catch the attention of grouse and the occasional wandering flock of waxwings.

On a bleak winter day, a family of chickadees emerging from the dense forest for the first time into the meadow must be cheered by their discovery. There, protruding from the side of a larch tree at the edge of the meadow, is a block of suet bigger than the birds themselves. And a gorp log hangs from a young spruce tree a few wing flaps and a glide away from the suet. The gorp log is one of Steve's gifts to the birds. He drilled holes in a piece of deadfall selected from the forest floor and filled the cavities with a peanut butter gorp.

"We have placed three feeders around the meadow's perimeter in as natural a manner as possible," Cristina says, "situating them where there are leafy overhangs and lots of perches."

"I keep my feeding minimal," Cristina explains, "because I want to maintain a natural habitat. Putting out a smorgasbord in front of the dining room window might have a negative effect on the birds in the long run."

Steve, Cristina, and their children, Alana and Bianca, aren't bothered by the feeders being a distance from the cabin. "I spend a lot of time in my woods," says Cristina. "And the girls, who do the counting and tallying for FeederWatch as a home-school project, like to break up their sessions watching with binoculars out the dining room window by going outside. "I go out on snowshoes and count birds," says eight-year-old Bianca.

"The circuit we make of our feeders is the highlight of our count days," says Cristina. "Even on the coldest, snowiest days, we spend an hour or two in the meadow with our field notebooks and binoculars, looking and listening." The girls have learned much more than which birds come to a feeder. They proudly identify birds by their calls and their flight pattern. More important, "They have learned to be still and have discovered that there is a wealth of information they can pick up simply by looking and listening," says a pleased Cristina.

Toward the end of winter, the Eisenbergs added a fourth feeder, a hanging basket they fill with a commercial suet studded with seeds and nuts. "Our

Alana (l) **and Bianca** (r) **Eisenberg** "talking" with the chickadees at their feeder.

A red-breasted nuthatch inspects some peanut butter pudding spread onto a tree stump before a winter storm.

*MONTANA
BIRD COOKIES*

*Mix:
1 c. softened butter
$^1/_3$ c. sugar
1 egg
2 c. flour
$^1/_2$ c. chopped nuts,
optional*

Shape dough into walnut-sized balls and place on a cookie sheet. Press cookies $^1/_4$ inch thick. Use a straw to poke a hole in the middle of each cookie. Bake at 350° F about 15 minutes until lightly browned. When cool, thread yarn or string through hole and hang from tree.

woodpeckers tend to be shy," Cristina explains, "so we hung the basket from a tree about 100 feet into the woods and visit it on our rounds."

In addition to downy and hairy woodpeckers, pileated woodpeckers and Williamson's sapsuckers come to the meadow. With snow still packed deep on the ground, all four species have started to drill nesting cavities at the meadow's edge. At the east end of the meadow, nearly opposite the cabin, a much more dramatic nest is taking shape. A pair of golden eagles is beginning construction of their elaborate nesting platform in the crown of an old Douglas fir.

The golden eagles course the meadow throughout the winter, and Cristina thinks that she knows why. "Wild turkeys come to feed on seeds dropped by the little birds. The golden eagles are in turn attracted by the turkeys." A pair of short-eared owls and a great northern owl also hunt in the meadow.

Alana and Bianca have learned that the songbirds usually feed in distinct sessions of a half-hour or so apiece. Besides the dawn and dusk sessions, they usually appear twice more over the course of the day, but when a snowstorm is coming, the birds become very active. "They'll clean out the gorp log in about 15 minutes," says Cristina.

Winter storms can last two or three days, so Cristina and the girls spread extra gorp and seeds on the ground for the birds. Bianca helps her daddy make the extra gorp. Alana, seven years old, sometimes helps her mama make bird cookies. "They seem to enjoy the bird cookies," says Cristina, "and I do that as a little boost for them."

And the birds give a little boost back to the Eisenbergs. Alana will long remember the black-capped chickadee that was the first bird she identified on her own. She has her own drawing of it in the personal field guide she is creating from her observations and from information gleaned from her parents' field guides.

Bianca thinks all kids should be FeederWatchers. "It's fun! Do you know what a red-breasted nuthatch looks like? Well, I do because I'm a FeederWatcher."

Bryan Pearson
Iquauit, Baffin Island, Nunavut Territory

FeederWatching in extreme conditions is the norm for those living in the Far North.

The nearest tree to bed-and-breakfast owner Bryan Pearson's bird-feeding site is 600 miles south. With no trees, frozen ground, and Arctic temps that can reach –50° F or lower, he's had to develop a special feeding strategy: he throws stuff on the snow.

More precisely, Bryan buys grocery-store mixed seed on occasion, although it is expensive on Baffin Island, and tosses it, along with chunks of bread, meat, and dog food mixed with bacon fat, on the ground outside his back door. The birds that remain during the winter months find it and have a feast.

"I really only get a couple of species up here in the winter — on occasion, the redpolls (common and hoary) and regularly, the ravens. Still, they're extraordinary birds to watch."

A couple of winters ago, during raging winds and well-below-zero temperatures, Bryan saw a flock of 15 to 20 redpolls land at his feeding site. But they didn't spend much time eating. Instead, he watched them disappear into a snowdrift. "Moving backwards, they just wiggled their little bums until they were out of sight. How the hell do they do that?"

He says he really gets a kick out of watching the ubiquitous ravens. They regularly visit his feeding site and make the rounds of the community's dog food dishes too. It's a kind of feeder watching.

"We get a good laugh around here about how these ravens outwit the dogs," says Bryan. "They operate in families. They'll land near a tied-up dog and break into smaller groups. One group distracts the dog. They'll sit screaming at him at a distance about an inch or two longer than the dog's chain. The dog then races to get them, but his chain brings him to an agonizing halt. Whilst he goes nuts, the other ravens casually eat the dog's food or fly away with it." Once he watched a raven mercilessly pull his English spaniel's tail. Adding insult to injury, another bird grabbed all the dog's food.

Snow buntings are an omen of spring for Bryan Pearson when they return in late March.

Bryan says he always looks forward to late March because he knows more bird species will show up at his ground-feeding site, including his favorite snow buntings, along with Lapland longspurs, wheatears, and horned larks.

"It's just great to see them when they first return. I'll see them all summer, of course, but there's something special about having them at my site just as they've come back north."

Wendy Hellstern, Classroom FeederWatching in Utah's Rocky Mountain Foothills

Can you imagine being a student and having your teacher ask you to look out the window and watch birds? That's one of Wendy Hellstern's first instructions to her Greeneville Elementary fifth graders at the start of each school year. "We're lucky. Our feeding station is in a courtyard just outside the classroom. I get them going on bird identification right away by simply having them watch the birds that come to the feeders near our windows."

She says her students' observation skills get better immediately. "Some of them have never really noticed one bird from another. Suddenly they're figuring out differences between male and female goldfinches and then house sparrows and female house finches, which can be tricky at first. Because the classroom is working on bird I.D. together, everyone's learning curve goes out of sight."

Wendy makes sure students know which birds are coming to the feeders before they start keeping tabs on them. The first thing she does is show them the parts of the bird. "I put up a big overhead transparency from the Classroom FeederWatch curriculum that has bird parts labeled. Right away I have students use some of the language of ornithology. They'll refer to the 'wing bars' on a goldfinch, or the colorful 'rumps' of male house finches. Just using the specific vocabulary helps them observe finer details."

She says what often happens after just a couple of days of learning about birds is that students come into class with stories about the birds they've seen at home or on their way to school. "Real connections to the natural world start being made once students have even a little bit of bird knowledge."

The feeding site isn't limited to Wendy's fifth graders. "Actually, the whole school is involved in watching birds now. My class has put up bird identification posters in the faculty room and the library. Even the lunchroom cooks sometimes stop by to talk to us about the feeder birds."

To help fund the feeder site and obtain a dozen pairs of binoculars, Wendy has received grants from the local chapter of the National Audubon Society and the Utah Science Teachers Association. She has fund-raised for plants and had them donated too.

But the first year she tried FeederWatching with her students, they got no birds, zero feeder visits.

"It was so disappointing. There were brand-new feeders full of food, and we had lots of hopes and dreams about doing the project." Wendy says students learned their local birds anyway. "We dutifully sent in our 'no data' to FeederWatch. We also tried to figure out why the birds didn't like us."

The conclusion? "There wasn't any bird habitat. All that was out there was hard ground, a few patches of grass, and our seed-filled birdfeeders."

The second year of FeederWatching, some bushes and a birdbath were added to the courtyard. The feeders got a few birds. "We had house sparrows, goldfinches, and house finches. It was so exciting. Students learned those three species very well."

Year three of the courtyard's habitat enhancement has proven phenomenal. "We get so many different birds now; we even had a deer. Adding the plants has clearly demonstrated to all of us the importance of having natural food, water, and shelter for the birds and other animals."

There have been mysteries at the feeders too. "Once we had an odd little bird at the feeders. It was small and mostly white and wasn't in any of our field guides. I had the students draw it and describe it. We invited local birders and even some professional biologists to come by for a look at what students were calling the 'Hellstern bird.'"

She says students were impressed with the outside interest. "It was a great learning experience for all of us. I was pleased that students met others not from our school who care for birds." The strange bird was identified as a partial albino house finch.

Wendy also has been impressed with how the students have applied their feeder bird experiences.

Students in Wendy Hellstern's fifth grade class fill the feeders in their school courtyard. From their classroom windows, they can watch birds use the feeders.

Thousands of school-children are enrolled in an inquiry-based education curriculum derived from Project Feeder-Watch. Students do "real science" and also pursue their own questions, such as:
• What are the effects of adding mealworms or popcorn to our feeder site? by the Nassau Spackenkill School, Poughkeepsie, New York
• How close do different species of birds get to each other on a power line? by the Southwest Middle School, Orlando, Florida

The Greeneville Elementary School courtyard is no longer a typical bare school playground. "A local nursery gave us Arctic willows, aspen, chokeberry, dogwood, and a wide array of flowers," says Wendy. "Parents have been great too, sharing their plants, especially flowers, and bringing in logs to sit on, picnic tables, and boulders."

"Our local newspaper carried a story with a photograph that was labeled 'sparrow.' The bird was really a house finch. My students noticed that and jumped all over it. They wrote the newspaper and got a correction printed. Talk about knowledge being empowering."

Stuart and Mary Houston
Urban Lot in Saskatoon, Saskatchewan

Stuart and Mary Houston have only a small urban backyard in which to indulge their love of birds, but do they ever make the most of it! In the winter of 1999–2000, they not only fed numerous birds but caught and banded 1,442 redpolls.

Both the Houstons are licensed banders. All the feeders, traps, and a birdbath are outside their dining room window. The feeders hang from a mountain ash tree and include a unique black-oil sunflower seed feeder constructed from a honeybee shipping case. A suet bag also adorns the tree, and the tree itself provides many clusters of red mountain ash berries at its top for the birds.

The honeybee-shipping-case bird feeder came from the local nature society. It is a totally enclosed box feeder that the birds must enter through a 1¼-inch hole, like the hole in a birdhouse. The small diameter keeps out the sparrows but lets in the chickadees and red-breasted nuthatches. "It makes a great feeder," says Mary, "and keeps the seed from spilling on the ground."

There is no thistle feeder hanging from the Houstons' mountain ash, at least not when redpolls are present. Niger seed is placed in seven traps and spread on the table in front of them.

Contrary to what some Americans might believe, Saskatoon is 600 miles south of the redpoll's Arctic nesting range. Redpolls begin arriving in mid-February and depart in April. Stuart says that more came in 2000 than anybody in Saskatchewan can ever remember seeing. "They were the most common bird at local feeders," Stuart exclaims, "and they came a month early. Clearly they were starved out of the Arctic."

Each trap has a front panel that raises and rests on a catch that is connected to a treadle covering the front third of the floor. When a redpoll walks on the treadle, its weight releases the catch and the door closes. Redpolls are so light and shuffle along so peacefully that it sometimes takes two of them to trip the catch.

"We don't trap in really cold weather, when the added stress might endanger them," Mary says. The redpolls are docile and don't seem at all stressed by trapping or handling. Where they come from, few ever encounter humans, and they are not frightened by people. "I am able to reach in the trap with my right hand," Mary says, "and easily slip my middle and index fingers over a redpoll's head." She then gently closes her hand over the quiet, unresisting bird and removes it from the trap.

Mary then transfers the bird to her left hand so that she can attach the band, actually a prenumbered split ring, with her right. She spreads the ring open with a pair of bander's pliers, slips it deftly over the bird's leg, and closes it. Job done.

Well, almost. Each bird also gets its wing chord (the distance from the bend of the wing to the tip) measured and gets weighed before being released.

"Wing chord length is the most common measurement of a bird's size," Stuart says. "In redpolls, it can help separate young males from females." Males don't get their rosy breasts until their second winter. In their first winter, they look like the dull brown females. "If the wing chord is long, the bird is more likely to be a male, although there is some size overlap."

Mary says the little females will usually weigh 13 to 15 grams. Most males run 16 to 18 grams. (It takes a little more than 28 grams to equal an ounce.) "When the birds first arrive, there are few that weigh more than 14 or 15 grams, but they quickly fatten up."

Purple finches, pine siskins, juncos, and others are occasionally trapped. They get banded too. The Houstons color-banded some local black-capped chickadees and, following their movements, discovered they moved hardly more than one city block!

Stuart has tips for bird-watchers searching through a flock of common redpolls for the elusive hoary redpoll. Of the 1,442 redpolls Mary and he banded in 2000, they identified 11 as hoaries, which is less than 1.3 percent of all the redpolls that they have averaged over the years. Stuart makes it clear that it is not always easy to separate a hoary from a common redpoll even with the bird in hand. "Some banders might have called only 6 or 7 of the birds hoaries," Stuart explains. "Others would have reported maybe 14 or 15 hoaries. On

A common redpoll rests calmly as Mary Houston attaches a band to its leg.

marginal birds, Mary and I frequently call each other and say, 'Hey, look at this one.'"

"First thing is to look at the head and upper body," Stuart advises. "Most common redpolls are heavily marked. Hoaries are noticeably whiter, with light markings on a white background. If the rump is pure white, you know you have a hoary, but some hoaries have a few dark streaks on the rump. Check the undertail coverts. They must be immaculately white if it is to be called a hoary."

What makes a birder become a bander? It happened to Stuart in 1943 when he was a 15-year-old in his first year of banding. Blue-winged teal that he had banded in Saskatchewan were recovered in faraway Cuba, Jamaica, and the Dominican Republic. "That'll turn a young guy on and hook him for life."

And what a life it has been. Stuart is 72 and still very active as the 21st century begins. In the 20th century, he and Mary banded over 117,000 birds of 202 species — all in Saskatchewan. He has had the second largest number of recoveries of all private banders, ever.

Seven traps containing redpolls waiting to be banded sit on a feeding table outside the Houstons' windows.

Why Band?

Banding reveals information about a bird's movements. It is the way scientists determine, among other things, whether migrants return to the same nesting or wintering site each year. But information is normally gathered in only those few cases when a band is recovered from a dead bird or a bird is trapped a second time. Although he has had an amazing recovery rate, so far, the only recovery of redpolls banded by the Houstons has been recaptures by Al Smith, Saskatoon's only other small-bird bander. He lives three miles away from the Houstons. But even those short-distance recaptures yield information. By analyzing the rates of recapture, the Houstons can estimate that there were between 10,000 and 50,000 redpolls in Saskatoon alone in the winter of 2000.

In November 1960, a common tern he banded was recovered in the Cook Islands, 2,000 miles south of Hawaii. "Until then, no one had a clue about common tern migration," says Stuart. "It was one of my most rewarding recoveries."

Ilse Gebhard
Rural Southwest Michigan

For FeederWatchers, relocating is more than getting adjusted to a new house and neighbors. There is the thrilling expectation of seeing new birds, alternating with a lurking fear that few birds will ever come to the new yard. Ilse Gebhard didn't really expect to see much change in her feeder visitors because she and her husband, Russ Schipper, were moving only 8 miles, from one part of Kalamazoo, Michigan, to another.

Surprise, surprise. "This winter (1999–2000) on one FeederWatch count day, I recorded 43 tree sparrows at our new place. On another count day, I saw 52!" Ilse enthuses. "At our old place, we would get a few tree sparrows maybe once or twice a year. Here we had large flocks all of January and February, with record numbers on the days it was snowing or bitter cold."

Success proved to have little to do with distance traveled and a lot to do with local habitat. The old home was set in hickory-oak woods. The new home enjoys a variety of habitats that attract birds, including open fields, a lot of scrub and shrubby areas, and an area of second-growth woods "with a lot of dead American elms that the woodpeckers like," Ilse explains. There are spruce and white cedars in the yard that the birds use for cover, and even a small stream and a pond.

"We use the same feeders and have pretty much the same feeder setup, but the only birds I see fewer of are blue jays and mourning doves," Ilse says of her new yard. Squirrels also are scarcer. "They were a problem when we lived near all the oaks.

Black netting provides positive protection for the birds against window strikes.

We strung wire between three poles and hung the feeders from the wire." Squirrels, she discovered, will walk on a wire. "We eventually had to put baffles on the posts and on the wire to defeat the squirrels."

The open habitat around the new home also affects the visiting hawks. "We haven't seen much feather evidence of kills here," states Ilse. At her old house, the sharp-shinned and Cooper's hawks hid in the trees to ambush the songbirds. At the new house, they are forced to use a different attack style with a lower rate of success. "They zoom over the house and down into the feeder area," Ilse explains.

The battery of feeders and choice of foods that Ilse employs are conventional, for the most part. One special device is a ground shelter that Russ made (see photo, lower left). When Ilse scatters millet on the ground, she also spreads some under the shelter. "The birds aren't real crazy about the shelter because of the low, angled roof and the three closed sides. I think they feel unsafe with only one side open should a hawk show up." But when snow falls and the seeds on the exposed ground are buried, the birds flock to the shelter. "There is always food in the open under there," Ilse explains.

Ilse provided a shallow bath with water, heated in winter, at her old place. It was often used. At her new home, she has stopped putting out water. "The birds didn't use it. Here they use the pond and the stream where it remains open and unfrozen. The stream tumbles over some rocks that form a small dam, and the sound of the running water seems to attract the birds."

Because they have a pond, Ilse and Russ put up nesting boxes for wood ducks in the summer. The boxes were left in place over the winter, and screech-owls unexpectedly took them over for roosting.

The feeders employed by Ilse and Russ are arranged on poles and wires. A ground shelter at left provides a snow-free ground-feeding area during storms.

"This winter we have one screech-owl, and we can sometimes see his gray face peeking out of the hole in the box," says Ilse. "Last year we had two screech-owls playing 'musical boxes' in the three wood duck boxes we had up." Ilse seldom sees screech-owls outside the roosting boxes — they don't emerge until it is nearly dark — but she often hears their whinnying calls at night.

Window strikes have been a discouraging part of feeding birds for Ilse at both locations. She and Russ tried silhouettes of owls on the windows. That didn't work. Fluttering streamers hanging in front of the windows didn't seem to help much either. They finally found the solution with black ⅝-inch mesh netting, the kind sold for placing over fruit trees and shrubs for protection from birds.

"It isn't very attractive, but it is effective," claims Ilse. "We suspend it from the eaves, and it hangs about one foot out from the window." The bottom is anchored to the ground. "We have also taped the netting directly over some windows. It isn't quite as effective that way, but it helps."

Ilse and Russ feed birds from mid-October to mid-May. "Part of our motivation is trying to help birds through the winter, but I don't know if they need it," she says. She and Russ enjoy watching them, of course, and Ilse states, "We like the scientific aspect. On my first FeederWatch day in each period, I monitor very intently from 8 to 11 a.m."

Steve Tracy
Wooded Lot in Gastonia, North Carolina

In January 2000, Steve Tracy reported 67 cardinals on his FeederWatch count — the FeederWatcher record for the year. "It was during a snowstorm," Steve recalls. "If it is not snowing, I rarely get over 40 at a time, usually less than 30."

Thirty cardinals? For all but a handful of Feeder-Watchers, any count over 30 at one time would be a yard record and a day to remember forever. So how does Steve do it? Well, his first smart decision was to buy a lot in wooded lowlands at the core of the cardinal's historical southeastern range.

"The things that interested me about this house were the mature trees and the wetlands in the backyard," says Steve. And if cardinals could talk, that's what they would say about Steve's property as well. The house sits near the front of the lot. In the back, there is a 20-foot drop to a marsh and a creek where there is dense cover. Red maples, white and red oaks, hickories, and many other mature deciduous trees provide canopy.

"Except for the marsh, the back was nearly all lawn when I moved in," says Steve. Since then, he has mulched about one-third of it and planted berry-producing native plants for the birds — blueberries, serviceberries, chokeberries, deciduous holly, wax myrtle, Oregon grape, and arrowwood viburnum.

A large hopper feeder protected by a cylindrical baffle in Steve Tracy's backyard holds mixed seeds. A common grackle enjoys a sample.

Steve got a little divine help in creating his cardinal oasis when Hurricane Hugo roared through Gastonia in 1989, opening up what was then a very closed canopy. However, his cardinal success is due ultimately to his feeding strategy. He doesn't cluster his feeders near a window. "I spread feeders out around the perimeter of the yard to take maximum advantage of the abundant natural cover available."

Avoiding a central feeding area also helps Steve combat the grackle problem. Grackles aren't as attracted to the small amounts of seed that fall under each feeder as they are to seed broadcast over a larger area. Yet his desired ground-feeders, such as white-throated sparrows, song sparrows, and juncos, find all the seed they want spilled under his feeders.

Although Steve attracts record numbers of cardinals (mourning doves also), his main intent is to bring in as many different species as possible rather than huge numbers of any one species. By the end of the 1999–2000 FeederWatch season, his yard list totaled 121 species. To attract the widest variety of birds, he provides simple advice: "Get a variety of feeders and offer a variety of foods."

Steve's own array of feeders and foods begins at the south end of his yard with a 4-by-4 post that supports a large hopper feeder holding 25 pounds of mixed seeds. He prepares his own seed mix in a 5-gallon bucket. "I add a lot of black-oil sunflower seed and some split peanuts to a commercial mix."

On a nearby post is a fly-through feeder filled with safflower seed. Steve also keeps a hopper feeder filled with safflower. "Safflower keeps the grackles and squirrels away," says Steve. His cardinals love it, and he says it attracts many other birds, such as titmice, chickadees, Carolina wrens, and nuthatches. "I have seen 12 purple finches feeding on safflower at one time. White-throated sparrows and wild mallards eat any that falls to the ground.

"Mallards come in late winter when the water level in the creek rises, and they eat almost anything I put out," says Steve. "They stop coming in early July after the ducklings are grown." He sometimes sees other wild ducks in his creek, but they don't come to his feeders like the mallards.

Spaced along the eastern perimeter of the yard are two hopper feeders with counterweights for defeating squirrels. "I have a lot of squirrels and use baffles on most of my poles," Steve says.

Four tube feeders are spaced around the perimeter of the yard in winter. Three are filled with niger seed; the fourth contains sunflower meats. "They pull in the finches and occasional pine siskin," says Steve. At the north end of the yard — the natural area — a mesh feeder hangs from one arm of a double shepherd's hook. "It was built for peanuts, but I keep it filled with black-oil sunflower seeds." The other arm of the shepherd's hook holds a suet feeder. "It was a regular stop for a ruby-crowned kinglet and a pine warbler this winter," Steve recalls.

To get the largest variety of birds, Steve keeps a bluebird feeder stocked with about 50 mealworms

each day. "I also put cups of mealworms on top of two posts that hold bluebird boxes." Bluebirds have yet to use Steve's boxes and rarely come for mealworms, but Carolina wrens, titmice, and chickadees enjoy the treat, he says. "One robin, one blue jay, and one red-bellied woodpecker also discovered the cups on the posts and returned regularly." Steve expects bluebirds to accept his hospitality soon.

His latest feeder is a gorp log. It has been a predictable success with the woodpeckers, among others. But he has one feeder that has yet to receive a single visitor, although it has been up for two winters. "I put a hummingbird feeder in a side yard outside our bedroom window, hoping to attract a western vagrant hummingbird."

Other yards in the Carolinas have hosted rare overwintering hummers from the West, and Steve sees no reason why a lost hummer shouldn't find his yard. He has attracted other rare birds from the West that migrated east rather than south to the tropics. "On January 16, 1999, I saw a western tanager at my large hopper feeder." The tanager returned for two more visits, and on the last visit, it was seen and confirmed by one of Steve's fellow birders.

Shelia and Katie Arnold
Cape Cod, Between the Ocean and the Bay

"I started with one feeder, then I had to have another one to share with the squirrels, then I had to have another one, and, well, I'm now up to over a dozen different feeders."

The bird feeders in Shelia Arnold's Cape Cod backyard began multiplying in 1995 when she and her family moved to the tree-filled half-acre site from their city home in Connecticut. Ever since then, Shelia has been bird-watching and "bird-scaping." Along the way, her teenage daughter, Katie, joined her.

Shelia's curiosity about birds transformed her life as well as her yard. "I couldn't watch the birds enough." She enrolled in an art class to help improve bird identification skills. "Drawing birds is absolutely the best way to learn them." She started a bird life list. "It's up to 89."

Brush piles were created for the birds. Water was added with birds in mind: four pedestal birdbaths, three hanging birdbaths, and a pond "that I put in myself." Then Shelia was introduced to the idea of bird-scaping.

"That was it. I had to plant for my birds." What went in the ground first were holly, viburnum, and cotoneasters. Next came dogwoods, then pear and apple trees. There are eight small perennial gardens around the house full of bird-favored flowers that Shelia lets go to seed: bee balm, coneflower, globe thistle. Shelia says the bird-scaping is working.

"In January, big flocks of robins show up. As many as 150 of them will cover my holly and viburnum. In one weekend, they can clean out all

The northern end of Steve Tracy's backyard in early spring, with feeders dotted along the perimeter. To the right, a hopper feeder holds safflower. Left of the swingset is a green counterweighted hopper feeder. At the far left, a bluebird box (home of a titmouse family) is mounted on a post with a cup of mealworms on top.

those red berries. It's a great sight."

The focal point of the Arnolds' bird-feeding site is a large homemade "feeder log." "As early as the first winter we had it, 20 or so blue jays claimed the log as theirs during certain times of the day. They would feast in one long row," all of them, that is, except an "alpha-acting blue jay," noticed by young Katie Arnold.

"This one blue jay has to have the log all to itself. It bullies the other jays and makes them wait to eat. But the moment it flies away, the others zoom in for food, *if* there is anything left."

In addition to the feeder log, birds in the Arnolds' yard can choose from an array of metal hanging feeders. Shelia fills certain feeders with a single type of seed — niger in one, striped sunflower seeds in another, sunflower hearts in yet another. In some feeders, she'll offer mixed seed. What Shelia doesn't serve at all are black-oil sunflower seeds in the shell. "The hulls just ruin the bird plants around the feeders."

Puddings are offered too, a mix of peanut butter with bacon fat and a little seed. Shelia and Katie spread the pudding mixture (gorp) in pine cones and then hang the cones on trees around the yard. "Most of our 'regulars' relish the gorp, but not our house sparrows. Even orioles and catbirds make gorp stops."

More likely to be found back at the feeder log than at the pudding are woodpeckers. Shelia says, "It's really funny. The downy and hairy woodpeckers and even the flickers and red-bellieds are constantly pecking under the feeder log and ranging over the wooden tripod legs."

During Shelia's first winter of watching birds in her Cape Cod yard, about all she got as regulars were blue jays. "There were six, and I could tell them apart by their coloring. So I named them. It helped me watch them more closely." Then one day a Cooper's hawk appeared on a branch near the bird feeders.

"I was marveling at the hawk's beauty when, whoosh! It swooped up Ralph. I was going, 'Oh-my-god, Ralph!' A couple of days later it was Alice, then Fred, then Ethyl. Within a few weeks, all of my blue jays had been eaten."

As devastating as Shelia says the experience was for her, by the same time next year, "I had 20 regular blue jays feeding. The hawk didn't dent the population." These days the hawk comes only once in a while, and Shelia says, "I've grown to realize it is a kind of pest, but it has to eat too. It is amazing to watch."

Shelia deals with some other bird pests by being especially kind. During spring and fall migration, when flocks of several hundred red-winged blackbirds, common grackles, and starlings descend, she puts up a special square platform feeder for them.

"It is made simply of screens and 2-by-4s and

The blue jays' favorite feeder in Shelia Arnold's yard is a split-log platform set atop a tree trunk that branches to form a tripod.

sits about 5 feet off the ground. I fill the screen with seed, and the birds go to the platform feeder instead of my regular feeders." Shelia says the blackbirds don't stay long, moving on in just two to three weeks. After they leave, she dismantles the platform until the next blackbird migration.

Shelia and Katie both say all the bird-watching they've done has changed the way they look at the world. Katie, who aspires to be a writer someday, says watching birds has helped her develop good observation skills. "I find that in everything I do now, I pay closer attention to all the little things."

Marilyn Hardy
Urban Lot on Seattle's Lake Washington
Life-long bird-watcher Marilyn Hardy doesn't mind confessing, "Birds run my life." Because of the birds,

Marilyn Hardy's backyard is terraced with plants that provide food and cover for the many birds that visit her feeders.

A deck overlooking Marilyn Hardy's backyard on Lake Washington is patrolled by a favorite crow looking for treats.

her Pacific Northwest yard is classified a National Wildlife Federation backyard habitat. Because of the birds, she has yet another reason to travel the world. Because of the birds, her days often have a bird focus to them. "Let's face it. I finagle my time so I can watch birds do what they do. I've been hooked since I was a kid."

When laid up sick for a while in Milwaukee, young Marilyn got her parents to throw bread crumbs to city birds in the vacant lot next door. She would sit at her bedroom window and watch the feeding frenzies. At age 11, she got more serious about bird study. "I trotted down to the local museum and introduced myself to the bird curator as a 'girl who wants to know everything about birds.' That kind gentleman became my mentor." She's been a birder ever since.

Now she watches the feeding frenzies of birds on another small urban lot, her backyard, only this one is overflowing with bird-friendly plants and located right across from Lake Washington and next to a strip of parkland. "It's a great space for birds, really. I feed them. I plant for them. They reward me with their presence."

Her deck and the feeders attached to it make up Marilyn's FeederWatch site, all of which she can see from her dining room. "On a FeederWatch count day, you can find me sitting at the table here, doors wide open, watching the birds. Sometimes they fly in here and watch me! I've had chickadees and house finches on my chairs, in my jade plant. It's extra excitement for me and my old cat."

Marilyn puts shelled peanuts on the deck railing for the Steller's jays and a favorite crow she affectionately calls The Hulk. "He's my alpha crow. He

always flies to the roof with the peanuts and proceeds to make a loud ruckus when he's messing around up there eating them." Ground-feeding birds such as juncos and song sparrows fly up to get mixed seed Marilyn scatters on the deck floor. The winter population of juncos in particular helps her out with a "piggy pine siskin" problem.

"I swear that my pine siskins, who commandeer the nylon thistle socks, pick just one seed out of six to eat. They toss the rest, which makes for an expensive mess. Niger seed isn't cheap. At least the juncos benefit by eating it all up."

The two nylon mesh thistle socks hang from the deck roof on each side of a small cylindrical hummingbird feeder, a configuration that has made for some interesting avian encounters. The feisty Anna's hummers that remain in her yard year-round don't let the siskins perch on their sugar feeder for long. And they have no compassion for sleeping house finches, either. "Early one morning, I noticed a house finch asleep on top of the hummer feeder. As soon as the male Anna's arrived for his first sugary sip of the day, he tried to knock the house finch off. They both went at it, wings out, beaks open. It was a sight."

The roof also supports a suet feeder, and attached to the outer edge of the deck railings are two swinging metal arms with a large squirrel-guarded tube feeder hanging from each. At these she gets a variety of finches — house finches in all the colors, from pale yellow to deep scarlet, pine siskins, goldfinches, and occasionally evening grosbeaks.

Her front yard is really a small courtyard with another bird-watching area. In the middle of the courtyard's brick terrace is a recirculating water fountain with a two-tiered birdbath. This is where the front yard action is. "I call this my 'bird spa.' I'll get robins, house sparrows, a dozen house finches, and chickadees, who like hanging around the scalloped edges where it's a little shallower."

Feeders hang in the front yard also, but it's bird plantings to which Marilyn attributes her increasingly diverse bird population. She also believes in letting almost everything go to seed.

"I tend to overplant. After planting this and that for the past 15 years, I've got stuff all over the place. I don't do much fall cleanup, which makes my ground-feeders especially happy. I'll see the towhees and song sparrows searching for insects in the leftover leaf mulch all year long." Her latest plant additions include the berry-producing red-flowering currant and seed-bearing coneflowers and cosmos. "Birds here love the cosmos." She's also added delphiniums and larkspurs for the hummers and maintains fuchsias and verbena for them too.

Among the other plants that don't get cleaned up are old-style roses in the backyard. "I let my roses develop rose hips. This pleases the chickadees.

They work these over for hours, looking for bugs and small seeds."

Marilyn gets avian help controlling gray squirrels and other pests like the Norway rats that sometimes live in her rock retaining wall and the "nuisance birds" that show up at her feeders. "The local red-tail hawk is my best rodent control. One of the peregrines who nests downtown, along with a local merlin, keep the pigeons in balance, and the sharpies and Cooper's hawks go after my house sparrows on a regular basis. I'm grateful to them all."

One day, having just refilled one of her hopper feeders, Marilyn walked back to shoo away an "unbelievably bold" gray squirrel. "Suddenly there was this huge shadow that the squirrel and I noticed at the same time."

An adult bald eagle swooped down, grabbed the squirrel by the back with its talons, and dropped it. The injured squirrel shot off under the deck. "The squirrel's wound turned into a wedge-shaped scar. From then on, I could keep track of the less-adventuresome Scar's whereabouts around my feeders."

It is that sort of excitement that keeps Marilyn glued to her feeder areas. "There's always a show going on here." She says the often gray and drizzly Seattle winter weather doesn't seem to lessen her feeder birds' activities. "The rain doesn't bother them or me. We all live with it."

Kathie Satterfield
San Diego Suburbs, Overlooking a Canyon

"In 1996, I pulled up every single plant in my yard. It was more work than I'd ever imagined but has been worth all the dimes and energy I spent."

Collaborating with a local native-plants landscaper, Kathie Satterfield replaced all of the plants at her previously owned home with those that are indigenous to the southern California area where she lives.

"I used to get four or five regular bird species here — house finches, mourning doves, scrub-jays, and towhees. My current yard list is up to 56 different kinds of birds. The plants and my feeders have made all the difference in the world in a relatively short time."

The plants provide both food and shelter for birds. Kathie credits five of them in particular for their bird-friendliness.

California lilac: "An insect magnet. The bushtits nest in here. When the beautiful purple flowers go to seed, towhees, goldfinches, house finches, and song sparrows are all over them."

Toyon, an evergreen, also known as the Hollywood bush: "The waxwings and the mockingbirds go wild over the red autumn berries."

Mexican elderberry: "Finches, mockingbirds, orioles love all of it — berries, flowers, and seeds."

Evening primrose: "When this goes to seed, it is covered in goldfinches."

California fuchsia: "Beautiful orange to red flowers. This plant comes with a hummer guarantee."

Kathie's FeederWatching takes place in a window-filled room with a view of her feeders and birdbath, overlooking a protected canyon park. "My two indoor cats and I curl up in my big chair and watch the birds together. I even keep window feeder bird lists for my cats. They've seen house finches, mourning doves, California towhees…"

The birdbath pond is located "next to one of the California lilacs to give the shier birds plenty of nearby cover." Not only do plenty of feeder and non-feeder birds visit the birdbath, but mammals such as

On the viewing window overlooking her "easy-to-install" Avian Aquatics recirculating bird bath, Kathie has mounted a tray and a suet feeder, which allow for up-close bird observations by her and the two cats that join her for FeederWatching.

gray foxes and coyotes show up too. The sound of running water made by the waterfall in the creek attracts birds and mammals, and the shallow pond is hard for animals in southern California to pass up.

Kathie says she was especially thankful she had her birdbath when, several years ago, a flock of two dozen red crossbills descended, landing in her birdbath all at once. "It is one of my most incredible bird memories." The crossbills were not there on a FeederWatch day, of course, but plenty of other birds make those days memorable too, she says.

The majority of Kathie's seed and suet feeders are located on or under a 75-foot-tall pine. "This tree is so important to my feeding site. It's a great place for my feeders and provides good shelter for birds from rain, wind, and hawks. Sharp-shinned, Cooper's, and kestrels are always on the hunt."

On one of the pine's lower branches hangs two-feeders-in-one. Attached to a mesh-style peanut feeder is a wooden suet feeder with perches. "The peanut feeder gets shelled peanuts, which is a favorite of the scrub-jays." The feeder is promoted as a woodpecker feeder, "but the only woodpeckers we get around here are Nuttall's, and they are not the least bit interested in my feeders."

The suet feeder that piggybacks onto the peanut feeder was purchased with one particular bird species in mind. "I fill the suet feeder with 'Bird Bug Bite,' Wild Birds Unlimited's suet. My Bewick's wrens love it."

Other feeders under the pine include a sunflower feeder mounted on a pole, similar to the wire-mesh peanut feeder. On the same pole is a painted metal tube feeder filled with more hulled sunflower seeds. Next to the sunflower feeders, a pole-supported Wild Birds Unlimited wood and Plexiglas hopper-style feeder offers a no-mess mix of hulled sunflower, safflower, and millet. This food is a hit with

Cascaded feeders hold shelled peanuts (top) and commercial suet cakes (bottom).

all the finches, sparrows, and grosbeaks.

An open tray feeder mounted high on a pole serves up a blend of red and white millet with hulled sunflower seed and is a favorite of mourning doves, towhees, and thrashers, but because it is up so high, it isn't a favorite of squirrels. Kathie considers this feeder one of her "squirrel success stories."

Ground squirrels go for the tray feeder, which sits about a foot off the ground, but so do white-crowned sparrows, golden-crowned sparrows, and California thrashers. For the ground-feeders, Kathie offers the same Wild Birds Unlimited millet and sunflower blend she uses in her above-ground tray feeder. Unwittingly, from the ground tray feeder, she once served a mouse. "I looked out one day to see a mouse who'd been feeding there picked up and carried away by a scrub-jay."

In addition to creating less mess, Kathie offers hulled sunflower seed for another reason: she doesn't want to buy the shell. Hulled sunflower seeds costs a bit more, but "in the long run, they really are a better bargain."

Kathie didn't know much about birds until she got laid off from her corporate accounting job. She decided to take a six-week training course at a local park, where she became a docent and learned about the natural world around her. "I started leading plant walks, bird walks. It changed my life totally." She became a birder, a FeederWatcher, a Wild Birds Unlimited store owner, and an author on southern California birds and native plants.

"I have gone from wanting to leave my home here in San Diego County for someplace greener to falling in love with the habitats here and never wanting to leave. My personal mission now is to open as many other eyes as I can to the wonders and the birds of their own backyard."

Under a large, sheltering pine tree (trunk at left) stand a battery of Kathie's feeders. The feeder tray is squirrel-friendly and also serves the occasional rabbit.

Raiders of the Unprotected Feeders:
All the Furry Freeloaders

"One of my earliest mistakes was not considering that anything other than birds would be interested in my feeder food," says Jane Calabria of Downington, Pennsylvania. If you are going to feed birds, you are going to feed other wildlife too, and you just never know who is going to show up.

More than 80 different species of mammals have been reported raiding FeederWatchers' feeding sites. They come in all sizes, from white-footed mice to moose and bear. In Texas, you might get armadillos; in Arizona, javelinas. The most frequent feeder raider? Is there any doubt?

Nearly 80 percent of eastern FeederWatchers report visits from eastern gray squirrels. Western grays show up at just under half of the feeders in West Coast regions.

If an average gray squirrel can jump 3 to 4 feet straight up, 10 to 12 feet from a sideways launch, and drop 15 feet straight down, clinging to the place it lands, where can you best locate feeders so they are out of the reach of these jumping masters? The answer for many people — nowhere.

"Squirrels are smart," concedes Dick Meyers of New Jersey. "They are like computer hackers. I can appreciate how good they are at what they do."

Dogs can help control squirrels and other raiders. "No squirrel has ever gotten to my feeders," says Jeanne Eberle of Libertytown, Maryland. "I think having a big dog at the bottom of the porch where I have my birdfeeders helps. He is an old dog and he does not like squirrels."

Often a FeederWatcher, tired of wars with the furry ones, will offer a truce. "Negotiation is the best policy," says one squirrel-savvy FeederWatcher, "or you end up feeling like Wile E. Coyote with his Acme gadgets." Janet Maynard of Hershey, Pennsylvania, makes a compromise by distracting them from the birdfeeders with a feeder just for them. "As long as I keep the tray feeder by 'their tree' full of sunflower seeds, squirrels leave the other feeders alone."

A Peabody, Massachusetts, FeederWatcher who lives in an urban area says, "Squirrels are the only wildlife I regularly get to see. After counting dozens of pigeons and house sparrows for FeederWatch, the squirrels are a welcome sight. I feed them peanuts every day."

At nearly every wild bird store, there is a section of **feeders and foods** just for squirrels. Feeders range from a simple snack box (shown, p. 33) to gizmos like spinning wheels of corn and nut-filled boxes they have to "engineer" to open. Ron Piper of Burlington, Iowa, gives his squirrels their own snack box "away from the other feeders. They open the lid and snack all the time."

Corn on the cob is what most FeederWatchers set out for squirrels. Black-oilers are what the rav-

A whirligig with ears of corn and a rest to sit on while eating — what more could a gray squirrel want?

enous rodents often prefer if they can get to them easily. Peanuts are popular treats.

Squirrels will cart off a whole corn cob if it is not nailed down, and Jane Blumenthal in Falls Church, Virginia, advises, "You need a screw rather than a nail. Squirrels can pull a cob off a nail, but not so easily off a screw."

In Connecticut, Merle Turkington uses a screw with an eye. The corn is then hung from a tree by a chain connected to the eye. "The squirrels will hang on the cob and eat. It's fun to watch and a lot cheaper than one of the wooden corn feeders."

The Tree Squirrels Around Us

- *Eastern or western gray squirrel (Sciurus carolinensis/griseus)*
  East; Pacific states. Generally gray. A black form is becoming more common in parts of the East. They are about 20 percent smaller than fox squirrels and have silver-tipped fur instead of tawny- or brown-tipped hairs.

- *Fox squirrel (Sciurus niger)*
  East, except New England; west to Rockies. Three color phases; only one is fox-colored. FeederWatchers find them more "laid back" than the grays.

- *Abert's squirrel (Sciurus aberti)*
  Limited to ponderosa pines of Southern Rocky Mountains. Has ear tassels.

- *Red or pine squirrel (Tamiasciurus hudsonicus)*
  Pine forests of Alaska, Canada, Rocky Mountains, and Northeast as far south as Virginia. A small but dominant squirrel. The color is usually reddish on the back, separated from a white or grayish belly by a thin black stripe.

- *Douglas squirrel (Tamiasciurus douglasii)*
  Conifers along Pacific Coast from British Columbia to California. Very similar to red or pine squirrels, and often called a pine squirrel.

- *Northern or southern flying squirrel (Glaucomys sabrinus/volans)*
  Most of Canada; eastern half of U.S.; parts of West. Small nocturnal squirrel with soft brown fur and big black eyes.

Jack Hoisington of Norfolk, Virginia, tried the compressed corn logs now available. They are used like corn on the cob but last much longer. "We got one to try for our furry four-legged friends, but we have also seen blue jays on it."

In the long run, FeederWatchers who feed squirrels note the inevitable — their squirrels are fat, and each year more of them come to the birdfeeders. Consequently, plenty of FeederWatchers have come up with ways to make life a little more challenging for the bushy-tailed bandits.

Not figuring out ways to deter squirrels and other raiders can prove more expensive than buying baffles, cages, or squirrel-resistant feeders. "You haven't lived until you've had a squirrel gnaw a hole in the side of your house and have babies in there," warns one FeederWatcher. "Do not encourage cute little squirrels to get comfy close to your house." An Ohio FeederWatcher had a resident squirrel bite him in the pocketbook. "Squirrels will eat engine mount harness straps on a car. I lifted the hood on the car, and out came a squirrel. Took it to a garage. My bill was $1,800."

One squirrel-control technique not only doesn't work but is dangerous to the squirrels. "No matter how many squirrels you **trap and transport,** there will always be more to take their place," observes Cathy Martens in Clarkston, Michigan. "Your newly squirrel-free yard — complete with fully stocked birdfeeders, even! — will be the perfect spot for a traveling squirrel to set up housekeeping."

University of Maryland mammalogist Vagn Flyger warns that "local squirrels harass or kill transported ones. The remaining young of relocated squirrels will end up dying." In some places, this sort of animal dumping is illegal.

An important factor in squirrel control can be the choice of **squirrel-proof feeders and foods.** Squirrel-foiling tactics, such as locating feeder poles

A nocturnal flying squirrel, its big eyes reflecting the camera's flash, starts dining soon after sunset.

at least 10 feet away from squirrel launching pads or attaching huge baffles to feeders, aren't practical for apartment dwellers like Sue Fuss of Rennselaer, New York. Her backyard consists of a small cement balcony. Sue highly recommends metal feeders with cages around them "to thwart the squirrels." She has a cage around her tube feeder and a cage around her suet feeder, which results in plenty of birds and frustrated squirrels. Wire cages and squirrel-proof (or at least squirrel-resistant) feeders are described beginning on p. 14.

Offering foods squirrels don't care for, like safflower seed (p. 12) and niger seed, helps discourage them, and red pepper is sometimes used to thwart them. In theory, the fiery compound capsaicin found in red pepper delivers a punch to squirrels but not to birds because birds' taste buds work differently.

Frank Davis of Mississippi adds red pepper to his gorp mixture. "Then when I fill the feeder with gorp, I sprinkle it with more pepper. It protects my gorp from squirrels." In Seattle, Washington, Marilyn Hardy found that "it worked for a little while, but after a few days, they seemed to mind it less. Maybe they developed a taste for spicy."

A formal study conducted by researchers at Cornell University looked at the consumption rate of black-oil sunflower seed shot through with capsaicin compared with that of untreated seed. The "hot" seeds seemed to reduce both the total amount of time *most* squirrels spent at the feeders and the amount of seed *most* squirrels consumed. Treated seeds didn't stop the chipmunks. They readily carried them away and no doubt received an unwelcome surprise when they eventually chowed down. How do opossums and raccoons react? "They will not even slow down when they come across cayenne-laced food," claims Ron Piper.

Carol Shillitto, near Portland, Oregon, squirrel-proofs her feeders with baffles. Two pole-mounted feeders "are protected by **shield-like baffles** that attach underneath the feeders," more than 5 feet

A red or pine squirrel does one of the things that squirrels do best — eats seeds.

above the ground. "The baffles have kept the jumpers at bay for years."

Carol also has a hanging tube feeder. "It has a dome baffle above it and always works fine. Newcomer squirrels give it a try and always slide off."

Success didn't come without trial. The failures included unprotected window-mounted feeders ("So I could watch birds up close. Ha! Forget it!"), hoppers on poles with baffles that were too low ("I had one champion leaper who cleared 5 feet to the top of a baffle — nooooo problem"), and platform feeders for ground birds ("Like they stood a chance, right!").

Big, wobbly baffles above or below feeders that block the path of a hungry squirrel are tried-and-true protection. The list of FeederWatchers' homemade baffles includes heavy-duty salad bowls, 2-liter plastic pop containers, and slick sheets of thin plastic fitted to feeder poles like tippy skirts. Commercial shield-like baffles are made for hanging or for mounting on poles and 4-by-4 posts. Baffles are included in the design of some hanging feeders.

In rare cases, baffles placed above hanging feeders might not do the job. Carol Takacs recalls living in Shaker Heights, Ohio, where the "'rats of Shaker' gnawed through the branches from which baffled feeders were suspended. Once on the ground, they could destroy the feeders conveniently."

Dick Meyers says he uses pole-mounted feeders with "commercial upside-down bowl-shaped baffles below them. There's one squirrel that will leap and smash into them and sometimes grab hold. I figure he's earned some free seeds."

Alice Topping of northern Illinois proclaims victory over squirrels using a **cylindrical baffle,** a 3-foot section of stovepipe attached to the bottom of her post-mounted feeders. "Sometimes they climb into the stovepipe with only their tails hanging out. It's funny to watch. You can only guess what they are thinking." Katherine Wolfthal of Weston, Massachusetts, agrees that cylindrical baffles impede the raids of both squirrels and raccoons.

Metal duct pipe or 6-inch-diameter PVC pipe can be used in place of stovepipe. Alice mounts her stovepipe firmly against the bottom of a wooden platform. Others close the top of the baffle with hardware cloth and hang it so that it will wobble.

There are several **other baffles** that some FeederWatchers use. Victoria Wegner of Somonauk, Illinois, is confident she has defeated squirrels and other raiders by putting sleeves of PVC pipe over all her poles. "Nothing climbs up those sleeves." Pipe with a diameter of at least 4 inches will defeat most raccoons. If a raccoon is able to get a grip, sand the surface and apply a hard (carnauba) wax. Vaseline, grease, and silicone spray collect dirt and grit and soon lose their effectiveness.

Walter Chaskel of Huntington Station, Long Island, New York, counted 14 squirrels at his feeders

A gray squirrel finds its trip to a feeder interrupted by a cylindrical baffle. "What to do now?"

one winter day. That was it. The fight was on. He hung all his feeders on small-gauge wire strung from his house to a tree. He won; no more squirrels! But one day he watched in disbelief as one "furball acrobat" slowly "tightroped" all the way to the feeders. "I hate squirrels being smarter than I am!" To defeat these high-wire artists, FeederWatchers have come up with baffles such as lightweight swimming pool floats, plastic juice containers, and LPs and CDs that they string along wire onto which feeders are hung.

Raccoons can create a lot more havoc than squirrels. They can be aggressive, dangerous animals and should not be fed or accommodated as squirrels often are. Rabies periodically runs rampant through their populations.

The husky, black-masked bandits will make off with whatever they can swipe, including entire feeders. "Our first winter here we left the feeders and suet out at night," says Catherine Fagan of Carlisle, Ohio. "A suet cage disappeared. It was cold and snowy at the time and so I didn't bother to look for it. I just bought a new one. Then the new one vanished. This went on all winter. In spring, I found the suet cages all together in a pile in the raccoons' 'picnic area.'"

Raccoons are especially attracted to suet because this high-energy food helps build their store of body fat for winter survival. They don't really hibernate. If temps are above 28° F at night, out they come, and any feeder they can reach is at peril.

One solution is to ration seed and suet so feeders are mostly empty by nightfall. A foolproof method is to bring all the feeders inside the house or a closed garage at night; a screened-in porch doesn't count. Or keep a large metal rodent- and raccoon-proof can that you can toss your feeders into overnight.

How We Cope With

A black bear attacks a tube feeder in Michigan. Ear tags are used to mark bears that are relocated. Two tags are often the limit before a bear is destroyed.

Baffles will deter raccoons, just as they do squirrels, if they are large enough.

Judy Kolo-Rose in Georgia baffled several trees to keep raccoons at bay. "We screwed together sections of curved metal duct into a loose ring around each tree trunk. The raccoons seem to have disappeared."

Opossums are one of the **other raiders** that visit feeders. They come at night like raccoons and pose the same problems with the same solutions. "One night I heard 'crunch, crunch, crunch,' says Shelly Ducharme of Auburn, Alabama. "A flashlight revealed a humongous 'possum up a tree eating one of my pine cones slathered with peanut butter."

Some FeederWatchers contend only with raiders, such as ground squirrels or mice, that eat on the ground below feeders or, in some cases, climb up to feeders to eat. Then there is that overly cute, small terrestrial squirrel, lover of sunflower seeds and bird eggs, that raids and raids — the chipmunk. Skunks, rats, and rabbits, too, make under-the-feeder visits. Minimizing ground spills deters these visitors.

Deer show up at feeders also. Bruce Robinson of Veradale, Washington, says he purposely feeds them. "Deer like to eat from the tray feeder and I let them." On the other hand, a FeederWatcher from California says, "The deer are so overly abundant in our yard, we have had to discontinue ground-feeding of corn. We created 'Rube Goldberg' devices to keep them out of our tall standing feeders."

"I have deer eating me out of house and seed,"

wails one anguished FeederWatcher. "I have tried everything, and nothing works for more than about one week." Caged feeders or feeders mounted beyond their reach are workable solutions, but deer damage to gardens and grounds can be so extensive that some people find they have to fence, even electrify, part of their property to keep the deer out.

As black bear populations rebound and people move into more rural areas, bear encounters become more frequent. "For every 100 calls I get about problems with bears, 80 of them involve a birdfeeder in one form or another," says New York big game biologist Dick Henry, who works in the Catskill Mountain area north of New York City.

Henry says a bear's sense of smell is 50 times greater than ours. "If you feed birds in bear country, do it only when the bears are denning, when it is cold. Even then, clean your feeding site up thoroughly and take your feeders inside every evening, leaving no residual seed on the ground. Bears don't really hibernate. They will come out on warm days." And do not, DO NOT store food on patios or porches.

One FeederWatcher in Minnesota recalls seeing a bear take one paw and swipe a Plexiglas feeder full of seed off a feeder post — in the middle of winter. A New Hampshire FeederWatcher expresses her amazement at watching a black bear "shaking sunflower seeds out of a tubular feeder."

Even if food is placed high enough so bears can't get to it, they will be attracted to your yard. As biologist Henry sees it, "Birdseed to a bear is like catnip to a cat. I call suet 'bear lollipops.'"

Predators from Above and Below: Hawks and Felines Ambushing Songbirds

Raiders make off only with seeds or suet. Predators like sharp-shinned and Cooper's **hawks** visit feeders to devour the birds. For many FeederWatchers, the first hawk attack is an unwelcome example of the Law of Unintended Consequences.

The hawk bears no moral responsibility for its actions — it is just being a proper hawk — but what about the FeederWatcher who feels that "I invited my songbirds into a trap!"

While the FeederWatcher is dismayed the first time a hawk strafes a backyard, the songbirds are not. They have seen it all before. Wherever they feed, it is the same. They know that the skies are always full of danger, and they stay close enough to cover to feel safe.

"I wish my hawks would feed elsewhere," says Michigan FeederWatcher Mike Ciaramitaro with the same resignation that the songbirds themselves must feel. Other FeederWatchers, perhaps most, are awed by the drama of a hawk attack and feel privileged to see it up close. "It is fascinating to watch a hawk sitting, observing, waiting, hunting, eating," says Dave Riffle of Ohio.

A description of the attack styles of hawks and the interplay of predator and prey is on p. 92.

The best hawk defense is to provide dense cover close to feeders for the songbirds. Some people welcome crows and jays because they harass hawks and disrupt their hunting. An anonymous Feeder-Watcher has a suggestion on how to select which birds are taken: "Put cracked corn on the ground in an open place far from your other feeders. The house sparrows will find it, and they make great hawk dinner."

Kestrels and some other hawks occasionally take songbirds. Red-tailed hawks will if they can but don't have the flying skill to succeed very often. Red-tails and red-shouldered hawks usually come to yards for squirrels, snakes, and the like. A California FeederWatcher watched a red-tailed hawk descend on a gopher snake intent on capturing a rodent that was busily eating birdseed. "The hawk and snake struggled for ten minutes. The snake won."

Shrikes also attack small songbirds (see p. 116). An Alberta FeederWatcher reported a northern shrike chasing a chickadee from a large willow. "I didn't see the outcome, but another chickadee remained in the bush and sat perfectly still for at least 5 minutes. I didn't know a chickadee could sit still like that."

Free-roaming feral and pet **cats** are major bird predators. Several wildlife studies conclude that cats kill millions of birds each year, with some of the bird kills happening at bird-feeding sites.

The American Bird Conservancy's Cats Indoors! campaign has researched the cat predator problem and offers many "cat relief" suggestions. But there is only one reliable way to control cats, says project director Linda Winter. "Keeping cats indoors is an easy way to help our native birds — and our cats."

Putting feeders out of a cat's "leap" may mean putting them too high to conveniently refill. "We saw one of the local feral cats make a vertical leap of 6 feet and grab a house sparrow at our feeder. Remarkable! We measured it," says Ed Campau of Greenfield, Indiana.

A Cooper's hawk displays its broad wings and powerful wing stroke while using its white-tipped tail as a rudder to change the direction of flight.

FeederWatchers deal with "attack cats" in numerous ways and not always successfully. Eliminating low bushes where cats can hide and lunge is a good idea but can be unrealistic, especially while at the same time trying to provide cover for birds.

Ground feeders can be protected be erecting chicken-wire fences around them. A green vinyl-coated version of chicken wire is widely available for yard use. Fencing also works around the bases of feeder posts by forcing the cat to leap a horizontal distance, reducing its vertical leaping range. One FeederWatcher discovered that she could stake fencing wire flat to the ground and the cats would avoid walking over it.

In Minneapolis, Minnesota, Sysliene Turpin says her neighborhood cats "think of my feeders as McDonald's." To discourage them, she uses a "SuperSoaker water gun filled with water and ammonia or vinegar." But this is a hard practice to keep up with on a regular basis.

Some FeederWatchers let dogs do the work. Karen Vizzi in Buffalo, New York, says, "Letting my two large dogs out without warning seems to do the trick. Birds come right back to the feeder once the cat is gone."

Judith Togher on Long Island, New York, had a problem with a "clever tomcat," a neighbor's pet, picking off feeder birds. "To deter him, I put rosebush and holly cuttings under my feeders."

Gaye Weisner on Staten Island, New York, chose a high-tech remedy. "I invested in one of those electronic sound machines that puts out a high-pitched tone, which is allegedly disturbing to dogs and cats and keeps them from hanging out. Works fairly well." Gaye enjoys cats and keeps hers indoors, "and that is the perspective from which they are allowed to enjoy their birding."

Wildlife rehabilitator and FeederWatcher Carol Ottomeier of Lake Almanor, California, has found that for rescued cat-caught birds "the outcomes are not good. Cat germs are virulent, and the wounds from claws and teeth are hard to find."

A young sharp-shinned hawk with dove remains. "Eat it where you catch it" is the sharpie's dining practice.

We Can Also Advise You About

Other Important Issues:
Window Strikes, Cleanliness, Diseases

Birds that whack themselves against glass are usually only stunned momentarily. Others need time to recover. Head-on collisions for some are fatal.

Estimates of the annual numbers of birds killed in collisions with towers, high-rise buildings, and other man-made structures are mind-boggling — some as high as 100 million. FeederWatchers have their share of **window strikes,** and they have devised some solutions.

"Startled birds fly to safety as quickly as possible," observes a Florida FeederWatcher. "Often they head straight for a window that mirrors the sky or nearby foliage." He recommends assessing your window problems and feeder locations.

Feeders might be too close or not close enough to problem windows. When feeders are very near a window, panicked songbirds can't gain enough speed to injure themselves. (Hawks might not be so lucky.) When feeders are far enough away from windows, birds are less likely to collide with them.

Go outside and look at your problem window just as a bird would. Can you see through it? So can a bird. Does the window reflect surrounding habitat? If so, how can a bird tell the difference between the mirrored image and the real thing?

Shades and curtains may solve the problem on windows that are not used for watching birds. Karen Fay of Baton Rouge, Louisiana, put up bamboo shades. "The window looks solid from the outside, but I can still see through it."

Jane Blumenthal offers her solution: "I don't wash my windows anymore — all in the interest of conservation, of course."

A powder down image on a glass door provides a ghostly record of a window strike by a mourning dove. The fine, waxy powder is a part of many birds' plumage.

FeederWatcher and wildlife rehabilitator Kieran Lindsey of Cedar Crest, New Mexico, deliberately smudges her windows: "Lessen the glare by spraying the outside window with a soapy or salty solution. The windows won't be clean and sparkly, but that's the point."

Stained-glass suncatchers, seasonal wreaths or garlands, decorative cutouts such as harvest themes and snowflakes, or commercially available decals like hawk- or owl-shaped silhouettes work primarily because they help break up reflections. Something as simple as strips of masking tape on the outside of a window have the same effect.

One of the decals marketed mimics a spiderweb. The idea is that birds might avoid spiderwebs as hazardous. Don McMordie of Coos Bay, Oregon, used a felt marker to draw spider webs on his floor-to-ceiling windows that kept getting hit by birds. "It worked for a while. Then they ignored them."

Long ribbons that blow in the breeze give birds the jitters. To exploit that, a rural Wyoming Feeder-Watcher says, "We tape lengths of surveyor's ribbon around the windows." A Delaware FeederWatcher finds that "green gardening ribbon works for me." Another choice is the red and silver "flash tape" sold by farm supply stores to protect crops from birds. The colors are supposed to make birds think "Fire!"

FeederWatchers also report success with moving items like hawk silhouettes hung from a string, mobiles, wind chimes, and hanging plants.

Some FeederWatchers can end window strikes only by hanging netting over the offending window. A Montana FeederWatcher stretched fishing net over her window. Fruit netting designed to keep birds from damaging crops is most often used. Pull it tightly over the problem window.

A FeederWatcher in Olympia, Washington, built a wood frame around her kitchen viewing window and covered it in black nylon tuille. A Carlinville, Illinois, FeederWatcher simply installed window screens. Others have put up garden trellises in front of their windows.

When building a new home or replacing windows, consider installing those that are angled downward; they'll reflect the ground instead of the surroundings.

Ron Piper heard the ominous "thump" at his window and found a hairy woodpecker in need of some **bird first-aid.** "When I picked her up, there was a strong heartbeat and some movement of the eyes. Since she didn't have her living will with her, I explained she would have to go to IC for observation, and I put her in a paper bag." When Ron checked a half hour later, the bird looked alert. "She flew away as if nothing had happened."

FeederWatchers who are also federally licensed wildlife rehabilitators offer comprehensive advice. Carol Ottomeier near Mount Lassen in northern California, says birds with slight concussions require warm, dark, safe, quiet places in which to recover, such as a clean cardboard box with small airholes poked in the lid. Betty Shannon of Sierra Wildlife Rescue says "quiet" means "quiet." No radios, TVs, pets, or children should be nearby.

Do not offer food or water or put anything else in the box except paper towels or tissue to cushion a bird that can't stand upright. Don't use terry cloth towels; talons can get tangled in the cloth loops. Keep the box away from air conditioning. After half an hour, peek inside the box. If the bird seems to have "come to," take the box outside into an open space facing away from windows and open it.

Louise Grider of New Brockton, Alabama, says when birds first come to, they are often disoriented and will "just sit kind of hunched for a while." She says if a bird doesn't appear normal, let it rest for an hour or so. Then, if it still seems off balance or can't fly, call a wild bird rehabilitator.

Several FeederWatcher/rehabilitators recommend that people who watch birds at home keep contact information for local rehabilitators. "Have rehabber phone numbers where you can find them quickly."

Kieran Lindsey runs Natural Assets Consulting in Cedar Crest, New Mexico, where she often talks about **cleanliness** with people who want to feed birds in a healthful way. She suggests once-a-week cleaning of feeders, water sources, and feeding grounds as a good rule of thumb. Change water daily. "If you see any mold or mildew at feeders or water sources, trash the food or water immediately where birds and other animals can't get to it. Clean everything thoroughly — right away."

Wind, rain, and sunshine can adequately cleanse some platform feeders, for instance. But tube feeders, in particular, are best scrubbed weekly, as Kieran advises, to prevent the growth of mold or mildew. Dunk them in hot, soapy water and scrub thoroughly. Brushes designed for tube feeders are available at bird supply stores. Rinse off the soap and then soak in a 10 percent solution of bleach to sterilize. Rinse again with warm water and allow to dry.

"The cleaning process will get to be routine after a while, like doing your dishes," assures Kieran. "Remember, your cleaning helps promote disease-free, healthy birds. Keeping up with it doesn't mean you won't see illness; it means you've done your best to prevent it."

Many FeederWatchers routinely rake built-up hulls and add them to their compost; others employ creative methods to keep feeding sites clean.

Don McMordie and others use lawn mowers to vacuum their sites. He mows under his safflower and sunflower feeders, but under his mixed bird-seed feeder he has an old window screen. "This lets the water through but catches the spilled seed. I clean the screen every few days and toss the seeds in the mulch pile." Under his niger feeder, he

Bonnie Campion of Texas hangs purple and silver ribbons in front of her windows to prevent bird strikes: "The colors of the Farmersville Fighting Farmers! I get the shiny Mylar used for football game decorations."

lays out a square of artificial turf. "This is easy to roll up and shake out every now and then."

A New England FeederWatcher, Charles S. Sylvia, put a bed of stone dust in his primary feeding area. "You still have to clean up the hulls, but it is much easier. You can hose it. You can use bleach right on it, plus Mother Nature cleans it too."

Birdbaths and other water features require the same cleaning and sterilization as feeders. One anonymous FeederWatcher, excusing herself for not changing water daily, says, "I see birds drink from far worse places than my watering hole, so I think they are doing fine."

Rehabbers, veterinarians, and other professionals couldn't disagree more strongly. "Imperfect water is not better than no water! The most prevalent cause of infections and disease is dirty water," asserts Jimmy Mech of Mt. Baldy, California.

All the seed hulls, bird droppings, feathers, bugs, dust, pollen, plant parts, and wind-borne debris that a birdbath accumulates in one day can create a perfect medium for growing and harboring things you don't want your birds to encounter — diseases like salmonella and trichomoniasis. "Water in a closed area can breed those bugs quicker than you can imagine," says Jimmy.

Some FeederWatchers are leery of chlorine in tap water, but it is very unstable and dissipates quickly. "If you are afraid this may hurt your birds," says Jimmy, "set out water late in the evening. There will be no chlorine left when the birds arrive in the morning. I have used this method with very sensitive fish, and it works."

Like humans, birds get a variety of **diseases.** They can suffer from avian forms of malaria, tuberculosis, the flu, and other infections. They can also be plagued by a long line of parasites.

Four of the diseases associated with backyard

If there is evidence of disease, consider wearing plastic gloves and a facial mask when cleaning or raking around your site. "Because I have emphysema, I always wear a paper face mask when filling or working with birdfeeders. Also, I always pull on a pair of disposable rubber gloves."

Claude Hall
Dandridge, Tennessee

Vacuuming outdoors. Sandy Belth keeps the ground under her feeders clean with a shop vacuum cleaner.

feeders may affect humans: salmonellosis, aspergillosis, histoplasmosis, and chlamydiosis.

Salmonellosis is the most common of the four. It is a bacterial infection of the intestines and is spread by infected droppings that contaminate food. Flocking species are particularly at risk. During the winter of 1997–98, a salmonellosis outbreak swept 18 states and eastern Canada. In most winters, small outbreaks of salmonellosis occur among house sparrows at backyard feeders, but the 1997–98 outbreak was heaviest among siskins, evening grosbeaks, purple finches, and especially common redpolls.

Affected birds are lethargic and easy to approach. "The pine siskins are all puffed up, like they're cold. They just sort of sit around" is the way one Feeder-Watcher described it. If you see this behavior, clean everything thoroughly and stop feeding for at least one week. Affected birds will disperse rather than

concentrating and transmitting the disease.

Aspergillosis and histoplasmosis are caused by fungi. The aspergillus fungus may grow in damp birdseed or hulls. Birds inhale the spores, develop problems breathing and walking, become emaciated, and die. Humans can inhale the spores and may become infected, but this is rare.

People are more at risk from histoplasmosis, which can grow in dirt where droppings have built up. If the fungus is disturbed when hulls are raked up, for instance, spores are released, which can cause infection in a small percentage of people if inhaled. Symptoms are fever, chest pains, or a cough. Death may result if the disease is untreated. Birds seem rarely affected by the fungus.

Chlamydiosis is a disease that often affects doves, pigeons, and poultry. It is caused by a bacterium. Infected birds have breathing problems, a swollen head, discharge from the eyes, and green diarrhea. People get the disease (not the same as chlamydia) by inhaling the bacterium or by ingesting it after contact with the birds or their secretions. Most people experience only a mild infection with fever and headaches, but the infection may lead to pneumonia and death. Antibiotics are effective treatment.

The most prevalent disease that is seen in birds but is not a threat to humans is house finch eye disease. Avian pox and trichomoniasis are other avian diseases sometimes seen at feeders.

House finch eye disease, a bacterial infection, is a highly communicable disease primarily affecting house finches in the East. The symptoms are crusty, swollen eyes that cause temporary blindness, leaving the birds helpless. Direct bird-to-bird contact is the primary cause. Discourage overcrowding by providing enough well-spaced feeders to keep the finches dispersed. Crowding can be a factor in spreading disease, and the stress it creates may also make birds more susceptible. Should an outbreak occur, discontinue feeding for at least a week and disinfect your feeders.

Avian pox is caused by a variety of pox viruses and is very noticeable in its more common external form. Wart-like growths appear on the bare parts of birds — around the eye, at the base of the beak, and on the legs and feet. This disease is spread by insects, as well as infected birds. Foods and feeders, if kept clean, are not common means of transmission. Feeding doesn't normally need to be interrupted.

Trichomoniasis is caused by a protozoan parasite. It most commonly affects pigeons and doves and the raptors that feed on them. Look for fluffed-up birds that gasp while flying and have diarrhea. Contaminated water is a primary means of distribution. If the disease is noted, clean water sources daily, especially stationary ones, or temporarily shut them down.

House Finch Eye Disease

FeederWatchers in the Washington, D.C., area first noticed house finches with crusty, swollen eyes during the winter of 1993–94. The disease, diagnosed as mycoplasmal conjunctivitis, is caused by a bacterium previously found only in domestic poultry. Since eastern house finches all descended from a few captive birds (see p. 78), they are genetically very similar and are similarly susceptible to the disease. Finch behavior doesn't help either. These birds forage in flocks and crowd birdfeeders, increasing the spread of the disease. In the autumn of 1994, the Cornell Lab of Ornithology launched the House Finch Disease Survey to track its spread. Reports showed it advancing steadily west, north, and south of the sites where it was first observed. By spring 2000, reports had leveled off.

Identifying

BIRDS

AT FEEDERS

Size differences in downy (l) and hairy (r) woodpeckers are obvious when the birds are seen together.

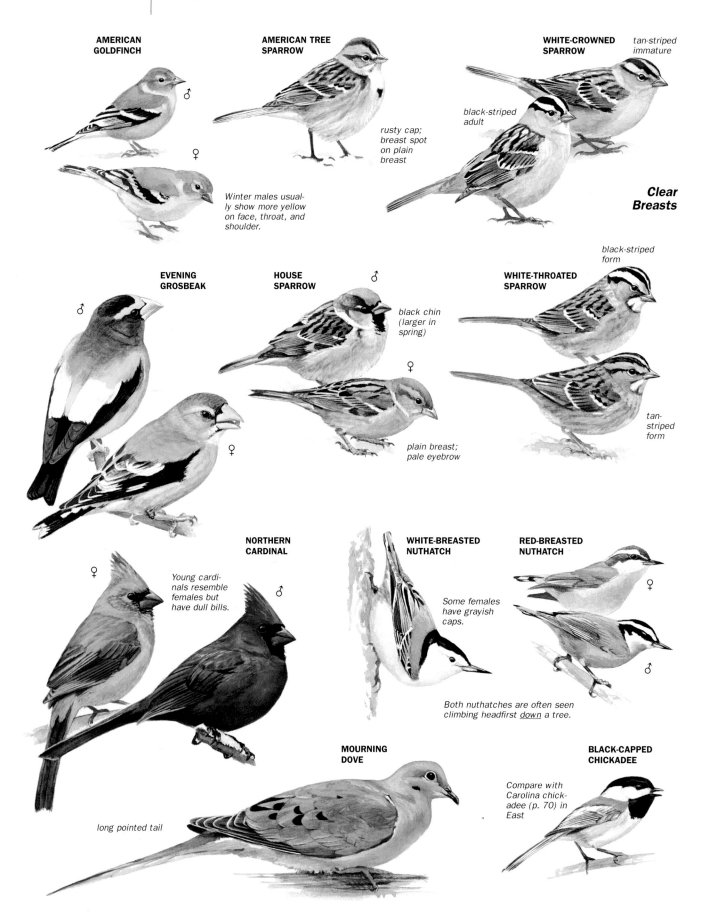

**AMERICAN
GOLDFINCH**

♂

♀

Winter males usually show more yellow on face, throat, and shoulder.

**AMERICAN TREE
SPARROW**

rusty cap; breast spot on plain breast

**WHITE-CROWNED
SPARROW**

tan-striped immature

black-striped adult

*Clear
Breasts*

**EVENING
GROSBEAK**

♂

♀

**HOUSE
SPARROW**

♂

black chin (larger in spring)

♀

plain breast; pale eyebrow

**WHITE-THROATED
SPARROW**

black-striped form

tan-striped form

**NORTHERN
CARDINAL**

♀

Young cardinals resemble females but have dull bills.

♂

**WHITE-BREASTED
NUTHATCH**

Some females have grayish caps.

**RED-BREASTED
NUTHATCH**

♀

♂

Both nuthatches are often seen climbing headfirst <u>down</u> a tree.

**MOURNING
DOVE**

long pointed tail

**BLACK-CAPPED
CHICKADEE**

Compare with Carolina chick-adee (p. 70) in East

♂ **HOUSE FINCH**

dark
streaks
on belly

plain
face

***Streaked
Breasts
or Sides***

♂ **PURPLE FINCH**

clear belly;
streaks on
sides only

*Difference in color
of male house and
purple finches is
not a reliable mark;
pattern of color is.*

♀

broad
white
eyebrow

♀ **HAIRY WOODPECKER**

*larger than downy
and with longer bill*

DOWNY WOODPECKER

♂

*Male has red
on its hind-
crown; female
doesn't.*

♂

♀

PINE SISKIN

*heavy mustache
marks; breast
streaks; breast
spot*

SONG SPARROW

FOX SPARROW

*rusty red
rump and
base of tail*

Yellow on wings and
rump is more promi-
nent in flight.

*Eastern birds have
redder back and
breast streaks; some
western birds much
darker overall.*

*Red shoulder patch
on male often hidden;
white or yellowish
border remains visible.*

♀

RED-WINGED BLACKBIRD

*Young male resem-
bles female but dark-
er with more red on
shoulders.*

♂

**EUROPEAN
STARLING**

*glossier in
summer*

*short
tail*

BROWN-HEADED COWBIRD

*short
conical
bill*

♂

♀

**AMERICAN
ROBIN**

**RED-SHAFTED
(NORTHERN)
FLICKER**
♂

*Male has red
mustache
lacking in female.*

♂ **DARK-EYED JUNCO**

OREGON FORM

PINK-SIDED FORM

♀

*pink bills;
white in tails*

**CHESTNUT-BACKED
CHICKADEE**

**MOUNTAIN
CHICKADEE**

white eyebrow

*Compare with house
and purple finches
(pp. 70–71)*

♀

**GOLDEN-
CROWNED
SPARROW**

♂

**CASSIN'S
FINCH**

**SPOTTED
TOWHEE**

*rusty red sides;
white spots on
backs*

♂

♀

♀

♂

*clear breast;
not all individuals
show gold on
crown*

♂

*female paler,
with grayish
breast band*

**VARIED
THRUSH**

**STELLER'S
JAY**

*brownish, with
white under chin
and dark eye*

**BREWER'S
BLACKBIRD**

♀

♂

*purple head
sheen; yellow
eye*

DARK-EYED JUNCO

SLATE-COLORED FORM

♀

♂

white outer
tail feathers

CAROLINA WREN

white
eyebrow

crest

RED-BELLIED WOODPECKER

Female lacks
red on top of
crown.

♀

♂

Faint red wash
on belly usually
not apparent.

CAROLINA CHICKADEE

*Compare with
black-capped
chickadee (p. 70)*

**TUFTED
TITMOUSE**

EASTERN TOWHEE

♂

♀

*rusty-colored
sides; female
brown above*

**YELLOW-SHAFTED
(NORTHERN)
FLICKER**

♀

*Male has black
mustache
lacking in female.*

♂

**COMMON
GRACKLE**

♀

♂

*appears black
in poor light*

**BLUE
JAY**

long tail

MALE FINCHES

HOUSE
FINCH

CASSIN'S FINCH

PURPLE
FINCH

Male house, purple, and Cassin's finches all show a lot of red and can be confusing to the inexperienced backyard birder. With a little experience, they can be distinguished easily. House finches are the most abundant of the three in most backyards, and males can be identified without paying much attention to the red area. Just check for extensive brown streaks on the breast and belly.

Cassin's and purple finches have clear underparts except for blurry brown or reddish streaks on the sides. Both birds are a bit larger and chunkier than the house finch and typically a different shade of red. The male purple finch is a deeper, wine-colored red than most house finches. Cassin's is a brighter red. But color is not a reliable mark, as house finches vary considerably. Most are an orange-tinged red, but they can range from deep red to pure yellow. The color is determined by various carotenoid pigments consumed in seeds and berries while feathers are being replaced.

On a red finch with a clear belly, note the pattern of the red. The red on the purple finch extends from the crown to the nape and onto the back. The pink or reddish wing bars are an excellent mark. On Cassin's, the red is brightest on the forehead; only a pale pink wash extends onto the brown-streaked back, and the wing bars are whitish or buffy. The pattern of color on the house finch is also distinctive, extending in a U shape around the front and sides of the crown but not on top.

Redpolls (p. 93) also show some red but are not likely to be confused with other red finches. They are smaller than a house finch, and the red on the head is confined to a cap. The chin is black.

BLACK-CAPPED & CAROLINA CHICKADEES

BLACK-CAPPED
CHICKADEE

CAROLINA
CHICKADEE

Ranges of the black-capped and Carolina chickadees have only a narrow band of overlap (see p. 94). Identification usually is based on range, without considering the details of appearance. However, the two birds can be separated by plumage as well as geography. The wings show the best marks. The black-capped chickadee has white in the folded wing and forming a bar on the wing coverts. The Carolina chickadee shows a lesser amount of white on the folded wing, none on the wing coverts.

Close up from below, the outside web of the outermost tail feathers can be seen to be white on the black-capped chickadee, gray on the Carolina. And the white cheek patch appears wider on the black-capped. Differences in bibs and buffy sides are not always noticeable, but the Carolina may show less buff on the sides and a smaller, neater bib.

At the zone of overlap, there is little noticeable size difference, but black-caps are larger the farther north they live. Carolina chickadees progressively decrease in size south of the zone. It is the more northern black-caps that occasionally irrupt, and they are noticeably larger (and brighter white) than the resident Carolinas whose range they invade.

The songs, best heard in spring, are unique. Black-capped chickadees whistle a two- or three-syllable *fee-bee* or *fee-bee-ee.* Carolinas give a four-syllable *fee-bee, fee-bay.* The *dee-dee-dee* call of the black-cap is slightly hoarser than the Carolina's.

FEMALE FINCHES

PURPLE
FINCH

CASSIN'S
FINCH

HOUSE FINCH

PINE SISKIN

For identification, the little brown birds with seed-crunching conical bills are usually first divided into those with breast streaks and those without. Female house, purple, and Cassin's finches all have breast streaks. So do pine siskins. Like their male counterparts, the female finches require a little experience to separate reliably.

Except for her breast streaks, the female house finch earns the right to be called nondescript. Some show a pale narrow eyebrow, but there are no other notable facial marks. By contrast, the female purple finch has two broad white marks on her face. (The female's white marks are repeated in pale red on male purple finches. It is easy to imagine males as being wine-stained females.)

The female Cassin's finch is an in-betweener. Her face marks are not as broad and distinctive as the purple finch's, but they are white, not pale, as sometimes seen in the house finch. Her breast streaks are not muddy like those of the house or purple finch, but fine brown streaks on a white breast. They extend over the entire underparts, including the coverts under the tail. The undertail is often easier to see than might be expected and is a good mark distinguishing Cassin's from the female purple finch, which has clear undertail coverts.

Pine siskins have yellow in their wings and tails, but the amount is small and it is often nearly invisible on a perched bird. They are smaller than the other streaked finches and have notably smaller and more sharply pointed bills. And if niger seed is available, pine siskins will be the streaked finches attached to the niger seed feeder.

BLACKBIRDS & GRACKLES

Not everyone feels the need to separately identify the various black birds that visit feeders. Feeder-Watchers must, and it presents a challenge. Male Brewer's blackbirds and common grackles of both sexes are iridescent black birds with bright eyes. (Female Brewer's are dingy brown with dark eyes and more likely to be confused with female cow-birds than grackles.)

The common grackle is the larger of the two, but better clues are the size of the bill and the size and shape of the tail. Bill and tail are noticeably larger in the common grackle, which, combined with the flatter forehead, gives the bird a more elongated look than in Brewer's blackbird.

Grackles have a multicolored sheen that varies with the region and is duller in females. The most notable gloss on Brewer's blackbird is a purple head sheen, but it is not apparent in bad light. Rusty blackbirds, which sometimes visit feeders bordering wetlands, show rusty barring in fall and early winter. By late winter or spring, they are usually flat black. Any gloss is typically greenish.

BREWER'S
BLACKBIRD

COMMON
GRACKLE

ACCIPITER HAWKS

SHARP-SHINNED HAWK — imm. / adult

COOPER'S HAWK — adult / imm.

GOSHAWK — adult / imm.

Sharp-shinned and Cooper's hawks are the most commonly seen birds of prey at feeders and two of the most difficult of all birds to separate. The third member of the genus *Accipiter,* the northern goshawk, is seen only occasionally at feeders, principally in northern areas. The adult goshawk is distinctive with its large size, pale gray underparts, and broad white eyebrow. It is the adult sharp-shinned and Cooper's hawks that are the identification problem. A second problem is separating the young brownish birds of all three species.

Adult sharpies and Cooper's hawks have fine rufous barring on their underparts except for the undertail coverts. It can be so prevalent that it obscures the white base color. The upperparts are blue-gray in males but often brownish in females. Tails are long, with several bands of approximately equal width and a narrow white tip.

There is a size difference in accipiters. Not only are the species separated by size, but the sexes are different sizes as well. Females are larger than males, resulting in six small but discrete size differences, without overlap, from male sharpie (smallest) to female goshawk (largest).

Distinguishing individuals two or three steps apart on the size scale is not too difficult. A male sharpie, for instance, is about the size of a blue jay or mourning dove and is noticeably smaller than the female Cooper's, which is about crow-sized. Using size to separate a female sharpie from a barely larger male Cooper's is another matter.

Fortunately, backyard birders often have the chance to study plumages while accipiters sit waiting for prey. Cooper's, both adult and young, have a slightly rounded tail with an obvious white tip.

Sharpies' tails are generally blunt or notched; the white tip can be apparent but is often so narrow as to be indistinct.

The head of an adult Cooper's, especially the male's, is subtly different from that of the adult sharpie. The adult male Cooper's has a dark cap that contrasts with its blue-gray nape, and most show gray on the cheek. Because the Cooper's head is larger than the sharpie's, the eye is more forward, giving the Cooper's a particularly fierce look.

Adult sharpies have no contrast between the crown and nape; there is no dark cap. The cheeks are rufous, and the eye is more centered in the small head, giving the bird a startled look.

Young accipiters wear brown plumage throughout their first winter, acquiring adult plumage in their second fall. There are several other brownish hawks with streaked underparts. The only ones likely to be seen at a feeder site are young red-tails and young red-shouldered hawks (p. 117). Neither of these hawks has the bright eyes of the young accipiters.

The different young accipiters offer several plumage clues to their identity. Young goshawks have a white eyebrow that flares broadly behind the eye. A narrow white eyebrow is usually seen on the sharpie, less often on a young Cooper's. A young Cooper's is often distinguished by its particularly tawny head. The streaking on a young bird's underparts is variable but generally less extensive on Cooper's, which often shows a clear belly. Some sharpies have reddish streaking.

An accipiter's eye color changes with age and can be used to distinguish individuals. Young birds have yellow eyes. In adults, the color deepens from yellow-orange to ruby red over four or five years.

About the Information in the Accounts of The Birds We Feed

The species accounts on the following pages include a wealth of information about the birds seen at feeders. Data from Project FeederWatch are provided along with a range map, photograph(s) of winter plumage, and written information. There is also space provided to make records of your sightings.

Data for the rankings are from the months of December, January, and February of the winters 1992–93 through 1998–99. Ties in the rankings are broken by standings in the most recent years.

Every species recorded by more than 1 percent of FeederWatchers continent-wide or by more than 5 percent within any one region is included, except the mallard; just over 1 percent of FeederWatchers report mallard ducks at their feeders. Several species of special interest, such as the rapidly spreading Eurasian collared-dove, are also included, even though only very small numbers are yet reported.

④ ③ ① ②

flock of 7, side yard   11/14/01 ☑ **CHIPPING SPARROW** 38

⑤
⑥

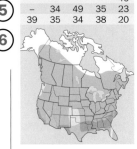

–		–	–	46
–	34	49	35	23
39	35	34	38	20

1. **Name** Most birds have separate accounts beginning with the bird's formal name. Some less common birds are combined with relatives and presented in group discussions (beginning on p. 116).

2. **Overall Rank** The top 50 feeder birds continent-wide are ranked by the number of FeederWatchers reporting them. The most commonly reported bird, the dark-eyed junco, is reported by nearly 83 percent of FeederWatchers. Number 50, the brown thrasher, is seen by just over 5 percent.

A species' rank does not reflect the number of individuals that visit a feeder or how often they visit. It is determined only by the percentage of FeederWatchers who report the species at least once.

3. **Checkbox** Check the birds you identify at your feeders. Watching your list of bird sightings grow is part of the fun of feeding birds.

4. **Title Bar** Use the title bar to record sighting information.

5. **Regional Rankings** In addition to the overall rank, a regional rankings chart is provided above each species' range map. It lists a bird's rank in every region where it is reported by more than 5 percent of FeederWatchers. To find the placement of your region's ranking on this chart, use the Region Map, at right, and the Chart Key in the margin directly above it.

Ohio residents, for instance, will find that the Region Map has their state, Illinois, Indiana, and Kentucky grouped as the East Central (EC) Region. The Chart Key shows that rankings for the EC Region are in the fourth position of the middle row.

The regional rankings chart for the chipping sparrow (next to the circled 5 above) shows that the chipping sparrow ranks 35th in the East Central region, ranks 34th in the Allegheny Region, and is most frequently reported in the Southeast, where it ranks 20th. A dash (–) indicates that it is reported in a region but by fewer than 5 percent of FeederWatchers and is therefore unranked. The absence of any mark for the Al-Can Region (AC) indicates that the chipping sparrow is absent or reported by less than one FeederWatcher in 200.

6. **Range Map** Seasonal ranges are indicated by colors on each species' range map.

▨ Summer   ▨ Winter
▨ All Year   ▨ Migration

Range maps provide a simplified picture of a species' distribution. They indicate the birds that can be expected in any local region.

Birds are not evenly distributed over their ranges. They are typically scarcest at their range limits, and to be present at all, they require suitable habitat. Weather and food availability also affect distribution in winter.

CHART KEY				
AC	NR	NP	CA	SW
NC	GL	MC	EC	SC
NA	NE	AL	MA	SE

REGION MAP

AC | Al-Can
AL | Allegheny
CA | California
EC | East Central
GL | Great Lakes
MA | Mid-Atlantic
MC | Mid-Central
NA | North Atlantic
NC | North Central
NE | New England
NP | North Pacific
NR | Northern Rockies
SC | South Central
SE | Southeast
SW | Southwest

1 DARK-EYED JUNCO ☐

7 9 1 2 1
7 6 1 3 8
7 4 3 3 9

The most widely seen winter backyard bird is, fittingly, the symbolic bird of winter in much of the United States and Canada — the dark-eyed junco, or "snowbird." Eighty-three percent of Feeder-Watchers record them, and the figure is even higher in rural areas and mature suburbs. Even if no food is set out for them, juncos might well appear in a backyard searching the ground or snow cover for wind-blown seeds.

Flocks at feeders are usually content to feed on mixed seeds scattered on the ground or fallen from hanging feeders. They do not scratch the ground to uncover food. Juncos will adapt to high platforms or hanging feeders if they have no choice, and they readily leave the ground for suet.

Some junco flocks are permanent residents from nearby nesting territories; others are migrants fleeing winter weather in the North or at high elevations. Females tend to migrate farther south than males, as they do in many species, and typically for the same reasons. Males like to stay as close as they can to their northern nesting territories so that they can arrive early in spring to stake their claim. Females find it advantageous to fly farther south, where they don't have to defer to as many dominant males. In many winter migrants, females in the southern portion of the range may outnumber males two or three to one. Junco flocks are fairly stable in winter, although they sometimes splinter or merge.

Identification "Dark-eyed" is too dull a name to comfortably describe the beautiful variations of the dark-eyed junco. Each form is commonly called by a specific name. In all forms, the pink bill, white belly, and white outer tail feathers are easy identifying marks — much better than the dark eyes.

The **SLATE-COLORED JUNCO** can be found across the continent in winter and is the only form found east of the Great Plains; males are slate gray above; females, browner and often with a back color that contrasts slightly with the hood. There is a form that winters on the central plains that resembles the slate-colored but has white wing bars and is called the **WHITE-WINGED JUNCO**.

The brown-hooded **OREGON JUNCO** winters over much of the West, often in mixed flocks with other western forms. A variation of the Oregon junco has a gray hood and extensive pink sides and is often called the **PINK-SIDED JUNCO**.

The **GRAY-HEADED JUNCO** also has gray sides and a rusty red back. It is most common in the Southwest.

The different forms all interbreed, which is why they aren't considered separate species any longer. Plumage variations of almost any combination are possible, particularly in the West. Even among flocks of eastern slate-colored juncos, much variation can be noted, especially among the browner females.

SLATE-COLORED JUNCO

SLATE-COLORED JUNCO

OREGON JUNCO

OREGON JUNCO

GRAY-HEADED JUNCO

☐ MOURNING DOVE 2

The mourning dove may be the most abundant bird on the continent. It is found everywhere except deep forest, areas of intense cold, and arid land without nearby water. Mourning dove populations ballooned during the centuries that Europeans colonized North America. And in the last half of the 1900s, the birds expanded range into the northern United States and southern Canada.

Some recent data show mourning doves decreasing, but FeederWatchers haven't noticed it. In the 1990s, a steadily increasing percentage of FeederWatchers reported them in the Mid-Central, Southwest, and South Central regions. In the North Central Region, the mourning dove ranked 8th in 1999, three spots higher than the 11th place average from 1993 to 1999.

Small songbirds often scatter when jays arrive — not the mourning doves. Even crows don't scare them. They are like squatters staging a sit-in and continue feeding contentedly on cracked corn, millet, and a variety of other seeds; birds often show individual preferences. Given the choice, they prefer to feed in fields on wasted grain, which is why FeederWatchers report them increasing on croplands in the South and Midwest. On uncultivated lands, they consume a wide variety of wild seeds.

In late fall, mourning doves gather in large flocks that are well known to FeederWatchers across nearly all of the United States and southern Canada. Many northern mourning doves migrate south in winter, but an increasing number remain as far north as the Gulf of St. Lawrence, huddling deep in sheltering conifers to roost. They come to feeders in the largest numbers when deep snow blankets the ground, covering their grains and wild seeds.

In many states, mourning doves are game birds. Maintained and fattened on farmers' grains, more mourning doves are harvested annually than all other game birds combined. It is a loss that the species is well prepared to sustain, as proven by the birds' increasing abundance. Other birds, small mammals, and reptiles have long preyed on mourning doves with as much enthusiasm as humans and four to five times as much success.

Mourning doves have adapted to predation by raising as many as six broods of two chicks each during a season. The nestlings grow rapidly and leave the nest in just 15 days — as soon as they can maintain their body temperature. Parents continue to feed them outside the nest for another 15 days. Often the hen will start laying her next clutch of eggs while still caring for her current brood. Heavy predation is an important part of keeping mourning dove populations in check.

WHITE-WINGED DOVES range from southern California to western Louisiana and sometimes flock with mourning doves. Most of them overwinter south of the U.S. but return to nesting grounds in Arizona and California in February. They rank 41st in the South Central Region, where winter flocks in southern Louisiana have been steadily increasing. In the Southwest, they rank 58th. There is an introduced population in Florida that visits feeders, but there are too few in the region to be ranked.

Identification No other large North American dove or pigeon has a long pointed tail. Females are a bit browner than males and have slightly less iridescence on the sides of their necks. The western subspecies is noticeably paler than eastern birds. Like all pigeons and doves, the mourning dove nods its head as it walks.

The white-winged dove has a long band of white in the wing that is apparent and diagnostic in both standing and flying birds. It is a slightly larger bird than the mourning dove and has a blunt, not pointed, tail with white in the corners.

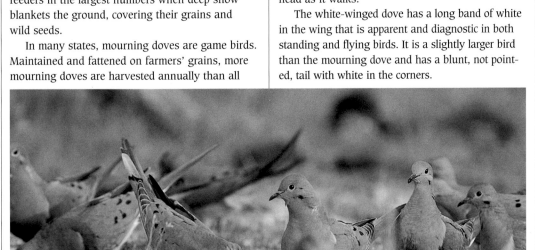

3 BLUE JAY ☐

6	–			30
3	2	3	6	2
2	2	5	6	4

Ravens and crows are commonly considered the most intelligent songbirds, but if a blue jay could talk, it would probably argue the point loudly. "I'm as canny, inquisitive, and resourceful as any crow or raven," the jay might squawk, "and I can spot danger and give my 'steel-cold scream' quicker than either of them." True, we would have to admit, though we might well wonder how a jay — however smart — could quote Thoreau's moving description of its alarm call.

Blue jays are smart enough, ornithologists suspect, that they may alter their behavior when they know they are being watched. Their intelligence and princely attire compensate for their bad manners. Blue jays always create a ruckus on arrival at a feeder and may emit a first-class imitation of a hawk's call to clear the whole area. If a flock of jays arrives, the dominant individual commandeers the prime feeding spot and the rest feed elsewhere or wait their turn.

FeederWatchers who enjoy watching jays' antics often lay out unshelled peanuts for them. Sunflower seeds, cracked or whole corn, and suet are also popular. Like all corvids, blue jays sometimes prey on the eggs and nestlings of other birds and have been widely disliked for it since Audubon's famous *Birds of America,* in which three blue jays are portrayed pillaging a nest. "Thieves, as I would call them," Audubon writes, "were it fit for me to pass judgment on their actions. See how each is enjoying the fruits of his knavery, sucking the egg which he has pilfered from the nest of some innocent Dove or harmless Partridge!"

In reality, eggs and young birds are a minor part of the blue jay's diet, which is heavily vegetarian. Nuts are staples in the wild, but the birds are omnivorous, which allows them to occupy various habitats, wild and developed. Blue jays in the wild tend to be shy, wary birds. Those that live around developed land, and most do, are bolder.

Blue jays seem to make individual decisions about migration, based partly on the food supply available. FeederWatchers in the northernmost part of their range see few of them in winter; most migrate. Many birds in the middle tier of states also migrate south in winter, to be replaced by the northern birds.

Migratory flocks in the East may include several hundred birds, and groups of a dozen or more may remain together all winter. Migrants usually return to the same area each winter, although perhaps half of a flock will be young birds replacing those that have died. Life is tough for a young jay, but those that master it can live for 10 or 15 years.

Identification Not all "blue" jays are "blue jays." The crest, gray underparts, and tail markings distinguish the blue jay from other jays and songbirds that are blue.

4 BLACK-CAPPED CHICKADEE ☐

1	1	2	55	10
1	1	6	9	
1	1	1	14	42

"This is one of our resident birds," wrote ornithologist Alexander Wilson in 1840, "active, noisy, and restless; hardy beyond any of his size, braving the severest cold of our continent as far north as the country round Hudson's Bay, and always appearing most lively in the coldest weather." Wilson also noted that black-capped chickadees were seen "in parties of six, eight, or more" and were "fond of sunflower seeds." We can add that they are bold at feeding stations and love hulled peanuts and suet as well as sunflower seeds.

Black-capped chickadees are ranked first in more FeederWatch Regions than any other bird. More than 99 percent of FeederWatchers in New England report them in some years. Feeders are a valuable resource

☐ DOWNY WOODPECKER 5

8	2	14	44	13
2	3	5	7	15
4	5	6	7	11

The smallest woodpecker, the downy, is also the most widespread and commonly seen. They are permanent residents that usually stay paired throughout the winter, although they may feed some distance apart.

Several downies may meet at a yard at the same time, particularly in harsh weather. Typically, one bird will dominate a feeder and the others will wait their turn. They thrive on suet and puddings and regularly take peanuts, sunflower seeds, and saf-flower seeds from platform feeders or the ground. Tube feeders don't intimidate them if that's where the desired food is.

Even in winter, they are able to uncover insect matter secreted in bark. Their small size permits them to inspect small branches and twigs as well as tree trunks. Downies also take nuts and berries in season and often feed on goldenrod galls and corn-stalks. They don't cache food.

When other feeder birds are alarmed and scram-ble for cover, the downy typically freezes on a tree trunk or slips around the tree to the opposite side of the apparent danger. FeederWatchers rarely report them bathing in winter; they are known to take snow baths, however. At night, each bird roosts in its own cavity, typically excavated in a snag. Occasionally they have been found roosting in bluebird boxes.

Identification The white back distinguishes the downy woodpecker from all except the hairy wood-pecker. The white plumage is noticeably grayer on some northwestern downies, and the white spotting in the wings is often greatly reduced in birds of the Rockies and the Northwest.

The details of the downy's black-and-white head pattern and the male's red crown spot are very indi-vidualistic. By checking these marks carefully and

taking notes, specific birds can be identified. People used to seeing three or four downies queued up at a time have discovered that a dozen or more were visiting at different times.

Similar Species The hairy woodpecker (p. 84) is nearly identical but larger and with a much longer bill. If making size comparisons seems difficult, do what Iowa FeederWatcher Ron Piper does and mark your tree or suet feeder pole so that you can gauge size accurately. Ron places thin strips of red tape 6 inches apart on his suet feeder pole.

I've had my downies eat from just about any of my feeders. They like the tube feeder with finch mix, probably because of the peanuts in it. They also will go to the sunflower hopper, but primarily they go to the suet feeder. They will also go to the water dish on the deck at times.

Merle Turkington
Hebron, Connecticut

for black-caps. Studies have determined that flocks fortunate enough to have a backyard feeding station in their territory survive hard winters better.

Chickadees are busy foragers, dangling acrobati-cally on trees and hanging feeders but rarely inspecting the ground. They are so successful at finding insect matter in the furrows, crevices, and crannies of trees that much of their diet is animal, even in winter. Chickadees seldom eat food at a feeder. Instead, they carry a seed to a spot where they can hold it with their feet and peck it open. They also cache food. Tests show that black-capped chickadees can recall cache locations for at least a month and even remember which caches hold choice bits. If a cache has been stolen, they replace it.

Black-capped chickadees seldom travel far from their natal nest. In summer, most fledglings disperse less than a mile and attach to a flock. Flocks are sea-sonal groupings built around a territorial pair. For the most part, members live together from late sum-mer through winter and maintain a regular territory. In some areas, black-caps migrate, and in winters when food gets scarce, some of the most northerly black-caps (mostly young birds) irrupt south.

Identification The black-capped chickadee's dis-tinctive white cheeks and black cap and bib are also characteristic of the Carolina chickadee. See Carolina chickadee, p. 94, and The Confusing Look-alikes, p. 70.

6 HOUSE FINCH ☐

The house finch was originally found only in dry lowlands in the West — arid scrub, canyons, yards, and towns. It is the species most commonly reported by California FeederWatchers and ranks second in the Southwest.

The eastern population of house finches reportedly grew from a few western birds set free on Long Island, New York, in 1940. Threatened with prosecution, dealers in illegally caged house finches let the evidence take wing. It is nearly certain that the male house finch reported near Jones Beach on Long Island on 11 April 1941 — the first eastern report of a house finch — was a survivor from unlawful captivity. Evidence of the crime was soon to be found in everyone's backyard.

In the 1960s, house finches began rapidly expanding range in the mid-Atlantic states and New England. They proved to be able to hold their own in competition with house sparrows for the right to live close to us and our houses. In the 1980s, house finches began to claim the Southeast and Midwest.

FeederWatcher data record the proliferation of the house finch across the plains in the 1990s and the ultimate joining of the eastern flock with its parent western population. Twenty percent or less of FeederWatchers reported them in any of the Central regions in 1989. By 1999, they had visited more than 60 percent of feeders in the North and South Central regions and a whopping 85 percent in the Mid-Central.

FeederWatchers also mapped the spread of house finch eye disease, which developed in eastern house finches after 1994 (p. 64). House finch eye disease has been very recently reported in western house finches but is still rare in the West. Avian pox is the more prevalent disease in western house finches.

House finches are year-round seedeaters. At feeders, they eagerly take black-oilers and a variety of other seeds. They also frequently drink and bathe if water is available. Yards with conifers for roosting are especially favored. They roost communally in the densest conifer tangles, sometimes with house sparrows.

Western house finches are typically resident, but some eastern birds in the northern tier of states have become migrants, perhaps in search of winter food. Females migrate farther south than males, resulting in smaller flocks of mostly males during winter in the North and larger flocks of predominantly females in many backyards across the South. There is banding evidence that some migrating birds return to the same wintering area in consecutive years.

Identification See pp. 70–71 for a full discussion of separating house, purple, and Cassin's finches.

House finches are familiar, but there is a lot of color variation in males, both in extent and shade, which causes confusion. Males sporting shades of yellow, orange, and red are possible. The colors come from carotenoid pigments ingested during feather development. Purple and Cassin's finches also get their color by ingesting pigment but show variations much less commonly.

Purple finches, pine siskins, and Cassin's finches are sometimes overlooked in flocks of house finches, concealed by the typical variations in a flock. Or more frequently a person unfamiliar with the less common finches will sort through a flock of house finches and "identify" the atypical ones as some other species, such as purple finch.

Most male house finches gain their bright colors the first year after hatching, but yearling males in the Great Basin look like females until their second year.

☐ AMERICAN GOLDFINCH 7

Goldfinches are nearly always in flocks. Even when nesting, they often feed in flocks. In winter, flocks can balloon to a hundred or more, and competition for a perch at a tube feeder filled with black-oilers or niger seed can get serious. Birds defend their perches and feed continuously until forced off by a more determined or hungrier individual. Feeding is particularly frenzied before a winter storm.

Goldfinches consume seeds almost exclusively, especially the seeds of composite plants like dandelions and thistles. Other seedeating birds often supplement their diet with insects; their nestlings require protein-rich animal matter to survive and grow. Young goldfinches manage to develop on the seeds their parents regurgitate to them.

In winter, flocks of goldfinches may search large areas for a feeding station or patch of exposed weed seeds. They are known to fly 5 miles or more just to get from one feeding spot to another — far enough to build up a good appetite!

Goldfinches are not as cold-hardy as many finches, and northern populations migrate. Even in the broad portion of the continent where they appear year-round, the flock that visits a feeding station in winter is often different from the one that comes in summer. The bulk of the population winters in a different region each year. Sometimes the largest concentrations are in the Southeast or South Central regions, and sometimes in the North Atlantic or Great Lakes regions.

Migration takes place in daylight (most songbirds migrate at night), with flocks of birds bouncing along in the characteristic deep, undulating flight of finches. Because goldfinches nest so much later than most songbirds, their "spring" migration lasts into June. After nesting, most birds leave their northern range by November, but southern migration continues into December.

The most repeated explanation for their unusually late nesting is that goldfinches wait for thistles, an important source of food, to flower. This may be true, but ornithologists also suspect that nesting is delayed because goldfinches molt in spring (they are the only finch that does) and the energy requirements for molting and nesting are too great for both events to occur at the same time.

Identification In summer plumage, goldfinches are easy to identify. Males are an eye-popping lemon yellow (the only yellow bird with a jet black forehead and wings). Females are mostly greenish yellow with an olive-brown back and brownish black (not jet black) wings and tail.

In winter, the plumage of both sexes is so brown that the birds are sometimes not recognized as goldfinches. Males retain their jet black wings and

are a bit brighter below than females, especially on the throat. Males also have a bright, often pure yellow shoulder patch in winter that contrasts well with their black wings.

The brightness of individuals varies considerably and so does the timing of their molts. Some males start putting out their first bright yellow in midwinter. There are times when a flock can contain nearly the complete range of plumage variations.

Similar Species In the West, lesser goldfinches (p. 114) can be confused with the American goldfinch. In the East, the pine warbler (p. 124) has similarly obscure plumage.

WINTER PLUMAGE

PARTIAL MOLT

NEAR-COMPLETE MOLT

8 NORTHERN CARDINAL ☐

				51
13	7	2	1	1
18	9	4	1	2

The possibility of attracting a cardinal is what prompts many people to set out their first offerings for birds. Chances of success are extremely good in the East and Midwest anywhere south of the Great Lakes in winter.

Dusk and dawn, when few other birds are around, are favorite feeding times for cardinals. Sunflower and safflower seeds are favorite foods. Peanut butter puddings are also relished. In the wild, their strong bills allow them to exploit a variety of seeds, as well as fruit, insects, and buds as available.

The steady northward push of the cardinal has been documented since the middle and late 1800s, when cardinals colonized northern Ohio and southern Michigan. From there, they expanded west into Iowa and Minnesota, reaching the Twin Cities by 1930. FeederWatchers now report them from most of northern Minnesota and southwest Ontario.

The expansion into the Northeast began in the 1900s. From Pennsylvania and New Jersey, they swept across New York and into southern Ontario, reaching Toronto by 1930. In the 1970s, they extended their reach to Maine and Ottawa, Canada. With the critical help of feeders, cardinals now over-winter in small numbers all the way to Nova Scotia.

The first cardinals in Arizona were reported in the 1870s. Expansion there has been limited by arid habitat and high elevations, where cardinals give way to their closest relatives, **PYRRHULOXIAS**. In the Southwest, pyrrhuloxias rank 53rd and are reported nearly as often as cardinals by FeederWatchers.

River valleys are the typical avenues of expansion and still hold the highest concentrations of cardinals. Yearling birds are the ones that usually colonize new territory; adults are sedentary. In winter, cardinals might wander a few miles to find food, and a yard may be graced with many of the brilliant red birds.

Identification The large bill and prominent crest make the brownish female cardinal as easy to identify as the brilliant red male. Cardinals have bright pink bills, except the youngsters, which have dull bills for their first two or three months. Otherwise, young birds resemble females.

Variations in color intensity and the black face pattern can sometimes be used to identify individual males. Females can show considerable variation. Birds in Arizona and southwest New Mexico are a larger, more outgoing race than the shy, eastern birds; males have crests as bright as their breasts and no black extending across the top of the bill.

Similar Species In the Southwest, female cardinals can be confused with pyrrhuloxias, but in addition to plumage differences, the pyrrhuloxia has a yellow parrot-like bill.

9 HOUSE SPARROW ☐

–	3	15	9	3
6	10	7	5	5
17	14	11	13	27

By 1851, when the first house sparrows were introduced in Brooklyn, New York, they had already had centuries of experience adapting to civilization in Europe. They easily established the same lifestyle across North America — attaching themselves to urban buildings and rural barns and living primarily on cereal grains scattered on the ground. Flocks of a dozen or more house sparrows often camp out at a feeder, and well-fed flocks will multiply.

Most FeederWatchers consider house sparrows to be pests but admit a grudging respect for their toughness and adaptability. They are considered non-native and can be legally destroyed. Many have been, and in most regions, the number of

☐ **WHITE-BREASTED NUTHATCH** 10

14	35	24	16
4	8	12	11	30
13	6	8	9	18

The white-breasted nuthatch is more than a little special. It appears to have a unique partnership with gravity that allows it a topsy-turvy view of the world. While clinging upside down to a tree trunk, the nuttie arcs its head outward and up until the bill is fully horizontal, calmly surveying its surroundings. Should it see anything worthy of comment, it honks once or twice, sounding much like a distant model-T Ford.

A white-breasted nuthatch remains bonded to its partner and their territory (a patch of deciduous or mixed woods) all year. They are spirited in their defense of territory from other nuthatches but generally mild-mannered in their relationships with birds at a feeder. They often associate with chickadees and other mixed-flocking species.

More often than not, white-breasted nuthatches are reported in pairs by FeederWatchers, and they are recorded all winter. Territorial bonds are sometimes lessened at feeders in the worst weather, and several pairs of white-breasted nutties may visit at different times of day, or a floater (typically a juvenile without a territory) may be allowed access.

The upside-down foraging style allows the nuthatch to find bits of larvae and other foods secreted in tree crevices that upward climbers miss. Even in winter, the white-breasted nuthatch fills about 25 percent of its diet with animal matter. Consequently, it often spends time at a backyard suet feeder if one is available. Or it scours the area beneath the suet feeder for tiny fallen morsels. White-breasted nuthatches will feed on the ground and from hanging feeders as well as tree trunks. Acorns and deciduous tree seeds account for the majority of food.

Puddings are as popular with nuthatches as suet, but seeds are the winter staple. At feeders, any seed or nut the size of safflower or larger is likely to be taken. Seeds in shells are jammed in a

bark crevice and hammered until the shell breaks. Unshelled seeds or nuts are often cached.

White-breasted nuthatches roost alone in a natural cavity or sometimes a woodpecker hole.

Identification The white-breasted nuthatch is larger than the other nuthatches (red-breasted, p. 86; brown-headed and pygmy, p. 127). Some females, especially in the Northeast, have a grayer cap than the male, and there is variation in the amount of rusty color on the flank. There are several different races. Some have distinctly different calls and may prove to be a different species.

feeders visited by house sparrows declined by 10 to 20 percent over the 1990s. It is unlikely that the decline is due entirely to aggressive control. At least some decline at feeders is probably due to passive methods such as feeding less cracked corn and other grains that attract house sparrows.

Winter flocks of house sparrows are casual aggregations of local birds and juveniles that have dispersed from nearby areas. They often take shelter and find roosting spots in buildings or under eaves and are seldom found any distance from man-made structures. Shopping malls may have a colony hanging out at the food court. Single birds will roost in any shielding cavity, including bluebird nest boxes

placed in their vicinity. Flocks also roost communally in evergreens or thick shrubs.

Identification The male house sparrow is especially distinctive with its black bib, gray crown, rusty nape, and white cheek. Females are more subtly marked; look for the plain breast, pale eyebrow, white wing bar, and pale bill. That combination is diagnostic.

Similar Species The EURASIAN TREE SPARROW is numerous but limited to St. Louis, Missouri, and nearby Illinois. Male and female are alike and similar to the male house sparrow but brown on the crown and rump and with a black ear patch.

11 EUROPEAN STARLING ☐

23	18	13	33	9
14	11	9	10	18
8	12	12	12	30

A year ago, we put a flicker box on our cottonwood tree. Soon a pair of flickers was doing some remodeling of the entrance hole. We were so excited! They spent days in and around the box, then a starling showed up. It waited, and when the flicker came out, the starling simply went in and stayed there. The flickers didn't even try to put up a fight.

Diane Bingeman
Southwest North Dakota

Starlings would be ranked in the top 10 if many FeederWatchers didn't discourage their visits. Often they are easily spooked and decide not to return to a feeding area after being scared away several times — especially when seeds are the only fare available. An opportunity to load up on suet or puddings may make them more persistent.

Much of starling behavior is opportunism, including an individual's diet. In general, they prefer bugs and other invertebrates when available, often patrolling a lawn in loose ranks. In winter, when animal food is scarce, they take quantities of fruit and berries. Seeds are a regular but usually smaller and less preferred component of their diet.

Their diverse behavior is displayed in other ways than individual feeding preferences. Many

starlings gather in huge flocks to roost at night in trees or on structures. Others take the opportunity to duck into a nest box or cavity by themselves or find a warm corner in a city. During the day, a flock of 100 or more starlings, sometimes mixed with blackbirds or robins, might overwhelm a feeder, but about one-third of the time, FeederWatcher data record them visiting in groups of one to three. Starlings that like the fare at a given feeder can be expected to return.

If 100 to 200 million starlings survive the winter to breed in spring, as has been estimated, then 50 to 100 million cavities will be usurped from native cavity nesters, including the woodpeckers that excavated many of them. That domination of nesting cavities has been disastrous for native cavity nesters, such as bluebirds and red-headed woodpeckers in the East and gilded flickers and Gila woodpeckers in the Southwest.

Identification The name would suggest an inspiringly beautiful bird. Instead, the European starling is rather dumpy, with a stubby tail, long beak, and flat head. The shape is its easiest mark. The plumage is basically blackish in adults but changes seasonally from glossy in spring and summer to dotted with small white spots in fall and winter. The bill color changes from black to a bright yellow in breeding birds. Some males begin showing yellow at the base of their bills as early as Christmas.

12 TUFTED TITMOUSE ☐

	22	13	12	7
25	7	9	4	3

The small groups of tufted titmice that visit a feeder in winter are composed primarily of family members. The core is a pair that typically maintains a permanent territory throughout the year. Often some of the offspring will remain with them over the winter and disperse later in spring. One youngster may even remain through the spring, helping at the nest.

Many young tufted titmice disperse shortly after fledging and flock with neighboring families. FeederWatcher data show that pairs are recorded about 40 percent of the time at feeding stations, while groups of three or more tufted titmice are seen slightly more than half the time. They come for seeds, hulled peanuts, and puddings. Sunflower seeds are carefully selected one at a time and taken to a sheltered spot for hammering the shell open and eating. Much food is cached.

Once a southern bird with a range similar to that of the Carolina chickadee, tufted titmice have steadily pressed northward and now share feeders in many locales with black-capped chickadees. Their newly

☐ AMERICAN CROW 13

38	18	35	24
15	17	19	14	21
14	11	13	16	25

Crows are part of a family, the corvids, that includes jays, magpies, and ravens. Corvids mate for life, maintain strong family bonds, are omnivorous, cache food, and have generally benefited from mankind in spite of frequent persecution.

Corvids are considered the most intelligent songbird family (parrots are not songbirds), and crows and ravens are at the head of the class. The most striking result of their intelligence is individual personality and adaptability. To a degree, crows are what we make of them, as they react logically to the treatment they receive. They can recognize a gun and learn its range as quickly as they can find scraps of food and learn to petition the provider for more.

Throughout the 1990s, American crows became more common at feeders, in some regions visiting nearly twice as many feeding stations at the end of the decade as they did at the beginning. The yearly rank for the North Central Region was in the top 10 by the end of the 1990s. Still, in many areas and at most times, crows do not usually come to feeders unless deliberately attracted.

They sometimes will nibble at corn kernels broadcast on the ground, but they prefer dried dog kibble, corn chips, peanuts in the shell, table scraps (especially meat on the bone), and bakery goods. Boiled egg yolks and canned pet food are special treats sometimes offered by FeederWatchers who delight in watching crows' sometimes charming, sometimes hilarious antics.

FeederWatchers distressed by hawk attacks at their feeders appreciate the way crows relentlessly mob hawks. A perched hawk frequently tries to ignore the harassment but eventually flies off — with a crow escort.

Crows are easily trained to visit at specific times. They learn to recognize and trust the humans who feed them. Small family groups usually forage together during the day, but larger flocks form as crows return from daytime foraging to their nighttime roosts. Late in the day especially, crows look for large trees in which to congregate.

Until the mid-1900s, roosts were typically in trees in isolated or rural areas. Crows have since become increasingly urban. One theory is that they are escap-

claimed range resembles their original strongholds, the Mississippi and Ohio river basins, in being lowland deciduous forest with significant rainfall and the presence of snags for nesting and roosting.

Feeders are likely a major reason for the northern range expansion of the tufted titmouse. Tests show what FeederWatchers know; tufted titmice thrive at feeders. Nearly two-thirds of FeederWatchers report seeing them during every count period.

Identification The crest and black forehead are great marks for the tufted titmouse, but it is the big black eye that imparts the better part of the bird's special look. The eye is made larger by the black ring surrounding it.

The black-crested race of the tufted titmouse is found in south Texas. It has a white forehead and black on the front of the crest.

Similar Species Oak and juniper titmice (p. 126) are western relatives of the tufted titmouse and are sometimes mistakenly called tufted titmice.

ing shooting. They are legal game in some states and commonly persecuted illegally in others. Many of the birds that roost in developed areas remain throughout the day to scavenge on delicacies such as roadkill and fast food remnants. Others travel tens of miles each day, flying with their steady, rowing wing beats, to reach rural feeding areas.

Similar Species Besides the American crow, there is a **FISH CROW** in the East, and there is a **NORTHWESTERN CROW** along the Pacific Coast (ranked 29th in the Al-Can Region). The three species cannot be reliably separated in the field visually.

All birds in the northwestern crow's range — along the Pacific Coast north from and including Seattle, Washington — are presumed to be northwestern crows.

Fish crows are numerous near water or at landfills in the Southeast and along the Atlantic Coast as far north as Maine. They are distinguished by call, a nasal, double-noted *eh, eh,* much different from the American crow's *cah.*

I have five crows. This is their second season with me, and I keep a journal just for them. They are THE most fascinating birds for me — intelligent, with language and their own society. I study them. Plus, they're hysterically funny.

Anne Mundstuk
North Reading,
Massachusetts

14 HAIRY WOODPECKER ☐

9	5	24	58	22
5	12	16	18	45
6	13	15	22	35

The hairy woodpecker comes to most of the same feeders that attract downy woodpeckers (p. 77), but they usually come much less frequently. They are not as bold as the little downy, and some Feeder-Watchers report better luck attracting them when feeders are placed away from the house and closer to surrounding woods. Urban FeederWatchers generally have to be contented with attracting only downies to their feeders.

FeederWatchers report pairs of hairy woodpeckers visiting their feeders almost as often as single birds. In the wild, the sexes tend to feed slightly differently, permitting them to accompany each other without competing for the same resources. Males more often search for insect larvae by drilling into the thin bark of the higher branches; females most frequently scour the deep bark crevices of the lower trunk. Downy woodpeckers behave similarly. In the worst of the winter weather, pairs may forage separately.

Insect matter is the hairy woodpecker's staple, but it also takes some berries and nuts or seeds. At feeders, the hairy makes the same choices as the downy — mostly suet and puddings. When hummingbird feeders are set out in spring, both species may attempt to drink the nectar. Hairies also roost like downies in carefully excavated individual cavities. Each bird may prepare several roosts.

Identification The white back distinguishes the hairy woodpecker from all except the downy. The sparkling white areas of plumage are noticeably grayer on some northwestern hairies, and the white spotting in the wings is often reduced in birds of the Rockies and the Northwest, following the same regional pattern of variation as in the downy.

Similar Species The hairy woodpecker can be readily distinguished from the downy by its much longer bill. Call notes are also diagnostic. The hairy woodpecker gives a different *peek!* than the downy, one that is easily recognized once noted.

15 RED-BELLIED WOODPECKER ☐

17	20	10	13	12
–	19	14	10	7

Red-bellied woodpeckers typically come to a feeder one or two at a time in winter and seldom stay long. A couple of days may pass between visits. As a result, the red-belly is one of the more appreciated regulars at an eastern feeder. It typically dominates other birds and even squirrels, but it doesn't bully everything else off a platform feeder.

A northern range expansion of the red-bellied woodpecker occurred throughout the late 1900s.

Most of the northern birds are residents that endure chilly winters. They are recorded by FeederWatchers right up to the northern limit of their range.

Rankings of the red-bellied woodpecker have improved over the 1990s in every northern region from the Great Plains eastward. In New England, the percentage of FeederWatchers reporting them increased from the low teens at the beginning of the 1990s to the mid-thirties by the years 1997, 1998, and 1999.

The red-belly is widespread and numerous, in part because it is a generalist, taking everything from insects to seeds, berries, and fruit in season. It feeds on the ground and in bushes, as well as on deciduous trees. It even catches bugs in flight, like a flycatcher.

At feeders, red-bellies are known to check out almost everything available, including the water. Suet, puddings, sunflower seeds, and peanuts get a lot of attention. In fall, much food is cached for the hard days of winter.

☐ PURPLE FINCH 16

	–	17	17	65
16	14	15	22	20
12	15	18	21	16

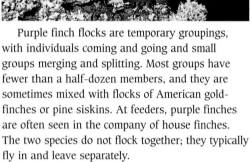

Purple finches are winter wanderers, especially in the East. Often their visits last only a few days. Attracting them one winter is no guarantee that these handsome little birds will visit again the next. And if purple finches do come two years in a row, chances are slim that any of the individuals are repeat visitors.

In some FeederWatch Regions, notably the Great Lakes and Mid-Atlantic, purple finch attendance at feeders in the 1990s often varied two-to-one from year to year.

Although many overwinter in the warm Gulf states, purple finches are cold-hardy birds, and some consistently brave the rigorous winters of Edmonton, Alberta, and southern Newfoundland. In the West, those nesting in northern or mountainous areas withdraw to winter in valleys, foothills, and coastal regions. They occasionally irrupt into the eastern lowlands and deserts of California and Arizona.

Identification The red-bellied woodpecker's barred back is unique throughout most of its range. The male is further distinguished by a brilliant red head stripe running from bill to hindneck. In the female, the red is restricted to the nape and above the bill.

Similar Species Two woodpeckers much like the red-bellied visit southwestern feeders. The **GOLDEN-FRONTED WOODPECKER'S** range is centered in Texas and overlaps slightly with that of the red-bellied. Too few golden-fronteds are reported for the bird to be ranked. The **GILA WOODPECKER** is widespread in southern Arizona and bordering areas of California. It ranks 52nd in the Southwest Region.

Both golden-fronted and Gila woodpeckers have backs like the red-bellied. The golden-fronted has a golden or orangish nape and a similarly colored small patch above the bill; males also have a small red crown patch. Gila woodpeckers are the plainest of the three species. Females have unmarked tawny heads; males have a small red crown patch.

Purple finch flocks are temporary groupings, with individuals coming and going and small groups merging and splitting. Most groups have fewer than a half-dozen members, and they are sometimes mixed with flocks of American goldfinches or pine siskins. At feeders, purple finches are often seen in the company of house finches. The two species do not flock together; they typically fly in and leave separately.

Although the purple finch is the larger bird, the house finch is dominant in 9 out of 10 encounters, according to one study. The invasion of the house finch in the East has been blamed for the large decline — greater than 50 percent — of eastern purple finches since 1966. However, the link is questionable because house finches stay near buildings in the East and do not compete with purple finches in the wild for food or nesting sites. Western populations have remained stable.

In the wild, purple finches usually forage in deciduous trees and only occasionally on the ground. They are especially fond of ash, box elder, and elm seeds. In backyards, they seem to readily accept low platform feeders or sunflower seeds strewn on the ground as well as on hanging feeders and high platforms. They typically roost in trees and especially like dense conifers.

As for most other small birds, the average life span of the purple finch is short, perhaps a couple of years, but one banded bird is known to have lived in the wild for 14 years.

Identification For those unfamiliar with them, the purple finch is easily confused with Cassin's finch (p. 112) or the house finch (p. 78). The differences are compared in detail on pp. 70–71.

With a little experience, all three finches (or six, as females differ from males) can be separated with confidence. Eventually the practiced eye wonders how the chunky-looking purple and Cassin's finches (larger bodies, shorter and more deeply notched tails) could ever be confused with the trim-looking house finch.

17 RED-BREASTED NUTHATCH ☐

6	10	9	41	25
9	15	24	26	35
11	16	20	28	41

The red-breasted nuthatch is the coniferous counterpart of the white-breasted nuthatch (p. 81), upside-down lifestyle included. However, it is more the size of a chickadee and, like a 'dee, investigates tree limbs more often than the tree trunks favored by the white-breasted nuthatch. It is also much bolder than the white-breasted, with very little fear of humans. It is especially fond of the seeds of spruce, fir, and other conifers and may hang acrobatically on a cone while extracting seeds.

Within its permanent northern range, the red-breasted nuthatch ranks in the top 10 annually. Over the rest of the continent, its yearly numbers fluctuate greatly in response to cone crop success in Canada and the western mountains of the United States.

The average ranking of 24 for the Mid-Central Region, for example, includes irruption years such as 1998, when the red-breasted nuttie ranked 15th, with nearly half of all FeederWatchers in the region reporting it. The following year, 1999, fewer than 5 percent of FeederWatchers saw one. Conifers are preferred in irruptions, but the birds also advance across the prairies eating weed seeds.

The red-breasted nuthatch is as territorial as the white-breasted, but in irruptions they usually don't defend a territory, and FeederWatchers occasionally report several at once. More often red-breasted nutties visit a feeder alone or in pairs, taking sunflower seeds or bits of suet or pudding. Like the 'dees and titmice, they carefully weigh seeds in their bills before selecting a heavy one and packing it off for shelling and eating.

Identification The "racing stripes" on the head and the rusty underparts are easy marks for the red-breasted nuthatch. On males, the crown is black and contrasts with the gray-blue back. On females, the crown is usually the same color as the back, and the rusty underparts are paler than the male's. The call is a higher-pitched version of the white-breasted nuthatch's and often likened to a tiny tin horn.

18 WHITE-THROATED SPARROW ☐

–	–	43	42	64
30	30	21	23	16
24	17	16	11	12

The white-throat is the most frequently reported sparrow (the house sparrow is not a true sparrow) at feeders in the South Central Region and in the eastern coastal regions from New England to the Southeast.

Until 1961, it was thought that the two forms of the white-throated sparrow represented sex or age differences. Males or adults were presumed to be the ones with the bright, white-striped crowns; females or immatures were the duller, tan-striped form. It was a fair assumption, true in every other case with similar birds.

Instead, it was found that males and females could be either form and that, in a quirky twist, individuals almost always mated with the opposite form! It is not a matter of opposites attracting, however. The white-striped females control the situation. Males of both forms prefer to mate with them, but they overwhelmingly accept only tan-striped suitors. The rejected males and females then accept each other. The mixed matings ensure that both forms continue.

In winter, the color of the sparrow's crown stripes ceases to affect status; only age and sex matter, with older males heading the hierarchy. One of the perks that comes with status is getting to feed closest to concealing hedges, shrubs, and brush piles.

White-throats dislike venturing far from cover; they feed underneath or at its edges, kicking up leaf litter and looking for the weed seeds that are their winter staple. At feeders, they will take millet or other small seeds placed on the ground or a platform near cover. They also take insects and berries in the wild when they can find them.

WHITE-STRIPED FORM

TAN-STRIPED FORM

☐ SONG SPARROW 19

Song sparrows are territorial. Even in winter when territorial boundaries can be relaxed, Feeder-Watchers usually see them alone or in pairs, unlike the flocks of other little brown birds that can carpet a feeding ground. They are a brush-loving, cold-hardy species, ranked in every region except the North Central in winter. Millet and mixed seeds satisfy them, but they might sample puddings or anything that's available to them from the ground.

Song sparrows often seem more furtive than the other sparrows and finches at a feeder, reluctant to come out from cover to feed and quick to take alarm. When in the open, they often feed near other ground-feeding flocks, taking advantage of the protection provided by all the eyes in a flock.

In the coldest regions, song sparrows abandon nesting territories to migrate south in winter. In more temperate regions, part of the population migrates, and in the mildest climates, all are sedentary. Young song sparrows do not remain with their parents in winter. Those that don't migrate disperse to nearby areas. Song sparrows that migrate generally return before the last snows melt. Males return before females and pick a high perch to give voice to the song for which they are named.

The song varies with each rendition but usually starts with two or three identical, clearly spaced notes and continues for several seconds with trilled and short notes. "He is not a great or showy musi-

cian, but a singer of songs, plain every-day home songs with the heart left in them," wrote Florence Miriam Bailey in her 1902 *Handbook of Birds of the Western United States.*

Identification The song sparrow is the most common sparrow to attend feeders that has a streaked breast and central spot, but there are three others described below that can show those marks.

Because of their sedentary nature, numerous regional races of the song sparrow have evolved varying in size and shade. Some northwestern birds are a dark chocolate brown; some birds in the arid Southwest are particularly pale. Size increases to the north, with the largest birds found in the Aleutian Islands.

Similar Species The fox sparrow (p. 100) is larger than the song sparrow and has a reddish square-tipped tail.

LINCOLN'S SPARROW is closely related to the song sparrow and has a similar long, rounded tail. It is a more delicate bird than the song sparrow, with finer brown breast streaks on a buff, not white, breast. The breast spot is usually small or nonexistent. Lincoln's sparrow is occasionally reported at feeders from California east to Texas.

The **SAVANNAH SPARROW** has a short notched tail and usually has yellow lores (between the bill and the eye). It is widespread but rare at feeders.

The small flocks of white-throats that Feeder-Watchers most often record at their feeders are aggregations of birds whose individual winter territories include the feeder site. Each bird has its own small (less than an acre) territory to which it returns each winter. How young birds disperse in fall and winter is not known.

The territory is not defended from other white-throats, although birds tend to keep a few feet from one another. Dominance relationships ensure that old-timers get preferred feeding spots.

Identification The crown stripes, whether tan and brown or black and white, separate white-throated sparrows from all but the white-crowned sparrow (p. 98); the namesake throat of the white-throated sparrow separates the two of them. A yellow spot before the eye is present on most white-throats.

In winter, the crown stripes of the white-striped form are often tinged with buff, but they are not as dull as the stripes on tan-striped birds. Tan-striped birds usually show faint brown streaking on their breasts. All first-winter birds are similar to the tan-striped form, but some show a white center stripe.

Our Great Backyard Bird Count route took us past a frozen slough. The mercury hovered around zero. There, perched atop a frozen cattail, seemingly impervious to the cold, was a song sparrow, loudly singing its spring song. We saw that sparrow perched on the same cattail for four days.

Cristina Eisenberg
The Swan Valley,
Montana

20 AMERICAN ROBIN ☐

27	21	11	10	7
26	27	17	20	10
27	25	25	25	14

In fall, when robins disappear from suburban lawns, they form flocks and switch from a diet of mostly bugs and earthworms to one primarily of berries and fruit. They don't necessarily migrate south. The traditional red-breasted harbinger of spring will remain throughout the winter if fruiting shrubs and trees are available in nearby woodlands. Wintering nearby makes it easier to arrive back on the lawn in time to welcome spring! Before the last snows are gone, robins are filling the predawn hours with their flute-like notes.

Small numbers of robins have always endured subzero temperatures and found food while the majority migrated south or to lowlands where fruits were more plentiful. More recently unusually large numbers of robins have remained north. Even in the frigid northern plains of the North Central Region, 40 percent of FeederWatchers reported robins in the winters of 1994–95 and 1998–99, ranking them in the low teens each year.

Robins are generally infrequent visitors to backyard feeders. Most often they come to drink or bathe. They may arrive in a flock, but FeederWatcher data show that two-thirds of the time only one or two birds put in an appearance. Fruiting shrubs and trees like pyracantha or crab apple will attract them if cedar waxwings or other competitors don't strip off the fruit first. Raisins or bits of dried fruit plumped up in a small amount of hot water are well-liked treats. Robins may also take suet, puddings, and seeds, especially in late winter or early spring when their supply of wild food may become exhausted.

At night, flocks of robins roost together in trees, sometimes with other species such as blackbirds.

Identification Although the robin is one of our most familiar birds, many people are unaware that the female is easily distinguished from the male. Males have black heads. Females have brownish heads and a duller orange breast. There is some regional variation in color intensity. Most eastern birds show white corners in the tail.

21 AMERICAN TREE SPARROW ☐

–	29	–	–	50
20	13	23	17	59
15	18	17	29	–

Over a wide swath of the continent, the American tree sparrow is the common winter *Spizella* — a genus of small, flocking sparrows with notched tails, white wing bars, and unstreaked breasts. In the Great Lakes Region, where they are most common, over 50 percent of FeederWatchers report them in some years.

In most areas, the tree sparrow arrives in fall just after its congener, the chipping sparrow (p. 100), migrates to the southern tier of states. The seasonal rotation of the similar-looking *Spizellas* (see also the field sparrow, p. 107) might go unnoticed were it not for the tree sparrow's distinctive dark breast spot.

Ninety percent of the tree sparrow's winter diet is small weed and grass seeds. Sometimes the birds cling to stalks and peck at the seed heads, but more often they forage on the ground or on top of the snow where seeds have blown or fallen. They are occasionally seen feeding in trees on catkins, but the "tree" in their name is misleading. They are primarily ground-feeders, like most sparrows.

At feeders, tree sparrows select the smaller seeds from a batch of mixed seed. Millet and niger seeds are favorites, although even those small grains are much larger than the wild seeds the birds typically consume. To make a meal out of small wild seeds, the tree sparrow and the other *Spizellas* forage almost constantly, much as we would if our diet were peas and we had to unshell each one individually.

Tree sparrows are successful enough at finding wild seeds in winter that they tend to be most common at feeders during the worst weather. Small numbers are usually recorded by FeederWatchers, although winter flocks can be a dozen or more and

☐ PINE SISKIN 22

10	13	4	12	5
11	18	22	30	22
16	31	33	40	34

FeederWatchers in the pine siskin's permanent northern range often get to see them every winter. In the North Pacific Region, where they are most common, pine siskins are ranked in the top 10 annually, sometimes trailing only the junco for the most frequently reported bird.

In the middle and southern tier of states, siskin sightings are marked by yearly fluctuations. In an extreme example, over 80 percent of California FeederWatchers reported siskins in 1993, ranking the bird in the top 5. In the winters before and after, siskins visited only about 10 percent of California feeders and barely ranked in the top 50.

At the turn of the century, it has been deceptively easy to predict when pine siskins will irrupt from their northern and western mountain forests and visit backyards across the continent — they most often come in alternating years. However, the pattern is not dependable. Invasions sometimes happen in consecutive years, and as many as three years have elapsed between invasions.

Southwestern siskin irruptions are frequently out of sync with eastern ones, with western birds retreating to the lowlands from their mountain forests in years when eastern siskins spend the winter in their northern conifers.

Banding studies have shown that siskin flocks wander seasonally. You may have the same flock at your yard all winter if food supplies are good, but it won't be the same flock you had a previous winter. Birds seldom return to the previous year's nest site, either. Their wanderings seem solely driven by food availability, and they have been known to linger on a wintering ground long enough to nest when food supplies are sufficient. They are opportunists, much like their larger cone-feeding kin, the crossbills (p. 129). Both species exhibit the same "cone-chasing" behavior.

Siskins prefer small-coned conifers when they irrupt in winter but regularly feed in deciduous trees, thickets, and weedy fields, taking a wide variety of seeds. It is suspected that the planting of conifers on the Great Plains is the cause of their increase across the Midwest.

At feeders, they are especially fond of niger seeds and sunflower hearts taken from the ground or hanging feeders. Their relatively small bill (for a seedeater) limits them to seeds with thin shells. Siskins often show up at feeders with flocks of goldfinches or redpolls.

Some siskins are so tame that a feeding bird will sometimes hop on a finger placed beneath it rather than interrupt its feeding, especially on a cold winter morning when they are greatly in need of food.

are sometimes mixed with other species.

Adults frequently return to a good wintering site year after year, but the flocks they form are unstable aggregations with changing membership. The winter range of one individual may be as small as a few acres; another may wander over a half-dozen miles. It is not known how juveniles disperse in fall and winter.

Tree sparrows usually roost individually in thick brush or conifers but have been known to roost communally, with groups sometimes taking nightly refuge in drifts of snow.

Identification The prominent spot in the center of an otherwise clear breast is the badge of the American tree sparrow. Especially on sunny winter days, groups of tree sparrows can be heard engaging in a song-like, "tinkling" chatter.

Similar Species Lark sparrows (p. 128) have a breast spot but do not share winter range with the tree sparrow. Tree sparrows also lack the white corners in the tail and the heavily patterned face and black mustache mark of the lark sparrow.

Identification The pine siskin is a goldfinch with lots of brown streaks and very little gold. At a glance, it can pass as a female house finch and might escape notice. However, its streaks are more pronounced than those of the house finch, and its tail is shorter. More important, there is a distinctive flash of gold in the wings and tail when the siskin flies. Close up at a feeder, it is often the distinctive sharply pointed bill that is first noticed.

Individual birds may vary significantly in the amount of yellow they show and in the darkness and width of their brown streaks.

23 NORTHERN FLICKER ☐

22	8	6	18	4
23	31	14	25	25
34	29	29	27	28

Two forms of the northern flicker exist in the United States and Canada — the red-shafted in the West and the yellow-shafted in the East. Both are widespread in woodlands that have open areas for foraging. The two forms meet and hybridize in a broad range across the central plains within the rain shadow of the eastern slope of the Rockies.

A third, closely related flicker, the gilded, inhabits the Sonoran Desert, primarily Arizona. At various times, all three have been considered separate species or have been lumped as a single species.

One form of the flicker or another is reported in every FeederWatch Region. Numbers are lowest in the North and highest in the West; nearly two-thirds of Southwestern Region FeederWatchers report them.

For most of the year, ants are the food of choice for flickers, and the birds more often collect them from the ground in open grassy areas than from trees. In winter, when ants and other bugs are less available, the diet switches to fruit and some seeds.

Attractive feeder foods are puddings, suet, and black-oilers. Mealworms or bird grub is a treat. Flickers visit feeders one or two at a time but seldom come as regularly as downy or red-bellied woodpeckers. Feeders in mature suburbs with lawns and shade trees attract the birds as often as rural feeders.

Attics are popular winter roosts for flickers if they can gain access, and with their woodpecker bills, access is often not a problem. Some people provide roosting boxes under their eaves or on trees in their yard to keep a determined flicker from damaging their house.

Flickers roost in cavities but aren't as dependent on them as other woodpeckers. They sometimes sleep with their head tucked under their feathers clinging to a vertical surface, often on the sheltered side of a tree or under the eaves of a building.

Identification Those unfamiliar with flickers may not recognize them as woodpeckers because of their ground-feeding habit. The most useful mark in the wild is usually the white rump seen when the flicker flushes from the ground and flies directly away from the viewer. At feeders, the complex and colorful plumage pattern can be seen clearly. The underwing color (red in western birds, yellow in eastern ones) is from the brightly colored feather shafts.

Males have a mustache (red in western birds, black in eastern ones) lacking in females. The yellow-shafted flicker, but not the red-shafted, has a red nape patch. Young birds are duller than adults. Hybrids can show any combination of features. The **GILDED FLICKER** of the desert combines the head pattern of the red-shafted with the underwing color of the yellow-shafted flicker.

RED-SHAFTED   YELLOW-SHAFTED

Wood Siding and Woodpeckers

Wood siding on a house can attract woodpeckers faster than suet. They peck to communicate, to uncover insect larvae, and to excavate a cavity. Drumming to communicate is a woodpecker's equivalent of song. It is noisy but seldom does damage. If siding is insect-infested, get rid of the insects, and the woodpecker disappears too. If large holes are being drilled, the bird is excavating a cavity for nesting (in spring) or roosting (in fall). Metallic ribbons hung from the eaves are often an effective deterrent, particularly if they are stiff and rustle in the wind. Netting and hanging balloons have been used effectively. Tapes of a hawk's call or the spray from a water hose might be tried on persistent individuals.

In view of the overall abundance of grackles on the continent, FeederWatchers are fortunate that their feeders are not overwhelmed by the birds. Just over a quarter of FeederWatchers continent-wide report them in winter. Most of those reports are in February and represent birds leaving their winter range and starting migration.

Only a little more than 5 percent of Feeder-Watchers report grackles in December and January, barely enough to keep the bird in the top 50. Most reports are of a half-dozen or fewer individuals, but large flocks mixed with blackbirds, starlings, and cowbirds can occur at feeders in their core range or in migration.

Waste grains gathered from agricultural fields are most grackles' preferred winter staple. Their destruction of grain and fruit crops in spring and summer has made them significant agricultural pests.

They take seeds and nuts in the wild, especially acorns. In urban areas, they scavenge, and everywhere they are opportunistic. At beaches, they are

☐ CAROLINA WREN 24

| – | – | 20 | 19 | 11 |
| – | 21 | 21 | 15 | 6 |

The Carolina is the wren most commonly attracted to feeders in eastern backyards. Look for it in shrubs or brushy cover, especially in moist areas. Though shy, it is tolerant of humans and is particularly fond of buildings. The spider eggs under eaves, on decks, and in garage corners can be more attractive to Carolina wrens than suet or puddings at a feeder. Carolina wrens live almost entirely on spiders and insects; seeds are seldom taken. They forage from the upper branches of trees to the leaf litter on the ground.

The roosting opportunities presented by buildings also attract Carolina wrens. They roost alone or in pairs in cavities or partly enclosed spaces of almost any type. FeederWatchers report them sleeping on door sills, hanging plant baskets, wood piles, and in an abandoned robin's nest that had been attached to a front door wreath. Nest boxes also are commonly used for roosting.

Pairs maintain a year-round territory — typically a few acres — for life, and FeederWatchers report seeing a couple together and separately almost exactly as often. In their southeastern stronghold, four out of five FeederWatchers report Carolina wrens in winter.

In more northern regions, their numbers track the winter weather. In years with mild winters, Carolina wrens increase in the New England and Allegheny regions, only to succumb in severe winters. In the winter of 1994–95, sightings in both regions dropped to about half that of the previous year. The following winter numbers increased, and then in 1996–97, they plummeted again. Through the last of the 1990s, the birds gradually increased.

Identification The broad white eyebrow separates the Carolina from all but **BEWICK'S WREN**, which has a grayish (not cinnamon) breast and white corners in its tail. Bewick's was once common in eastern backyards but is now rare east of Texas and Oklahoma. It is most common in the North Pacific Region, where it is reported by about 15 percent of FeederWatchers and ranks 32nd. It ranks 39th in California, 44th in the South Central, and 54th in the Southwest Region.

Two other wrens, the **HOUSE WREN** and the **WINTER WREN**, are seen in backyard brush but rarely come to feeders. Both are small, mousy-looking, drab wrens without obvious plumage marks other than their short, finely barred tails. The winter wren is the tiniest, about the size of a kinglet, and has a particularly stubby tail.

☐ COMMON GRACKLE 25

| 28 | 28 | 18 | 16 | 14 |
| 28 | 24 | 22 | 19 | 17 |

often seen patrolling wrack lines for anything edible.

Grackles have become pests forming huge overnight winter roosts in some areas. They gather by the thousands with starlings, blackbirds, and cowbirds to roost in trees, thickets, or urban areas. A fungus harmful to humans can develop at roost sites and has been the common justification for the organized destruction of birds at some sites.

But as some eastern grackles come under control, others are spreading west. The Great Plains once stopped their advance by depriving them of trees. Shelterbelts planted by man now dot the plains, and grackles dot the shelterbelts.

Identification The flashy iridescence of the common grackle is usually visible at backyard viewing distances. Otherwise, the bird appears all black except for the yellow eyes. See p. 71 for a detailed comparison with Brewer's and rusty blackbirds.

The **BOAT-TAILED GRACKLE** is occasionally reported at feeders in Florida and along the Atlantic and Gulf coasts. It ranks 51st in the Southeast Region. Males are larger (and noisier) than the common grackle, with very long, full tails. Females are very different — smaller than males and tawny brown.

The **GREAT-TAILED GRACKLE** is nearly identical to the boat-tailed and replaces it in the South Central (where it is ranked 39th), Southwestern (60th), and California regions. There is range overlap in coastal western Louisiana and eastern Texas, where all three grackles can occur locally in the same yard.

26 SHARP-SHINNED HAWK ☐

28	28	19	23	19
29	21	27	29	32
21	23	23	26	37

I have had a hawk out here almost daily during the winter. I have been in awe of his patience, speed, and beauty. I used to hate having him around, and I still hate to lose my other birds, but he is magnificent to watch.

Rita McLochlin
Logansport, Indiana

Some birds eat other birds, and the one that most often attacks fellow birds at feeders is the sharp-shinned hawk. Sharpies, as they are commonly called, are reported by 20 to 30 percent of FeederWatchers in most regions. They nearly always come alone, and they might return several times over a period of days or weeks, refining their attack skills while the songbirds perfect their escapes. Some people root for the songbirds, a few root for the hawk, most are conflicted. Everyone is amazed at the action.

The visits almost inevitably end after a period of time. Experienced hawks sometimes make a few kills before leaving; inexperienced ones often don't. Depending upon the size of the prey, a sharpie needs one or two kills a day to survive. Overall, few of those kills seem to take place at feeders.

Most of the time, a sharpie will try to secrete itself into a tree overlooking the feeding area. Often the feeder birds see it approach and "freeze" or take cover. The hawk typically waits patiently for some birds to venture back to the feeder. If it locates a songbird too far from cover to save itself, the attack begins.

A sharpie is like a dragster. From a standing start, it can beat almost any bird over a short course. Its paddle-like wings capture large volumes of air the way a dragster's fat tires grip broad stretches of tarmac.

The comparison fails when a sharpie's maneuverability is taken into account. A sharpie can chase a songbird through a maze of limbs at full speed. It can pluck prey from midair or from the perch of a hanging feeder. Some FeederWatchers swear they have seen sharpies deliberately drive songbirds into a window and catch them on the bounce. But if a fleeing bird can escape a sharpie's initial rush, it is likely safe. Sharpies do not engage in long tail-chases.

In open spaces, sharpies often hunt by flying low to the ground or coursing among trees at midlevel, hoping to surprise a songbird. They occasionally attack at feeders by coursing, using the house or trees to hide their approach. Many FeederWatchers report an attack style seldom noticed elsewhere. After biding time in a tree while all the little songbirds hide in brush or shrubbery, sharpies are regularly seen diving into the tangles of vegetation after them. The songbirds seldom break out of their hiding spot, knowing they can be overtaken in flight. The tactic succeeds at least some of the time but is not without risk. At least one sharpie has been found deep in songbird cover impaled on a thorn.

Starlings and house sparrows are among the most frequent hawk victims at feeders. Mourning doves, jays, juncos, siskins, and house finches are also favored prey, according to a FeederWatch study. Sharpies typically eat near the spot of the kill, leaving feathers but little else in a pile. FeederWatchers have also noted sharpies playing with their prey, cat-like, freeing it and catching it time after time.

Squirrels typically ignore sharpies and occasionally harass them. Crows, jays, and even chickadees will often mob a sharpie until it leaves.

Identification See p. 72 for a complete discussion of sharp-shinned hawk identification.

ADULT

IMMATURE

"They come with the snowflakes out of the dun sky of November and leave as spring approaches," wrote E. H. Forbush in a description of redpolls in his classic 1925 book, *Birds of Massachusetts and other New England States.* He went on to note, "They are such hardy, boreal birds that probably they leave the northern wilderness in great numbers only when driven south by lack of food."

The northern tier of states and southern Canada can count on many snowflakes every year; redpolls are more dicey. In every region except the Al-Can, redpolls are cyclical. In irruptive years, twittering flocks of the tame, trusting birds can swamp feeders; in between irruptions, few venture south. The boom-or-bust nature of redpoll irruptions is illustrated by the figures for New England. In 1995, 1997, and 1999, a scant 1 percent of FeederWatchers in the region reported them. In 1996 and 1998, they were seen by 25 percent of FeederWatchers, and in 1994 by over 50 percent.

Today's FeederWatchers report few redpolls arriving as early as November, as recorded by Forbush in

☐ RED-WINGED BLACKBIRD 27

27	22	40	23	
–	32	25	28	17
39	30	27	23	21

Winter flocks of red-winged blackbirds behave much like the common grackles (pp. 90–91) with which they often flock and roost in the southeastern U.S. Both are abundant birds that ignore most feeders in early winter but frequent them in February and March as they begin early spring migration.

One notable difference between the two birds in the East is that the red-winged blackbird is more common at rural feeders, while the grackle is recorded most often in urban yards. Clearly, grackles have adapted better than red-wings to scavenging in urban surroundings. In the West, red-wings often flock with Brewer's blackbirds (p. 113).

It is also interesting that red-wing flocks are often segregated, at least partially, by sex. Males are the ones most often seen at feeders, eating a variety of small grains from the ground. Red-winged blackbirds prefer to feed heavily on waste grains in agricultural fields. They also take many wild seeds. Insects are only a small part of their winter diet.

Identification A band of cream or yellow is usually all of the shoulder epaulet seen on a male red-winged blackbird at rest. It is enough to guarantee the identification. The bright scarlet is revealed when the bird is displaying or in flight.

Female red-winged blackbirds look like very large, heavily streaked sparrows except for their long, narrow bills. A reddish blush on the face or shoulder can sometimes be seen, especially on young males, which resemble females throughout the winter.

☐ COMMON REDPOLL 28

2	7	37	–	
10	16	–	38	
9	22	24	41	–

1925. Large numbers aren't seen typically until January or February. It is the search for food that drives irruptions, as Forbush speculated. Tiny seeds of birches and alders are the redpoll's winter staple in the North. Trees produce seeds cyclically, and in years of low production, redpolls head south searching for seeds in weed fields and at backyard feeders. Niger and hulled sunflower seeds are favorite foods at feeders.

Seeds provide oils that redpolls metabolize especially rapidly to keep their bodies warm. It takes so much energy to combat the coldest Arctic nights that they must take a supply of seeds with them when they roost in order to survive until morning. A pouch in their esophagus contains the cache.

Identification Redpolls have the brown streaks characteristic of many finches. Their red caps and black chins are their most distinctive marks. Males usually have a pink breast.

HOARY REDPOLLS are sometimes identified in flocks of common redpolls. They are paler than the common redpoll but difficult to identify with certainty because some common redpolls are very pale. A redpoll can be identified with certainty as a hoary only if the undertail coverts and center of the rump have no dark streaking, if the bill is especially short and stout, giving the face a pushed-in appearance, and if the color on the breast is no more than a rosy wash.

Hoary redpolls are ranked 14th in the Al-Can, 22nd in the Northern Rockies, 24th in the North Central, 35th in the North Atlantic, and 39th in the Great Lakes Region.

29 CAROLINA CHICKADEE ☐

26	21	6
36	17	5

The Carolina chickadee is the southern counterpart of the black-capped chickadee (p. 76) and is nearly as common in its range as the black-capped is in the North and West. It has the same charm and bibbed throat as its northern sister species, and the two behave much the same. Both visit feeders in small flocks and are very common in their respective FeederWatch Regions.

Sometimes Carolina chickadees will have a variety of other small bug-eaters flocking with them — nuthatches, kinglets, brown creepers, yellow-rumped warblers, and downy woodpeckers. The different species can hunt insect matter in different ways or in different places on a tree and don't have to directly compete with one another. When a mixed flock arrives at a feeding station, many of the bug-eaters remain outside the feeding area, scouring the shrubbery for bugs. The chickadees head for the black-oil sunflower seeds.

Identification See Confusing Look-alikes (p. 70) to separate the Carolina from the black-capped

BLACK-CAPPED CHICKADEE

CONTACT ZONE

CAROLINA CHICKADEE

30 NORTHERN MOCKINGBIRD ☐

		15	48	
–	30	33	9	
–	26	28	20	13

In spring and summer, the mockingbird is famous for its inventive song and loud, tireless singing. In winter, it is renowned for jealously guarding "its" bush or tree of berries. Not until overwhelmed by a flock of cedar waxwings or robins will a mocker relinquish exclusive claim to a chokecherry tree or a bush of hawthorn berries. Multiflora rose hips are a favorite, and the proliferation of this plant is one explanation given for the steady northward expansion of the mocker's range.

The mocker is not a very cold-hardy bird, so the warming trend in the late 1900s is also considered a likely cause for the northward winter range expansion in the eastern seaboard states. Many northern mockingbirds still migrate south in winter, some traveling over 500 miles, but over 20 percent of FeederWatchers in New England report overwintering mockingbirds.

In its core region, the South Central including Texas, where it is the state bird, the mockingbird is recorded by over two-thirds of FeederWatchers. Pairs are observed about 20 percent of the time; single birds are the norm.

Most pairs of mockingbirds hold a territory year-round, although their winter territory might be smaller than their nesting range and not vigorously defended against roving bands of youngsters. Some

A Bird TKOY

Yes, mockingbirds have bad habits, which include chasing cats; attacking crows, red-tail hawks, and squirrels; screaming at snakes; and pestering dogs nonstop. I once watched while a single mockingbird was transformed into a feathered fury attacking a Cooper's hawk that had the audacity to come into her territory and launch a sneak assault on the other birds — birds that she cannot stand to be near her gold mine of privet berries. The whirlwind battle raged on for no more than 60 seconds and looked like Mohammed Ali in his heyday shadow-boxing an elephant. The mocker quickly won on a TKOY (technically kicked out of yard).
Keith Kridler, Mt. Pleasant, Texas

chickadee visually or by voice. Practical identification is almost always made by the location of the birds. Those seen north of the contact zone shown on the map or high in the Appalachians (the dividing line is around 1,800 feet in winter, 3,500 feet in summer) are black-capped chickadees; others are Carolinas. The notable exception is in winter, when some of the northernmost black-caps occasionally experience food shortages and irrupt south. Some may travel well into the Carolina's range.

Backyard birders within the contact zone (a swath about 20 miles wide) see hybrids with intermediate marks. Some individuals may have plumage marks characteristic of one parent species or the other, but it is unsafe to call any chickadee seen in the contact zone anything but a hybrid. Chickadees are sedentary, and black-caps and Carolinas interbreed so freely that in the contact zone, a mixed parentage has to be presumed.

Differences in song are often used to separate Carolina and black-capped chickadees. However, songs are learned, and a hybrid in the contact zone may learn the Carolina's four-noted *fee-bee, fee-bay* or the black-capped's two- or three-noted *fee-bee* or *fee-bee-ee.*

individuals may live a lifetime in one area with a single mate, but mockers experience divorce, death, and a cheatin' heart, just like people.

A pair of mockingbirds may split after raising young, or sometimes they merely divide up the territory and live side by side, defending separate territories. If the resources within a territory change, the boundaries are likely to change too. Some young claim territories immediately on dispersal; some gather in winter flocks and wait to claim territories until spring. A principal ingredient in all the social instability is a skewed sex ratio — males outnumber females.

Puddings, suet, fresh fruit, or simmered dried fruits are the feeder foods that most attract mockers. Apples, grapes, and plumped raisins are proven choices. Mockers often come for water as well.

In areas of the South where insects are available during winter, they feed in lawns in their characteristic wing-flashing manner. The bright white in the wings is presumed to startle insects, causing them to move and reveal themselves to the hungry mocker, but no one knows for sure.

Identification The northern mockingbird is a jay-sized gray bird with distinctive white patches in its wings and tail. Only shrikes (p. 116) resemble it.

☐ BROWN-HEADED COWBIRD 31

		–	54	–
–	29	33	24	19
32	33	26	24	29

In winter, cowbirds gather in large foraging flocks, ever-changing aggregations of individuals that often include starlings, red-winged blackbirds, and common grackles. "Trash birds" a lot of people call them, but popular disdain has not stopped the flocks from prospering. At feeders, there is not much to distinguish a cowbird's behavior or visiting schedule from that of the common grackle, described on pp. 90–91.

In the Southeast and bordering regions (Mid-Atlantic, East Central, and South Central), better than one-third of FeederWatchers report cowbirds at their feeders in winter. Most of the visits occur in February as spring migration begins and cowbirds leave the agricultural fields that provided the bulk of their winter food supplies.

Spring is when the cowbird creates problems. The female deposits her eggs in the nests of other birds and abandons the chores of incubation and chick-raising to the unwitting hosts. It is a habit developed when cowbirds (then known as "buffalo birds") foraged beside wandering herds of buffalo and could not afford to remain with a nest. Cowbird chicks usually hatch before the host's chicks, grow faster, and outcompete the host's hatchlings for food. Some populations of songbirds are at risk due in part to cowbird parasitism.

Identification The brown-headed cowbird is a small member of the blackbird family with a conical bill. It typically struts with its wings drooping and its tail stiffly held above horizontal while it feeds. The contrast of the male's coffee-colored head with its black body is an easy mark in good light. Females are gray-brown, paler below with indistinct breast streaks; the throat can be quite pale, nearly white.

32 SPOTTED AND EASTERN TOWHEES ☐

–	5	11	18
–	42	36	42
–	43	34	15

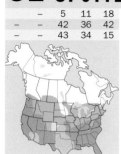

SPOTTED TOWHEE

EASTERN TOWHEE

EASTERN TOWHEE

Over 50 percent of FeederWatchers in the Pacific states and British Columbia report the spotted towhee, and the same number see the eastern towhee in the Southeast Region. In Texas and Oklahoma in the South Central Region, both species occur and overlap (hence, the combined statistics).

The two species were lumped together as the rufous-sided towhee as recently as 1995 because they interbreed in a contact zone centered in the Dakotas and Nebraska. It is the continued presence of pure parental types among the hybrids that has resulted in each type being recognized as a species.

Spotted and eastern towhees are shy brush- and shrub-loving birds that feed and behave much like fox sparrows (p. 100), especially at feeders. Neither towhee generally remains in the open very long.

Under their protective cover, spotted and eastern towhees noisily rake leaf litter with their feet to uncover seeds or insects. Seeds are the core of their winter diet, but berries and insects are taken when found. At feeders, they prefer the smaller seeds and grains strewn on the ground. Often they will drink or bathe if a water source is available for them.

In the wild, one or two spotted or eastern towhees may travel in loose flocks with other ground-feeding species in winter. At feeders, they are reported alone or in pairs most often. Small groups are reported about 20 percent of the time. Feeding stations that attract eastern or spotted towhees with the right combination of food and cover often see them repeatedly throughout the winter.

The few reports that exist on the roosting habits of spotted and eastern towhees have them, not surprisingly, roosting alone in dense foliage.

Identification Males of both species have broad rufous sides and black hoods and upperparts. Brown replaces black in females. Eastern females are a warm brown; spotted females vary in shade but are darker than eastern females, nearer the male in color. As its name implies, the spotted towhee has spots — white ones in the wings and sometimes on the back.

Bird Names

The lumping and splitting of species is decided by a committee of the American Ornithologists' Union. New evidence on vexing problems like the eastern and spotted towhees is regularly reviewed, with the birds' status being altered periodically. The eastern and spotted towhees were physically divided and kept apart by the prairies for thousands of years, allowing them to diverge genetically. The planting of shelterbelts across the prairies has permitted the birds to rejoin, and where they do, they interbreed. Are the offspring hybrids or proof that divergence has not proceeded far enough to justify separate species status? Getting answers is complicated. Several other "pairs" of birds have a similar history, including myrtle and Audubon's warblers, which are now lumped together as the yellow-rumped warbler.

☐ EVENING GROSBEAK 33

A flock of evening grosbeaks settling in for a sunflower seed snack at a backyard feeder is like a Christmas present for most FeederWatchers. Those who live in or near the birds' year-round range often receive the gift of their winter presence regularly. Everyone else must put out sunflower seeds on the ground or a platform like good little girls and boys and hope that the festive birds come and decorate their yards. Rural feeding stations are the most frequently favored.

In some winters, few evening grosbeaks irrupt out of their forest haunts in the western mountains or eastern Canada. In others, the birds are common in western lowlands, and eastern birds are seen as far south as Florida.

A banding study reported by the Cornell Lab of Ornithology found that, in consecutive winters, only 10 percent of birds returned to the same location. FeederWatchers report that flocks are as likely to visit early in winter as late and may vary in size from a handful of birds to 50 or more. Sometimes one or two birds precede a flock at a feeder.

Their huge bills and bulky, short-tailed bodies impart a particular presence to evening grosbeaks. These are not the hyperactive little finches that more commonly irrupt south in winter. And their appetite is legendary. In just a few minutes, an evening grosbeak can crack dozens of sunflower shells, scoop out the seeds with its purple tongue, and swallow them whole. Feeding a flock is like feeding a family of teenage boys, and a large flock can be just as expensive.

A western bird, the evening grosbeak is a relative newcomer to the East. The first recorded major

flight east of the Great Lakes was in the winter of 1889–90. It wasn't until the middle of the 1900s that the bird became widely established in the East.

Since the mid-1980s, eastern counts have been steadily declining, but whether due to fewer birds or more of them remaining far north is not known. At the beginning of the 1990s, 30 to 40 percent of FeederWatchers in New England reported evening grosbeaks annually. Over the course of the decade, the percentages dropped, especially in odd years. The decade ended in 1999 with only 6 percent of FeederWatchers hosting an evening grosbeak.

Identification Females and young evening grosbeaks are much less eye-catching than the golden-hued males, but both sexes have distinctive large white wing patches and, most significantly, enormous bills. The bills are a pale horn color in winter. In March, just before the birds depart their irruptive winter range, the bill becomes increasingly colorful — a delicate lime green. A whistled *peurr* call may be the first indication of a flock in the vicinity.

☐ COOPER'S HAWK 34

ADULT

IMM.

Cooper's hawk looks and behaves very much like the sharp-shinned (p. 92). Because the two can be very difficult to distinguish from each other, the data for each are less certain than they are for most other species. Overall, Cooper's is reported less often than the sharpie in every region except the East Central (Ohio, Indiana, Illinois, and Kentucky).

Cooper's captures fewer birds and takes more prey, such as chipmunks and frogs, than the sharpie does. In some yards, squirrels seem to respect Cooper's; in others, they don't. Cooper's favorite prey species at feeders are much the same as the sharpie's, although it has a decided preference for mourning doves (p. 75).

Identification See p. 72 for a complete discussion of how to distinguish Cooper's hawk from the similar sharp-shinned.

35 WHITE-CROWNED SPARROW ☐

21	–	26	6	15
–	–	32	31	29
–	38	37	33	44

The white-crowned sparrow ranges across much of the continent in winter but is most common in the West. In California, where it is reported by three out of four FeederWatchers, it is the most common backyard sparrow, ignoring for the moment that the junco is part of the sparrow family.

In most areas, wintering white-crowned sparrows are migrants. Flocks of up to 150 individuals may occupy a winter territory, but they don't defend it, and the members often feed separately.

Most flocks are smaller. White-crowns usually visit feeders in low numbers; 50 percent of the time they are alone or in pairs. Except for wandering youngsters, the individuals in a winter territory are mostly returnees from previous years.

One race of the white-crowned sparrow (there are five recognized races) does not migrate. Pairs of Nuttall's race, which lives along the California coast, maintain their territories year-round but do not defend them in winter. A pair is often joined by juveniles and migrant white-crowns over winter.

Golden-crowned sparrows (p. 108) and white-throated sparrows (p. 86) also commonly flock with white-crowns in winter; all feed primarily on weed seeds uncovered by scratching the leaf litter. The white-crowned will feed a bit farther from cover than the other two but often seems nervous about it.

Individuals in a feeding flock preserve relative peace by observing a pecking order — "dominance hierarchy," ornithologists call it. Most species that flock have dominance hierarchies, and the dominance relationships can be observed at feeding stations if the birds are watched carefully. In white-crowns, the interactions have been well studied.

Among white-crowns, as in many other flocking songbirds, males dominate females and older birds dominate younger ones. A dominant white-crown demonstrates its rank by usurping the space of a subordinate. The lower-ranking bird seldom resists. Time spent squabbling is time lost from feeding.

36 BROWN CREEPER ☐

20	31	39	–	43
25	33	29	32	43
26	27	32	30	48

Brown creepers are much cooler than their name. Their "brown" is an intricate camouflage of mottled earth tones on their backs that renders them nearly invisible against the tree trunks on which they forage. Often the first notice of a brown creeper is when it glides, with an occasional flap, from the upper portion of the trunk of one large tree to the base of another nearby.

Their "creep" is a hitch — a short, two-footed hop by which brown creepers climb up a tree trunk in their characteristic spiral. As they climb, they carefully inspect the bark crevices for insect matter. It is a very narrow ecological niche they fill, but it permits brown creepers to be one of the few exclusively bug-eating birds capable of surviving winters in northern regions. The bird's unique look and behavior draw most FeederWatchers to a window to watch for the brief time that a brown creeper typically visits.

Creepers can arrive anytime at a backyard that has large shade trees or borders a woodland with large trees. The bigger the tree trunk, the more

25	42	47	51	39
37	25	41	34	48
20	28	31	32	47

Many of the things learned about the well-studied white-crowned sparrow may apply to less-studied sparrows and to songbirds in general. For instance, science has rendered it a fact that white-crowns prefer to feed in mornings and evenings but will also feed a good bit in midday on cloudy days.

You may not have needed a scientist to tell you that, but scientists have also discovered that after the evening feeding, white-crowns are on their night roosts (dense vegetation of trees or shrubs) within 30 minutes and have already begun to allow their body temperature to lower if necessary. They can reduce their body temperature as much as 10° F and their oxygen consumption by more than 75 percent to withstand periods of cold and food deprivation.

White-crowns are especially social prior to roosting and often engage in much calling and even singing at dusk throughout the winter.

Identification The gray (not white) throat distinguishes both the black-and-white striped adults and the brown-and-tan striped young birds from similar white-throated sparrows. Some young golden-crowns may lack obvious golden crown stripes and therefore suggest a white-crowned, but only the white-crowned has a bright bill. The color varies from yellow to pink, orange, or reddish brown.

On some races of the white-crowned, the black eye stripe extends through the eye to the bill. Other races are white in front of the eye.

The pigeons that abound in cities are the feral descendants of birds that have been domesticated by man for an estimated 5,000 years. The original stock of wild birds are called rock doves, and ornithologists use the same name to describe the somewhat different feral pigeon.

North America's first pigeons were brought as domesticated birds by early European settlers in 1603–07. Feral flocks of escapees and released birds materialized soon afterward and have since spread across the continent.

Pigeons are primarily an urban bird. Feeder-Watchers in rural areas report far fewer of them than do their urban or suburban counterparts. Birds that do live in rural areas prefer open habitat and generally avoid the trees and shrubs in which most feeding stations are nestled.

Pigeon flocks can be large, but they don't swoop down on a feeding station en masse like mourning doves or red-winged blackbirds. In winter, pigeons are often breeding, and only part of a flock, typically a half-dozen or less, come to most feeders at a time. They eat mixed seeds of many types, including cracked corn and sunflower seeds. Their diet changes with the seasons and, interestingly, from one individual to another.

likely a creeper is to visit. Only in California are they so scarce that they are unranked. In most other regions, 10 to 20 percent of FeederWatchers report attracting brown creepers in winter.

FeederWatchers report them alone or sometimes in pairs, but they often travel with small bands of other birds, including chickadees and titmice. The sudden arrival of a twittering flock of hungry little 'dees is a good time to check for a creeper on any tree trunks in the feeding area.

Like other insect-eaters, creepers come to feeders for suet and puddings. Frequently they'll eat the fallen crumbs underneath a suet feeder rather than go to the feeder itself, especially if other birds are present. They can't crack seed shells, but sometimes creepers will eat broken bits of sunflower seeds and peanuts.

Identification The cryptic back pattern, curved bill, and distinctive habit of spiraling up tree trunks all combine to make the brown creeper easy to identify — if it is seen.

Identification Feral pigeons are likely to be confused only with the band-tailed pigeon (p. 112).

The many color variations seen in pigeons are the result of prior selective domestic breeding. It is remarkable that feral flocks retain these color variations and haven't reverted to their wild condition — a single plumage type — within a few generations.

No other domesticated animal has maintained any of its exotic colors or patterns after returning to a feral condition. As this is being written, the Cornell Lab of Ornithology is conducting an international research program, Project PigeonWatch, that is marshaling the efforts of thousands of volunteers, many of them children, in an attempt to discover why.

38 CHIPPING SPARROW ☐

				46
–	34	40	35	23
40	35	34	38	20

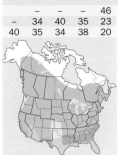

Chipping sparrows are summer visitors over most of the U.S. and Canada, but in the southern tier of states, year-round residents are joined in winter by flocks of northern-nesting birds. Over 30 percent of FeederWatchers in the South Central Region report them, and nearly 40 percent of southeastern FeederWatchers see the unassuming little sparrows.

However, some chippies overwinter in northern regions, especially along the eastern seaboard. In Maine and eastern Canada, some 5 percent of FeederWatchers report them.

Chippies feed in short-grass fields or partially barren areas, taking weed and grass seeds in winter. They are not grass- or brushland birds, however. They like wooded meadows, orchards, or backyards in rural areas and mature developments that provide a mix of tall trees and open ground. Like waxwings, a flock of chippies typically gathers in the upper branches of a tree near a feeding area before descending, one by one, to the ground.

Flocks of several dozen chippies are common in the wild, where they often wander in flocks with bluebirds, yellow-rumped warblers, and pine warblers. Smaller groups, often only one or two birds, typically show up at feeders, and those are frequently attracted by the wild seeds they can glean from a driveway or similar bare patch. Small mixed grains spread on the ground are their favorite feeder foods.

It is not yet known whether migrant chippies return to the same wintering site each year, whether they join resident flocks, or how juveniles disperse. Roosting habits have also gone unstudied.

Identification The chipping sparrow has the small size, clear breast, notched tail, and wing bars characteristic of *Spizella* sparrows (see American tree sparrow, p. 88, and field sparrow, p. 107). In winter, only a reddish brown remnant remains of its distinctive red summer cap. The best head mark in winter is the black eye line, extending from well behind the eye all the way to the bill.

39 FOX SPARROW ☐

19	–	16	27	–
–	–	39	37	50
–	36	38	31	39

A large furtive member of its family, the fox sparrow makes relatively few appearances at feeders but visits enough continent-wide to earn a ranking. It is most common in the North Pacific Region, where over one-third of FeederWatchers report it.

Fox sparrows are denizens of the underbrush, vigorously kicking up leaf litter towhee-fashion in quest of seeds. Berries and bugs are also consumed when discovered. At feeders, they prefer the same small millet-sized seeds that the little sparrows take. They most often show up alone.

Like many of the birds that live in underbrush, fox sparrows are reluctant to expose themselves. And in spite of their size, they often defer to other, smaller ground-feeders. Some FeederWatchers attract them and other shy birds by spreading small seeds or cracked corn near hedges or brush away from the hanging feeders and the flocks that they attract.

Surprisingly, fox sparrows can be rather brazen around people. They quickly come out of hiding to investigate squeaking or *pssshing* sounds, and FeederWatchers have reported them rushing out to collect ground feed while it is still being scattered.

Identification There are 18 regional races of the fox sparrow, and there is growing evidence that four different species may exist. All variations are bulky sparrows with heavy bills, long, blunt tails, and considerable streaking on their underparts that merges into a messy breast spot.

RED FOX SPARROW

SLATE-COLORED FOX SPARROW

☐ CEDAR WAXWING 40

–	35	–	34	37
32	37	38	–	27
42	37	39	42	38

FeederWatchers able to attract cedar waxwings seldom report them more than once or twice a winter, the time it takes a wandering flock to strip the fruit or berries from whatever bush or tree they discover. If water is available in a feeding area, they'll sometimes come for a bath or a drink, but they don't take seeds or suet. They manage almost exclusively on a high-sugar, low-protein diet in winter, obtained primarily from sugary fruits and berries. Sapsucker wells and tree buds are other sources of sugar they exploit when available.

At one time, cedar waxwings depended entirely on the wild berries of cedars, junipers, mountain ash, and other wild native plants to sustain themselves through winter. Ornamental plants such as crabapples and hawthorns have provided abundant new sources of food and contributed to a steady increase in waxwing numbers in the last half of the 1900s. Developed residential areas, which have the largest concentrations of ornamental plantings, also attract the largest flocks of waxwings. Hundreds of the beautiful birds can assemble. In some cases, the fruiting plants have been on highway medians, with catastrophes resulting.

One ornamental plant, Morrow's honeysuckle, has caused orange tail tips on some birds seen in the northeastern United States and southeastern Canada. Pigments in the fruit cause the shift from yellow if ingested when the feathers are developing.

A visit by waxwings is a special experience. Typically the birds arrive quietly, filtering into the top of a tall tree near the intended feeding spot. They perch with a very military bearing, erectly at attention and often facing the same way. When convinced it is safe, they descend one by one to the fruit they will enjoy. At close range, their impeccably sleek plumage — each bird must be at least a colonel — and high-pitched, lisping calls can be enjoyed.

FeederWatchers report cedar waxwings roosting in dense clumps of holly and conifers or on the bare upper limbs of deciduous trees. No formal study is available on their nighttime roosting habits at this writing.

In the Al-Can and Northern Rockies regions, the **BOHEMIAN WAXWING** is more common than the cedar waxwing, ranking 16th and 20th respectively. It is sometimes seen in flocks with cedar waxwings, and both species occasionally flock with overwintering robins. The Bohemian waxwing also makes the rankings in the North Central (36) and North Atlantic (38) regions.

Identification There is little about a cedar waxwing that would allow it to be confused with any other bird. The yellow tail tip is perhaps the easiest single mark. Bohemian waxwings are a little larger, have gray (not yellow) bellies, reddish undertail coverts, and a different pattern of white in the wings than the cedar waxwing. Both species display the red wax-like drops at the tips of their secondaries, for which they are named. Older cedar waxwings have nine or more red dots; younger birds, fewer.

The **RED FOX SPARROW** is the race seen throughout the East. The wings, tail, and streaks on the underparts are all a distinctive bright rusty (fox) color.

It can be impossible to identify a bird as one of the three potential species in the West because of variations and intergrades. The **SOOTY FOX SPARROW** is dark chocolate above with only a tinge of red in the wings and on the rump. The breast streaking is brown and the base of the lower mandible is yellow.

The **SLATE-COLORED FOX SPARROW** also has brown streaking on its breast, but its upperparts are gray and the rusty red in its wings and tail are obvious.

The **THICK-BILLED FOX SPARROW** is found only from southwest Oregon to southern California. The thicker bill is not always apparent. It is grayish brown with little red in the wings or tail. The base of the lower mandible is a pale horn color sometimes lightly washed with gray, green, or blue.

Similar Species Song sparrows (p. 87), especially the large dark race seen in the Northwest, resemble fox sparrows. On all but the darkest fox sparrows, the wings, rump, and base of the tail show some rusty color. The fox sparrow's head is more rounded than the song sparrow's, the spotting on its underparts is often chevron-shaped, and the tail tip is squared off.

We had Bohemian waxwings in Saskatoon, Saskatchewan, where I grew up. Winter temperatures reached 30 below without figuring in the wind chill, and they would sit outside on the trees and eat whatever berries were available. One crisp, clear morning we looked outside the dining room and saw birds attached to the tree limbs hanging upside down, dead. They had frozen on the branches, and it broke my heart.

Catherine Fagan
Southwest Ohio

41 PILEATED WOODPECKER ☐

	30	36	–	
18	35	44	39	49
36	40	41	39	36

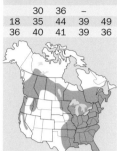

Pileated woodpeckers need large trees, dead or alive, for nesting and shelter. As old forests with mature trees were cleared in years past, the birds declined until, by the mid-1900s, they were rare in the East and scarce in much of the West. Since then, second-growth forest from earlier abandoned farmlands in the East has matured, and the pileated woodpecker has recovered with the regrowth. The disastrous Dutch elm disease has aided pileateds and other woodpeckers by providing them with dead trees and the insects living within.

Excavating a nest cavity typically takes several weeks for a pileated (PIE-le-at-ed or PILL-e-at-ed) woodpecker. One will sometimes roost in a nest cavity, but typically a pileated uses a hollow tree, drilling several entrance and exit holes so it can escape from predators. Numerous small mammals, birds, reptiles, and insects depend on holes excavated by the pileated woodpecker for their own nests and shelter.

Some pileated woodpeckers maintain close pair bonds and defend their territory year-round. FeederWatchers report pairs feeding together about one-quarter of the time. Other pairs relax their bonds in winter and sometimes accept floaters in their territory. In the wild, the birds feed heavily on wood-boring beetle larvae and carpenter ants in live and decaying wood. Decaying fallen logs provide good concentrations of the insects. Pileateds also take fruit, nuts, and berries in season.

They come to feeders for puddings and suet but seem to have a stronger preference for game (see pp. 19–20). Some FeederWatchers attract them by placing logs to rot at the edges of their yards. It may take several years for enough insects to infest a log to attract pileated woodpeckers, but they tend to return regularly to a good food source.

Identification Although largely black and crow-sized, pileated woodpeckers are unlikely to be confused with crows or anything else. Only males have the red mustache mark. White underwings are visible in flight, and a *wuk-wuk-wuk* call is often given.

42 STELLER'S JAY ☐

12	23	7	19	17
		–		

You throw it out, and a Steller's jay will cart it off if it is edible and big enough to be of interest. In the wild, pine seeds and acorns are an important part of their diet; at feeders, they typically load up on sunflower seeds and peanuts. Suet and puddings disappear rapidly if the jays can get to them. Much of the food apparently wolfed down by Steller's jays is

actually stored in a pouch under the tongue and cached in trees or on the ground for later use.

Steller's jay is the western counterpart of the blue jay (p. 76). A pair usually lives year-round in the same locality within coniferous or mixed coniferous forests. Because of its attachment to forests, Steller's jay is not as prevalent a feeder visitor as the blue jay is in the East. Blue jays are noted by 80 to 90 percent of FeederWatchers in their core eastern range. Two-thirds of FeederWatchers in the North Pacific Region note Steller's jays — still a very sizable number.

A pair of Steller's jays is rarely very far apart from each other. They will share much of their range with other pairs, as long as none get too close to the nest in summer. Some birds that nest at high elevations winter in lowlands, and occasionally, when food gets scarce in winter, some jays will irrupt south in a flock. Young birds typically disperse only a few miles from their parents to establish their own territories.

☐ EASTERN BLUEBIRD 43

It's not just southern FeederWatchers who get to see eastern bluebirds in winter. The bird is ranked regionally (seen by more than 5 percent of Feeder-Watchers) as far north as Pennsylvania and New York. It misses being ranked in the New England Region by the narrowest of margins — 4.99 percent of FeederWatchers report it. Many of the northern nesting bluebirds do migrate south in winter, especially in severe ones, but obviously some individuals endure hard weather.

Eastern bluebirds that don't migrate often remain near their nesting areas. They gather in flocks where fruiting plants are found, often low woodlands, and survive on berries. Insects are eaten when available. They are often seen with pine warblers and chipping sparrows in the Southeast, and they sometimes flock with robins.

Most FeederWatchers report only sporadic visits from small flocks of eastern bluebirds. They sometimes come for water but may be attracted primarily by the other feeding birds. Members of Cornell's Birdhouse Network provide nesting boxes in summer and report that "their" bluebirds sometimes return in winter to use the nest boxes for roosting, particularly in the heaviest weather. The bluebirders plug the vents in the nest boxes or sometimes provide boxes specifically for roosting A dozen or more bluebirds may share a box — and body heat.

Bluebirds that are used to being fed mealworms or other treats when nesting in summer will some-

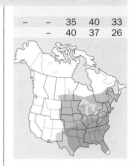

| – | – | 35 | 40 | 33 |
| – | 40 | 37 | 26 | |

♀

♂

times return in winter to the same feeding spot, obviously hoping a meal will magically appear. Scrambled eggs, shredded cheese, softened raisins and currants, or bits of suet or peanuts will satisfy them. Red berries attract them (see p. 23).

WESTERN BLUEBIRDS are not as commonly seen at feeders as eastern bluebirds. They are reported by barely more than 5 percent of FeederWatchers in California, placing them in 56th place in the regional rankings. **MOUNTAIN BLUEBIRDS** are even scarcer at feeders. Less than 2 percent of FeederWatchers in the Southwest, their core winter region, report them.

Identification The blue upperparts, rusty breast, and white belly of male eastern and western bluebirds can be inspiringly beautiful. Females are duller but have the same plumage pattern and cheery character. Scientists would argue that a bird cannot be accurately called "cheery," but bluebirds seem so.

On eastern bluebirds, the red breast extends to the chin. The throat is blue on western males, grayish on females. Male mountain bluebirds are all blue except for some white on the lower belly and under the tail; females are mostly gray, with blue being apparent only in the wings and tail.

Identification Steller's jay has a dramatic crest similar to that of the blue jay. It is sometimes called a blue jay by westerners, and with good logic, as it shows as much blue or more than the eastern bird formally named the blue jay.

Because Steller's is sedentary, forms have evolved in different localities with minor plumage differences. The foreparts (head, upper back, and breast) can be evenly blackish, or there may be noticeable contrast between portions of the head and back. Small streaks on the forehead and chin can be white, blue, or absent. Some birds have a small white crescent over the eye; a few also have a fleck of white below the eye. Young birds are duller, grayer than adults.

The intense cobalt blue in the wing and tail feathers of Steller's jays is a refraction of light caused by the structural detail of the feather. Blue pigment does not occur in birds. Pick up a fallen wing or tail feather from a Steller's jay, crush it, and the blue disappears.

The FeederWatch data server challenged my count for western bluebirds. I was really surprised, as for this area my count wasn't all that large — 24. At my Mom's house, I have seen well over 100 at a time. They cover the junipers, waiting for their turn at the water.

Susan Brians
Silver City, New Mexico

44 YELLOW-RUMPED WARBLER ☐

–	50	16	49	
	–	–	26	
–	–	–	44	23

MYRTLE FORM

AUDUBON'S FORM

Not all warblers leave the United States in winter. Yellow-rumped warblers abound in the Southeastern, South Central, and California regions, often in large flocks with other bug-eaters or ground-foragers. Enough of them visit feeders that about one-third of FeederWatchers in those regions report them. If they were more drawn to feeders, they would be commonly reported in the East as far north as Nova Scotia.

When individuals or small flocks of yellow-rumps do come to backyards, they are likely to investigate everything, including the eaves of the house (for spider eggs or other insect matter) and any shrubbery. Suet and puddings are their common feeder food preferences, but they will occasionally take broken bits of seeds and peanut hearts. Water often captures their attention if it is offered.

Insects are an important part of the yellow-rump's winter diet where they are available, but the staple in colder regions is berries. The yellow-rump's rare ability to metabolize the waxy lipids in bayberries and wax myrtle make it the most common winter bird in some areas along the eastern seaboard where these shrubs are plentiful.

Banding evidence tells us that some yellow-rumps return to the same area each winter, but the issue has not been well studied. Roosting habits are unclear as well, with evidence of both individual and communal roosts.

Identification It isn't often that a bird is named for its best field mark, but the yellow-rumped is the only warbler regularly overwintering in the United States that has a brightly contrasting yellow rump. "Butter-butt" is its popular nickname. A good confirming mark is the patch of yellow on the sides of the breast near the bend of the wing.

In winter, yellow-rumps vary greatly in brightness. Most are dull, brownish, streaky birds that, at first glance, might be taken for a sparrow if the yellow marks and thin bill are not noted.

The eastern form (myrtle warbler) has a white throat and a distinct face patch; it is also present in parts of the West. The western form (Audubon's warbler) often shows some yellow on the throat. The two forms hybridize in the Canadian Rockies.

45 RUBY-CROWNED KINGLET ☐

–	–	30	20	32
	–	–	–	28
–	–	–	–	33

SHOWING CROWN PATCH

Barely larger than a hummingbird, ruby-crowned kinglets are as busy as they are tiny. They often forage at branch tips, places larger birds can't exploit, often hovering to inspect a cluster of leaves or pine needles for tiny insect eggs. As they flit from branch to branch, they flick their wings in a manner that is often the first clue to their identity.

The ruby-crowned kinglet is common in winter in the southern tier of states, occurring in a variety of habitats from forest to scrub. Like most bug-eaters, it tends to be a sporadic visitor to feeders. Several will sometimes join wandering winter flocks

of small birds (see black-capped chickadee, p. 76), but ruby-crowns most often maintain a winter territory and are seen singly. They often revisit the same territory year after year.

More than one-third of California FeederWatchers attract them to feeders. They come for suet and puddings but could well take a sunflower heart or bits of fallen seed, as they do include some seeds in their winter diet.

Although less common than the ruby-crowned, the **GOLDEN-CROWNED KINGLET** is more widespread in winter, occuring in cold northern states that ruby-crowns avoid. A few are reported from every FeederWatch Region. Only in the North Pacific Region are they ranked (45th), with slightly more than 7 percent of FeederWatchers reporting them.

Golden-crowned kinglets are not the loners that ruby-crowns are. They forage in flocks, typically mixed, and they roost in flocks, often huddled on a limb on the sheltered side of a tree. They occupy the same varied winter habitat as ruby-crowns, and their foraging niche overlaps considerably with that of both the ruby-crowned kinglet and the black-

☐ YELLOW-BELLIED SAPSUCKER 46

–	–	–
34	42	34
44	36	32

Yellow-bellied sapsuckers are quiet and shy compared with other woodpeckers. They typically visit feeders one at a time, as the red-bellied woodpecker does, but they are far less regular. FeederWatchers report them most often taking puddings or suet in December and January, when trees produce little or no sap. Sapsuckers rarely take seeds but can be good customers for the grape jelly and oranges set out for orioles in spring.

In the wild, sapsuckers are well known for drilling small, shallow holes in trees — sap wells. They visit producing wells often, collecting the oozing sap and any insects attracted by it. They also consume the cambium and soft inner layers of bark through which they drill.

Numerous other birds, such as hummers, kinglets, and some warblers, are attracted to sapsucker wells. When a sapsucker drills wells on a backyard tree, it is like hanging out a new feeder.

Wells are in neat horizontal or vertical rows, and bands of them often girdle a limb or tree trunk as the bird drills new wells to replace older ones that stop producing. Only sapsuckers — no insects — produce such evenly spaced patterns of quarter-inch holes. Trees can be damaged or diseased by the process, but few are.

Ornithologists don't know how much sap yellow-bellied sapsuckers gather in winter months, when deciduous trees produce little and the birds rely

heavily on fruit and berries. Lumbermen report that wood harvested from southern forests inhabited by the birds in winter, especially hickory and yellow poplar, often shows rows of dark spots that they call "bird peck" (which ruins the lumber for use as veneer, cabinets, or fine furniture). Much of the drilling could occur in early spring before the birds leave their wintering grounds. Sapsuckers can be discouraged from drilling in shade trees by wrapping a damaged area with burlap or other material.

Identification No other woodpecker in its range has a plumage pattern similar to that of the adult yellow-bellied sapsucker. Males can be distinguished from females by throat color. Males have red throats; females, white. First-winter birds lack the adult's finery and have a dull brown head and breast with a narrow white facial stripe below the eye.

Similar Species There are three other species of sapsuckers in North America, all in the West, but they tend to ignore feeders. One, the **RED-NAPED SAPSUCKER**, winters in the Southwest and is very similar to the yellow-bellied except for a red spot on the nape of both the male and female.

All male sapsuckers and all but one female can be distinguished from other woodpeckers by their white shoulder stripe. Other woodpeckers may show patches of white in the primaries or secondaries, but not as a stripe on the shoulder.

capped chickadee. Small differences in bill size and the length and structure of their legs and toes create some differences in foraging preferences. They often hang upside down on branch tips, whereas ruby-crowns will commonly hover.

Identification Kinglets often are first thought to be warblers or vireos because of their small size, wing bars, and active behavior. For golden-crowned kinglets, the crown stripes are easy and sure marks, although the yellow center stripe of the female can be pale in winter.

The useful marks for ruby-crowns are subtler and include distinctive wing flicking. The male's scarlet crown patch is revealed only when the bird displays. The heads of males and females usually appear unmarked except for a white eye-ring, broken at the top. The area before the eye (lores) often appears white, creating a spectacled look.

All kinglets have a broad white wing bar with a contrasting dark patch (the "kinglet patch") beneath it. For a real test of the binoculars, check the yellow on the toes.

Flickers and the hairy, downy, and pileated woodpeckers all use the birdbath or eat gorp (puddings) that I put out for them. However, my red-naped sapsucker does not. He feeds daily at sap wells on the trees where the feeders hang, but won't come to the feeders.

Lori Stackow
St. Maries, Idaho

47 WESTERN SCRUB-JAY ☐

28	3	12
		57

Widely known as the scrub jay, the bird acquired its "western" prefix and the hyphen in 1995 when ornithologists determined that subspecies in Florida and on Santa Cruz Island, off California, deserved full species status. North America acquired two more breeding species — for now. Decisions on species status of birds as closely related as these three have a long history of being reversed and re-reversed quicker than the books that describe the birds go out of print.

Four out of five California FeederWatchers report the western scrub-jay, making it the third most widely reported bird in the state. They most frequently visit feeders in pairs, scarfing up peanuts,

sunflower seeds, suet, puddings, and about any other edible they can carry.

Adults are permanent residents. Youngsters typically gather in small flocks over winter and wander before establishing nest sites the following spring. Adults also may wander when winter food supplies, mostly acorns, in their territory are depleted.

The scrub-jay has most of the traits of its crested congeners. The most notable difference is its choice of thick, low, brushy habitat — especially scrub oaks — to live in. Where its range overlaps that of the blue jay (p. 76) or Steller's jay (p. 102), the scrub-jay usually commands first place at the feeder.

Identification The absence of a crest distinguishes the western scrub-jay from blue and Steller's jays. The long tail and gray underparts separate it from the pinyon jay (p. 120).

Western scrub-jays in the western portion of the range (generally west of central Nevada) are the most colorful, showing the strongest contrast between the gray-brown back patch and the blue upperparts. Young birds lack the necklace and streaks on the throat and have little blue on their upperparts.

48 PINE GROSBEAK ☐

3	16	48	–
22	26	–	–
22	–	–	

The "mope" is the name given the pine grosbeak by some for its habit of remaining motionless and seemingly bored for extended periods. It is a mild-mannered, tame finch of northern and high western conifers that irrupts south in some winters.

Berries and fruit seeds are favorite foods in winter. It also takes the buds and seeds of conifers and such deciduous trees as maples, ash, and elms. At feeders, pine grosbeaks come for sunflower seeds and water. Feeders hung in evergreens are most likely to be investigated.

Pine grosbeaks typically visit feeding stations in flocks of a half-dozen birds or so, although large

flocks are occasionally reported. Sometimes a flock will remain in one area for weeks. It is not known whether flocks are casual associations or family groups, but the colorful adult males are much less numerous in irruptive flocks than females and young birds.

Pine grosbeaks seem less interested in feeders and more content with wild foods than evening grosbeaks or other winter finches. They defer to evening grosbeaks at feeders, and there is speculation that pine grosbeak numbers have declined in the East as a result of competition for food from the more recently arrived evening grosbeaks (p. 97).

Identification Pine grosbeaks are the largest of the red winter finches and rather portly, half again the length and double the bulk of the purple finch or the crossbills. The pinkish red males have two white wing bars, narrower than in the white-winged crossbill (p. 129), and of course, they lack the crossbill's distinctive crossed bill tips.

Female and young pine grosbeaks are dark gray below. Young males have pink-red crowns; females lack any red and are capped with coppery gold.

Even in the dead of winter, a pine grosbeak will often perch on a treetop and whistle a sweet song similar to a robin's but shorter and richer.

☐ FIELD SPARROW 49

Field sparrows are shier than the other *Spizella* sparrows and often avoid backyards. Only in the South Central and Southeast regions do more than 10 percent of FeederWatchers record them, and both regions experienced a decline of greater than 25 percent over the 1990s.

Although some field sparrows overwinter as far north as Ontario, Canada, the bulk of the population migrates south in winter. It is not known if the flocks they form are casual groupings or have organized social structures. The flocks do not maintain winter territories.

Pastures and fencerows are the field sparrow's preferred foraging grounds. Like other *Spizella* sparrows (see the American tree sparrow, p. 88, and the chipping sparrow, p. 100), the field sparrow spends most of its day accumulating enough small grass and weed seeds to satisfy its needs.

At feeders, field sparrows are reported alone or in pairs, as well as in small, sometimes mixed flocks. They generally remain on the ground, gathering small or broken seeds scattered for them or dropped from overhead feeders.

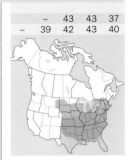

| | 43 | 43 | 37 |
| – | 39 | 42 | 43 | 40 |

Identification The plain breast, notched tail, and wing bars mark this small sparrow as a *Spizella*. The bright pink bill, distinctive plain gray face, and white eye-ring identify it as the field sparrow. The reddish streaking on the crown will be more prominent in summer. "There is something winning in his appearance," wrote Frank Chapman in 1899 in the ground-breaking *Birds of Eastern North America*. "He seems such a gentle, innocent, dove-like little bird."

☐ BROWN THRASHER 50

Reported by 5.06 percent of all FeederWatchers, the brown thrasher just makes the overall rankings at 50. In the Southeast Region, it is a common visitor, with 40 percent of FeederWatchers reporting one, either singly or sometimes two at a time. Brown thrashers maintain territories in winter, often the same ones from year to year, and are quite aggressive toward interlopers. They'll also sometimes lunge at other birds feeding on the ground at feeders but are generally more worried about being out in the open themselves.

Brown thrashers are another of the brush-loving species, like towhees (p. 96) and fox sparrows (p. 100), that make a living underneath and at the edges of brush and shrubs. Unlike the others, which kick the leaf litter to expose edibles, thrashers rake it with their bills. Both methods are equally noisy. They eat a varying diet of bugs, berries, nuts, and seeds in the wild. At feeders, crumbled bits of suet or puddings spread on the ground or a deck are readily taken if not placed too far from cover. Brown thrashers also take seeds and may well stop by for a drink or to bathe.

Identification The brown thrasher is long (12 inches) and slim, with a long, slightly curved bill and bright yellow eyes. The upperparts are rusty brown; the underparts, white with heavy brown streaking on the breast and sides.

Similar Species The breast streaks can cause confusion with the smaller hermit thrush (p. 122), the only spotted thrush to overwinter in North America. Most other thrashers (p. 122) are clear-breasted or have much less distinct streaks on their underparts.

In southern Texas, there is a thrasher that looks very similar to the brown thrasher. Known as the **LONG-BILLED THRASHER,** it is darker-backed than the brown thrasher, its bill is larger and all black, and it has orange (not yellow) eyes.

			–	
	–	–	31
–		–	19

COMMON RAVEN □

11	24	38	49	26
34	38			–
31	–	–	–	

Since 1988, there has been a yearly Christmas count of the birds at Prudhoe Bay on the coast of northern Alaska. So far, the only bird tallied has been the common raven. Other birds might be capable of surviving the bitter cold, but they would die of hunger. Ravens (68 were counted in 1998) scavenge on animals that fall to the hostile environment or are killed by predators. They also take any bit of garbage or dog food they can find at villages. Small prey gets swallowed whole. Like a hawk, ravens regurgitate any indigestible parts in a pellet.

Scavenging for animal remains is a favorite foraging style for ravens throughout their range. However, they are not limited to scavenging. Like other corvids, they are omnivorous opportunists. Coyotes and other predators sometimes have a few ravens in attendance as they hunt.

Ravens and crows behave much alike and compete for the same resources. Consequently, the two species seldom occupy the same precise area. Ravens usually choose wilder areas than crows, including deserts and mountains, and it is people at the edge of wilderness, Alaskans in particular, who have the best chance of seeing them at feeders. Table scraps, especially meat and bread, are favored offerings. Ravens usually visit singly or in small groups.

At night in winter, ravens typically roost communally, like crows.

Identification Ravens are a third again the size of most crows (p. 83) but are best distinguished by their larger bills, wedge-shaped tails, and hoarse croaking. The feathers on the throat often appear very shaggy.

In the air, ravens display flight skills that are considerably more developed than a crow's, and on the ground, they often hop; crows walk.

GOLDEN-CROWNED SPARROW □

–		21	8	–

If there were as many FeederWatchers on the West Coast as there are on the East, the golden-crowned sparrow would join its congeners, the white-crowned and white-throated sparrows, in the top 50 continent-wide. Twenty-five percent of FeederWatchers in the North Pacific Region and 58 percent of those in California enjoy these colorfully crowned sparrows. Flocks of a dozen or more are not uncommon at feeders, often mixed with numbers of white-crowned sparrows and/or juncos.

The winter behavior of the golden-crowned sparrow is much like that of the white-crowned (p. 98), to the extent that it is known. The most notable difference is that the golden-crowned likes its seeds best after they have sprouted. It therefore prefers wetter habitat than the white-crowned, areas where seeds are most likely to sprout.

Buds and flowers are relished as much as sprouts, and flocks of golden-crowns are capable of doing damage to emerging crops in spring. At feeders, they take millet and small grains placed on the ground or low platforms near cover.

Identification There is much variation in the crowns of wintering golden-crowned sparrows. First-winter birds lack crown stripes almost entirely. Their crowns are finely streaked, with some faint gold on the forehead bordered on either side by the hint of a brown stripe. Second-year birds show more definition, but there is much overlap. Even some older adults can be as drab as first-winter birds.

Individuals lacking any detectable head pattern can be confused with white-crowned sparrows. It helps to note the bill color. Golden-crowns have a dusky upper mandible and a pinkish gray lower one. Don't be surprised if the bill is stained green from eating sprouting weeds and grasses.

MATURE ADULT

FIRST WINTER

□ BLACK-BILLED MAGPIE

Black-billed magpies were once associated with bison herds, feeding on the remains of the great animals that perished, ticks from their backs, and small animals and insects stirred up by the grazing herds. Their intelligence and adaptability have allowed them to continue to flourish in spite of the loss of the bison, extensive shooting, and baiting with poisoned grain and carrion.

Some farmers shoot magpies because of the damage they cause. Animals with sores, for example, are walking carrion to magpies and may be consumed alive until the animal dies.

Meat, in the form of pet food or scraps from the table, is also a magpie's preferred meal at a feeder. But they aren't choosy; dog feces come close enough. Suet, puddings, and unshelled peanuts are more traditional items consumed by these omnivorous opportunists. They visit singly or in small, swaggering groups; occasionally in flocks of a handful or more. Over 50 percent of FeederWatchers in the Al-Can and Northern Rockies regions report them.

When a carcass or other large quantity of food is discovered, magpies busily cache bits of it nearby. Caches are consumed within a few days. The most dominant birds in a flock compete for the right to the carcass, adroitly dodging among coyotes and any other scavengers present. Subordinate individuals have it easier; they raid the caches.

Oddly, it is the juvenile males that are dominant. They first flock together in the fall and use their numbers to prevail over the paired adults. Adults often travel with a flock of juveniles in winter and put up with rude treatment because of the superior feeding opportunities afforded a flock. Some birds in a flock may distract successful predators from their kill long enough for others to carry off pieces or the whole animal if it is small enough.

Identification In both shape and color, the magpie is distinctive, as illustrated. Young birds resemble adults but show small differences, such as white on their bill tips and a varying amount of bare skin on their faces. The **YELLOW-BILLED MAGPIE**, a distinct species with a yellow bill, occurs in much of the Central Valley and central-coastal California.

□ BUSHTIT

Suet-feeder fights may be the norm for other birds, but a flock of tiny bushtits will blanket a block of suet and feed together happily, softly chattering among themselves. These very social birds are always in flocks except when nesting. Even then, a dozen or more pairs may hang their sock-like nests in a single tree. Puddings are appreciated as much as suet at feeders, and water also attracts them.

A bushtit flock is a related group. The birds flutter acrobatically through shrubs and low foliage, checking for insects, sometimes inspecting leaf litter on the ground. On cold nights, they huddle together for warmth as they roost in protective branches.

In early winter, flocks average about 15 bushtits and can be much larger. They are sometimes joined by other small species. In mid-January, birds begin to pair off for courtship, and flock size starts to decrease, until by the end of February only a half-dozen or so remain in the average flock.

Identification Their behavior, size, and plainness are bushtits' best marks. They are small, long-tailed, gray-brown birds with no crest, no wing bars, no eye-rings or other obvious marks except for a black face patch on a few males in the southern interior.

Coastal birds have slightly contrasting brown caps; interior birds are gray above except for a brown face patch. Females have pale eyes; males, dark ones.

Similar Species The **VERDIN** is common in desert scrub from southern California through central Texas. It ranks 57th in the Southwest Region. A bright wash of yellow over the face and chin distinguishes it from the bushtit.

ANNA'S HUMMINGBIRD ☐

41   5   40

I love to watch my young male Anna's wake up in the morning. He usually roosts in my hawthorn tree. When it gets light he starts to shake himself, zips to a close branch as kind of a test, and then generally shoots straight up into the air 15 to 20 feet, settles back on his perch, thinks about it a bit, and finally buzzes over to the feeder to tank up.

Marilyn Hardy
Seattle, Washington

California FeederWatchers get to enjoy hummers throughout the winter. Seventy-five percent of FeederWatchers host one or more Anna's hummingbirds. The number attracted frequently depends only on how many feeders and flowering plants are made available. If each hummer doesn't have a separate feeder, there is a fight. Besides a feeder with a four-to-one solution of sugar-water for drinking, nothing attracts a hummer like a fine spray of water for bathing. They love to dance in the mist.

Anna's hummingbird winters almost entirely in the United States, the only hummer to do so. Since the mid-1900s, it has expanded its range from California north to southern British Columbia and from coastal southern California inland through southern Arizona. Winter-blooming ornamentals and feeders have permitted the range expansion.

In its historic California range, winter is the rainy season. That's when wild plants like currant and gooseberry blossom and a reliable food supply is assured. So winter is when Anna's nests. It doesn't seem to matter that in some of their recently acquired northern range, snow might still be on the ground.

The tiny size of Anna's hummers can't be equated with frailty. They are hardy little birds that could make a living in a refrigerator and probably would if they knew that was where the nectar was kept. Even on bitterly cold days, when FeederWatchers keep a nectar feeder from freezing with heat from an electric lamp, Anna's refuels and survives.

To withstand long cold nights without feeding every 15 or 20 minutes as it does during the day, Anna's enters a state somewhere beyond sleep but short of death, known as torpor. The body temperature is lowered, breathing reduced, and metabolic activity minimized so that the bird can survive until morning without starving. It sleeps unmoving, with its bill pointed up and its feathers fluffed.

Site preferences for roosting haven't been studied.

Seventeen percent of California FeederWatchers record either rufous or Allen's hummingbirds (ranked 37th combined in the California Region, 54th in the South Central).

A nonmigratory race of **ALLEN'S HUMMINGBIRD** has long existed on the Channel Islands, off the California coast. It has more recently colonized the nearby mainland and by the end of the 20th century was common in coastal Los Angeles and Orange counties, where landscaped yards provide hummer havens. It and the **RUFOUS HUMMINGBIRD** are also seen in early migration throughout much of southern California.

Identification Compared to other North American hummers (except winter rarities), Anna's is noticeably larger, bulkier. The rose-red gorget of the adult male covers not only the throat but the crown. Females are green-backed like all female hummers, but their underparts are a dirtier gray and there are usually red spots on the throat, sometimes forming a small red patch. Details of the male's gorget shape and of the female's throat spotting can be used to help identify individuals.

Anna's is loud and talkative. It is the only hummer to sing a song — a distinctive jumble of raspy, buzzy notes. Unlike many other hummers, it seldom pumps its tail when feeding.

Rufous and Allen's hummingbirds have a distinctive wash of rusty red (rufous) on their sides and in their undertails. Males have identical orange-red gorgets. The male Allen's has a predominantly green back; the back of the male rufous is the same rusty color as its sides. Female rufous and Allen's hummers generally are impossible to distinguish from each other, except in hand. The data on the two hummers are lumped because females of both species are seen together and are inseparable in early spring migration.

☐ VARIED THRUSH

17   –   10   48

Thrushes are birds of the forest understory. The varied thrush specializes in the cool understory of the northwestern rain forests. There in the shade of dripping conifers, it rakes the ground litter with its feet and feeds on the bugs and seeds it uncovers. Berries and acorns are also eaten. A shy bird, it tends to remain in deep forest rather than invading towns and suburbs in spring and summer like its relative, the robin.

In its northwestern stronghold, the varied thrush ranks 10th, just ahead of the robin, as a winter feeder visitor. However, varied thrushes seldom come regularly. Unless a feeding station offers shrubs with winter berries, it is generally treated as a last resort.

During the worst of the winter weather, when snowfall threatens to cover the ground, is when varied thrushes are most likely to come to a feeding station. They usually show up one or two at a time and investigate whatever seeds or other foods are on or near the ground.

Some years are better for attracting varied thrushes than others. In boom years, they are reported by up to two-thirds of North Pacific Region FeederWatchers. In bust years, as few as a quarter of reports from the region include a sighting. It is not clear whether these fluctuations reflect changes in overall abundance of varied thrushes or simply periodic differences in their usage of feeders. Scattered reports of varied thrushes far outside their normal range occur every winter, even from the East Coast. These out-of-range birds are often spotted at feeders.

Identification The varied thrush is as handsome as a robin and has similar orange underparts except for a prominent black band on the male's breast. Females are duller than males and usually have a gray-brown breast band, but it can be absent. The orange wing bars and eyebrow on both sexes are easy marks.

☐ SNOW BUNTING

–   –   –
–   40   –
30   –   –

Subzero (F) temperatures and a blanket of snow don't discourage snow buntings. They can withstand exposure to –60° F for up to an hour before their body temperature starts to drop. In winter, snow buntings flock together, sometimes with a few horned larks or longspurs, on frozen fields and agricultural stubble swept free of snow by the wind. Sandy dunes with seed-bearing grasses are another example of the barren habitats they prefer.

Snow buntings are reluctant feeder visitors, not even ranking in the North Central Region, where they are fairly common overall. They most often show up before and after snowstorms, when a flock may camp out for a day or so, taking sunflower and other seeds tossed onto the snow.

Flocks are apparently stable and may follow daily routines, but they aren't territorial. At night, they may seek the shelter of a snowdrift for protection from winds but often roost dotted about in open scrapes in the snow. They have never been seen to huddle, whatever the weather.

Identification In winter, snow buntings have dark-streaked backs and rusty patches on their heads, backs, and wing coverts. Large white patches in their black wings are obvious when they fly.

CASSIN'S FINCH ☐

26   40   46   14

♂

♀

Cassin's is a regular at feeders in the high, open coniferous forests of the West, but most Feeder-Watch reports are of small flocks that have descended to low-lying regions for the winter. These birds are most attracted to rural feeding stations situated among conifers, but they aren't often repeat visitors. Some years they come; some years they don't.

In California and the North Pacific regions, the yearly percentage of feeders visited varies from less than 5 to more than 10 percent. Southwestern sightings also vary by more than two to one. An example of the extreme variation possible occurred in California when 31 percent of FeederWatchers recorded Cassin's finches in the bumper year of 1998 and only 5 percent saw them in 1999 — a bust year.

Cassin's wander in shifting flocks searching for seeds. They also take some berries, and in spring, tree buds become a favorite as they become available. At feeding stations, black-oilers are a staple. Cassin's finches sometimes arrive in mixed flocks with pine siskins or other winter finches. At night, they are thought to roost in dense conifers.

Although flocks of Cassin's finches are temporary assemblages, they have a consistent and unusual dominance hierarchy — females typically dominate males. Within each sex, older birds dominate young ones.

BAND-TAILED PIGEON ☐

33   38   –
–

A flock of band-tailed pigeons may be too quickly dismissed as just more city pigeons, but try to imagine a city pigeon clambering through the treetops collecting acorns or clinging sideways on an elderberry bush. For a bulky bird, the band-tail's agility is amazing. They will readily feed on high platforms or feeders that other pigeons may ignore.

In the wild, band-tails favor fruits and nuts, especially acorns, which they swallow shell and all. Cracked corn and red milo are favorite foods at

feeders, but they take many different seeds. The largest numbers of birds — flocks of 20 or more are not unusual — are seen in midwinter around Monterey, California. Smaller flocks are usually seen in other areas and during migration.

A different acorn-eating pigeon once blanketed the extensive original eastern hardwood forest. Had Project FeederWatch been conducted 150 years ago, it would have generated data that could have been used to help save the passenger pigeon from its eventual extinction.

People, especially those with guns, have not been good for band-tails, either. They were nearly extirpated before hunting became regulated. They have since recovered but are now thought to be decreasing in the Northwest, although there has been no change in their usage of feeding stations as reported by FeederWatchers over the decade of the 1990s.

Although not as prolific as many other doves and pigeons, band-tails share other characteristics with their congeners that help protect them from predators. Perhaps most important, they feed together in flocks and fly rapidly. Flocks have more

☐ **BREWER'S BLACKBIRD**

–	49	31	59
–	–	–	46
			–

Among most birds, dominance is typically established by bright colors, but the brightest, most vigorous male in a flock of Cassin's finches may well defer to the youngest and most drab female. This behavior has been noted also in house finches and is suggested to occur in purple finches. At feeders, dominance is often expressed in competition for food.

Interestingly, sex ratios are skewed in Cassin's, purple, and house finches. Males typically outnumber females, in some areas by as much as two to one or more. Speculation arises that the male's deference to females is related to the imbalance of the sexes. By deferring, the male improves the chances of the female's survival. And the more females that survive, the better chance a male has for mating. It is logical but unproven. Nor is it understood why the sex ratio is skewed in the first place.

Identification The differences between Cassin's, purple, and house finches are examined in detail in Confusing Look-alikes, pp. 70–71.

Male Cassin's finches don't acquire their red plumage until their second year. Yearling males look like females and are responsible for the mistaken impression that both males and females sing full songs.

Brewer's blackbirds sometimes mingle with the flocks of mixed blackbirds and starlings that roam agricultural lands in winter, but they often distance themselves. They also distance themselves from feeders for the most part. Only 20 percent of California FeederWatchers report them, and Californians see nearly twice as many as do Feeder-Watchers from any other region — low rankings for a bird that is abundant in much of the West, including towns, in winter. In the East, Brewer's blackbird is scarce and a relative newcomer.

Winter flocks of Brewer's blackbirds can be large, but the birds are more often seen at feeders in early migration (February), when flocks become smaller. FeederWatchers report four birds or fewer in half their sightings. Their typical diet is waste grains, wild seeds, and insects. In towns, they scavenge, and at feeders, they favor the same small seeds preferred by other blackbirds.

eyes to watch for predators. If a falcon or other hawk does attack successfully, it is usually a weaker pigeon that falls prey. The most vigorous individuals protect themselves by working their way to the center of the flock.

It is during feeding and drinking that pigeons and doves are most often exposed to predators, so they have adaptations to speed up both of these activities. They rapidly collect food when feeding, store it in their crops, and then retire to a safe haven to digest their meal. To drink, they use their bills like a straw instead of raising their heads to swallow, like most other birds. Studies on mourning doves revealed that in less than a minute and with only one or two drafts, a bird can suck up a day's supply or more of water.

Identification As the name implies, there is a pale band on the tail that distinguishes the band-tailed pigeon from a rock dove. The black-tipped yellow bill, yellow legs, and dark rump (white in the rock dove) are also good marks. The white collar band is sometimes absent on females and young birds. The cooing is a low *whoo-whooo.*

Identification Male Brewer's blackbirds are a yellow-eyed black bird that can be confused with common grackles (p. 91). The differences are described in detail on p. 71. Female Brewer's blackbirds are brown, grayish below, with a pale throat. Their dark eyes make them easy to distinguish from the yellow-eyed males and common grackles.

LESSER GOLDFINCH ☐

22 34
58

Lesser goldfinches are similar in many ways, including flocking and feeding habits, to their much more common relative, the American goldfinch (p. 79). Both choose similar open habitats, but lesser goldfinches show a preference for more arid lands as long as water is nearby. They drink frequently throughout the day and may come to a yard for water even when no food is present.

Even in their mapped range, lesser goldfinches are found only locally. Their largest concentration is in California, where about one-third of Feeder-Watchers report them. However, the number of southwestern FeederWatchers seeing lesser goldfinches more than doubled over the 1990s, reaching 18 percent in 1999.

In areas where both birds are present, Feeder-Watchers report that lesser goldfinches visit yards less frequently than do American goldfinches, and that they come in smaller numbers. A few are sometimes mixed with flocks of American goldfinches or pine siskins (p. 89).

Some lesser goldfinches migrate north of their winter range to nest, and there are some movements in elevation with the seasons, but most individuals restrict their wanderings to a limited area in which they can be considered permanent residents.

Identification There are two subspecies of lesser goldfinch in the U.S. Males of the subspecies found in most of the West have green backs. Males of the subspecies in Texas and eastern New Mexico generally have black backs, but some are as green-backed as the birds farther west. Intergrades are found in western New Mexico and eastern Arizona.

Similar Species In winter, female American goldfinches are dull and generally as nondescript as female lesser goldfinches. The lesser goldfinch has the greener back, but the sure mark is the color of the feathers under the tail. The American goldfinch has white undertail coverts; the lesser goldfinch has yellow ones.

BLACK-BACKED FORM ♂

GREEN-BACKED FORM ♂

♀

EURASIAN COLLARED-DOVE ☐

In the early 1980s, Floridians began noticing an increasing number of ringed turtle-doves, a popular cage bird, at their feeders. Serious birders, largely uninterested in escaped cage birds and their feral descendants, paid scant attention until it was dis-

covered that the birds weren't turtle-doves at all, but a similar-looking and closely related species, the Eurasian collared-dove, previously unknown in North America.

The Florida newcomers apparently arrived, unannounced, from the neighboring Bahamas, where they had been introduced in the 1970s. Sensing the start of a major invasion, nearly everyone interested in wild birds started looking in mature suburbs from coast to coast for Eurasian collared-doves. After all, this was a bird that began spreading from Asia Minor in the early 1900s and had reached the British Isles in less than 50 years. No one particularly wanted the bird in their area, but if it came, everyone wanted to be the first to report it.

□ INCA DOVE

– 38
24

Arid regions of Texas and the Southwest are the Inca dove's habitat. It long ago adapted to towns and cities, presumably for access to that most precious resource in arid lands, water. Inca doves like the dining opportunities in towns as well, with feeders providing most of the grains and seeds a bird consumes in some cases. Almost 30 percent of FeederWatchers in the South Central Region report Inca doves, nearly all sightings coming from Texas.

With civilization providing the habitat, Inca doves have spread slowly across the Southwest and into arid parts of California for more than a century, even into some areas of Texas and Louisiana that are not arid. This dove is built for heat, handling temperatures of 100° F without bothering to flutter its throat to create a cooling evaporation.

Cold it doesn't handle so well, and that limits the northward advance of Inca doves. On cold nights when roosting in trees or shrubs, they will sometimes protect themselves by huddling and allowing their body temperature to drop slightly. If they encounter harsh conditions while deprived of food or water, they can go into torpor like a hummingbird (p. 110). During the day, they may combat a cold snap by finding a sunny location and stacking themselves into a pyramid two or three layers deep.

Winter is the one season that Inca doves aren't paired off and reproducing. Groups of a half-dozen or fewer birds are typically reported by Feeder-Watchers, although flocks can get much larger, especially in the afternoon. Single birds and pairs are also reported. Flocks scour lawns as well as feeders for seeds.

Identification The long tail, about the length of the body, is an easy mark for the Inca dove. The tail is

not pointed, as in the much larger mourning dove. Both breast and back have a scaled look caused by dark feather edges. In flight, the rusty-colored outer wings are obvious. Females are slightly duller and grayer than males, which often have a pinkish tinge to the breast. The call is a monotonous lament, *no hope.*

Similar Species Inca doves share much of their range with **COMMON GROUND-DOVES**, which can be found across the southern part of the U.S. from California to Florida. They are reported at feeders in all southern regions, but only in the Southeast are

ground-doves seen by more than a very small percentage of FeederWatchers. Nearly 10 percent of southeastern FeederWatchers report them, ranking them 46th in the region.

The common ground-dove lacks the Inca dove's long tail but otherwise is about the same size and similar in appearance. The bill is pink at the base, not black as in the Inca dove, and the back is not so distinctly scaled.

By 1992, collared-doves were reported on Christmas Bird Counts in Louisiana and Alabama. Individuals reached Tennessee by 1995, Colorado and Illinois by 1996. The following year Montana and New York reported their first sightings, and after that, a collared-dove might be expected in populated areas anywhere across the continent, even very cold regions. In Europe, they have expanded north into Scandinavia and now live above the Arctic Circle.

The core population in the cities and suburbs of Florida and the Gulf Coast continues to increase and spread. Eurasian collared-doves visited more than 1 percent of feeders in the Southeast Region in 1999, and the percentage is expected to grow rapidly. FeederWatchers in the area report that col-

lared-doves visit feeders often and eat the same wide variety of grains and seeds as other doves. They can even manage whole unshelled peanuts.

Identification The Eurasian collared-dove shares its most prominent mark, the half collar on its hind neck, with the ringed turtle-dove. Escaped or feral turtle-doves might be found at any feeder. The collared-dove has gray underparts and is large, a little larger than a mourning dove. Turtle-doves are smaller than a mourning dove and are white below. The two species are frequently separated by their calls. The collared-dove gives a loud *coo-COO-coo* quite unlike the rolling or bubbling cooing of the turtle-dove. Collared-doves also make a distinctive braying noise when they alight.

SHRIKES AND HAWKS

Shrikes are very unusual songbirds. They don't come to backyard feeders for suet or seeds. They come for birds, as a sharp-shinned hawk does. They typically hunt from a perch — a fence post, the top of a tree, or a similar vantage point overlooking a grassland or pasture. When prey, such as a large insect, rodent, or small bird, is sighted, the shrike slips from its perch and attacks. Prey is ambushed or overtaken in flight.

Either the **LOGGERHEAD SHRIKE** or the **NORTHERN SHRIKE** is reported in every FeederWatch Region except the Mid-Atlantic but typically in very small numbers. For most FeederWatchers, that's just fine. Only in the Al-Can Region, where 7 percent of FeederWatchers report the northern shrike, is either

NORTHERN SHRIKE

26	–	–	–
–	–	–	–
–			

LOGGERHEAD SHRIKE

	–
	–
	–

of the shrikes ranked. In the East, loggerhead shrikes are seriously declining.

Shrikes don't have the powerful talons of a hawk. Prey is captured and dispatched with the formidable hooked bill. Loggerheads take large insects and other small prey more often than birds. The northern shrike is a little larger than a loggerhead, has a heavier bill, and tends to take more birds. The "butcher bird," as the shrike is often called, often impales its kill on a thorn or barb before dismembering it. Captured prey may hang for days before being eaten.

The color and pattern of the shrikes, including the white wing patches flashed in flight, suggest the much more common mockingbird (p. 94). However, shrikes do not share the mockingbird's lanky look. They are big-headed, compact birds. The distinctive black mask over the eyes and the broad, hooked bill are good marks. Any "mockingbird" seen swooping down from its perch and flying with rapid wing beats interspersed with glides deserves a close look, for that is the sterotypical flight style of a shrike.

The winter range of the northern shrike overlaps the summer nesting range of the loggerhead, but the two species rarely occupy an area simultaneously. The northern shrikes that occasionally migrate far enough south to be seen in the winter range of the loggerhead are usually young birds still in their brownish immature plumage with extensive barring on their underparts. They hold their immature plumage all winter. Young loggerheads in winter look much like adults.

The northern shrike is a little larger than the loggerhead, and adults are slightly paler with more conspicuous barring below. The black mask of the northern shrike does not extend across the bridge of the bill, as it does in the loggerhead.

Far and away the most common large hawk continent-wide is the versatile **RED-TAILED HAWK.** They are reported at some feeders in every Feeder-Watch Region except the Al-Can. They are not ranked in any region but come close in most eastern regions and in California and the Southwest, where between 4 and 5 percent of FeederWatchers report seeing one in their yards.

Red-tailed hawks are more likely to visit a backyard for chipmunks, squirrels, or snakes than for birds. Some probably stop for nothing more than a brief rest at a convenient perch. A red-tail will take a songbird if it gets the chance, but it doesn't have the flying skills to capture birds in most circumstances. Both the hawk and the smaller songbirds recognize this and generally ignore one another. Jays and crows, however, characteristically harass red-tails persistently.

The most common and widespread adult form of the red-tailed hawk has an easily seen and unique red tail (pink on the underside) with a dark subterminal band, as illustrated. Many western birds have additional fine dark bars on their red tails and can be dark-bodied rather than mostly pale on their chests and bellies.

Young red-tails don't have red tails and are harder to identify. Their tails are brown on top, white below, with fine dark bands on both sides.

The only other large hawk to be recorded by more than 1 percent of FeederWatchers continent-wide is the **RED-SHOULDERED HAWK.** Its eastern strongholds are southern swamps. In California, it is common along streams or roadsides, where it frequently hunts over the grassy margins or median. Like the red-tailed hawk, it is more likely interested in squirrels at a feeding station than fast-moving prey like birds.

The red shoulder and black-and-white checkered wings are obvious on most perched adult red-shouldered hawks. The tail has several dark and white bands. California birds are dark overall; those in Florida, much paler. Young birds show a hint of a red shoulder but are streaked with brown on their breasts, not barred with rusty red as in the adult. Their tails are dark with narrow white bands. Both adults and young birds have a distinctive loud *kee-ah* call that they often give repeatedly and other birds sometimes imitate.

In the Al-Can Region, **BALD EAGLES** and **NORTHERN GOSHAWKS** rank 24th and 30th, respectively. The bald eagle is not illustrated. The northern goshawk is shown on p. 72.

The **AMERICAN KESTREL** is the smallest of the falcons and was once known as the sparrow hawk. It takes small birds in winter and also feeds heavily on mice and other small animals. Where winters are warm and large insects available, it takes them as well. The kestrel often is seen perched on a utility wire scanning an open grassy area below for signs of movement. A productive patch of ground is revisited on a regular schedule. Kestrels also course over open areas, where they use their falcon speed to overtake small songbirds as well as ground prey.

Male and female kestrels are different sizes and differently marked. Both are small falcons, but the male is the smallest. He has colorful blue-gray wings that contrast with the dark-barred rusty red back. On the female, the entire topside — back, wings, and tail — is rusty red with dark barring. Both sexes have a white throat and cheeks with two vertical black streaks.

Ranked in California and the Southwest, the kestrel is most numerous in warmer climates but is not a common backyard bird anywhere.

RED-TAILED HAWK

	–	–	–	–
	–	–	–	–

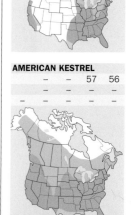

RED-SHOULDERED HAWK

			–	
		–		–

AMERICAN KESTREL

	–	–	57	56
	–	–	–	–
		–		–

GAME BIRDS

Pheasants, quail, turkeys, and grouse are all in the gallinaceous bird family. Like pigeons and doves, they have especially large breast muscles that make them preferred prey for many predators — man included. There are legal hunting seasons for each of these game birds, and many individuals are harvested annually. Large broods replace the birds taken, and as is almost always the case with birds, each species' continued success depends upon its ability to nest and fledge their young rather than on predation during the rest of the year.

Ring-necked pheasants, California quail, and Gambel's quail are common enough for each to be ranked in at least one FeederWatch Region. The

wild turkey and ruffed grouse are not ranked in any region but are widespread and seen at more than 1 percent of feeders continent-wide.

The most widespread gallinaceous bird at feeders is the **RING-NECKED PHEASANT**, introduced over 100 years ago from stock originating in China. There have been thousands of introductions of at least 70 different game birds in North America. The pheasant is one of the very few successes, although local populations often boom and bust and in some places require continuous restocking.

Pheasants feed heavily on waste cereal grains in agricultural fields, so it is rural FeederWatchers who most often report them. FeederWatcher data show the likelihood of a visit increases gradually throughout the winter. If males are in the neighborhood, it is likely that their loud crowing will be heard, especially in mornings.

All male ring-necked pheasants have a red eye patch, but the rest of their plumage can vary. Some have green bodies; others have white wings; some lack the neck ring. The female is not nearly as showy as the handsome male. She is a mottled brown but has the same general shape and distinctive long tail.

 FeederWatchers in snowy northern regions have the best chance of attracting pheasants, although less than 10 percent report these shy, wary birds. The deep snow drives the birds to feeders. Pheasants can scratch through several inches of snow to uncover food, but when heavy drifts cover fields, feeders become a useful alternative. Corn or other grains will be taken at feeders if spread at the edge of a feeding area, close to cover.

Pheasants form flocks in winter, usually segregated by sex. However, flocks often split up to forage, and only one or two birds typically visit a feeder at a time. At night, flocks may roost on the ground in protected areas like brush piles and briar patches, or they might roost in trees.

WILD TURKEYS are much too wary to visit most feeders, but they are seen by small numbers of FeederWatchers in every region except the Al-Can (Alaska and Arctic Canada). They were once unknown west of South Dakota, Colorado, and Arizona but have responded so well to transplanting and management that they now flourish from coast to coast. Their increase has been consistent since the early 1900s, when effective management began. Four million were thriving at the beginning of the 21st century, according to estimate.

Slimmer than domesticated birds, both male and female wild turkeys are dark and finely patterned with a bronze iridescence. Males are larger, with colorful wattles on the head and neck and a more prominent breast plume or beard. Some forms of

RING-NECKED PHEASANT

–	34	42	–	–
31	–	–	–	
33	–	–	–	

WILD TURKEY

–		–		
–		–		
–	–	–		

the wild turkey have white tail tips; others, buff.

Turkeys are birds of open woodlands. In winter, they feed heavily on nuts scratched up from under leaf litter on the ground. Seeds, berries, grasses, buds, and whatever large insects can be found are also taken. Flocks are typically segregated by sex, with adult males also separating themselves from first-year males. Flocks may split up to forage. Morning and evening feeding times are the rule. After filling their crops with food in the evening, they retreat to tall trees to digest their meal and roost for the night.

CALIFORNIA QUAIL and GAMBEL'S QUAIL are much more attracted to feeders than are pheasants, turkeys, or ruffed grouse. Half of Arizona Feeder-Watchers report coveys of Gambel's quail at their feeders, and a quarter of California FeederWatchers see California quail in their yards. In the wild, quail populations fluctuate widely from year to year, but the number of FeederWatchers who report them each year is very consistent.

Gambel's quail is a bird of desert scrub. California quail can be found anywhere from dry chaparral to wet coastal brush. Both birds like areas near water, cultivated fields, or developments and are very much alike in their behavior. Some coveys make a home in parks and suburbs, where cats may replace coyotes as the principal predator. As much as possible, they remain on the ground, running rather than flying from danger, but at night, they roost in dense shrubs or trees.

The curved head plumes are a fitting crown to the elaborately detailed plumage of the male California and Gambel's quail. Females have smaller but just as distinctive head plumes. Where ranges of the two species overlap, it is the birds' bellies that best separate them. The California quail has a scaled belly. Gambel's belly is pale, buff-colored in the male with a large black splotch at the center. The buff forehead of the male California quail is another good mark.

Winter quail flocks are amalgamations of smaller coveys and family groups and can include dozens of birds, with rural flocks being the largest. They usually forage in the early morning and late afternoon. The covey approaches a feeder cautiously, typically posting a sentinel to watch while the rest of the group feeds. Quail regularly return to a reliable source of mixed seeds, cracked corn, or water. In the wild, besides seeds and grains, they take greenery such as grasses, shoots, and leaves. The desert-loving Gambel's quail can get all the water it needs from green vegetation.

The RUFFED GROUSE is the most common North American grouse but is reported by barely more than 1 percent of FeederWatchers. It is seen most often by FeederWatchers in the Northern Rockies and North Atlantic regions. Ruffed grouse winter in coniferous or mixed coniferous and deciduous woodlands, feeding on berries, fruits, nuts, and seeds. They are cold-hardy loners that only occasionally come together in winter, and then to roost in small groups in dense conifers.

There are rusty red and gray forms of the ruffed grouse. The easiest field marks for either are a peaked crest and a barred tail with a wide band near the tip. In hand or with a favorable view, the tail band on female and young birds can be seen to be interrupted in the center.

GAMBEL'S QUAIL   – 35

CALIFORNIA QUAIL   – 34 28 –

RUFFED GROUSE   – – –
    – –

JAYS AND WOODPECKERS

There are three jays and four woodpeckers that are ranked in the top 50 in one or more regions but not continent-wide. None of the jays have crests.

For the **PINYON JAY**, feeders are a second, or perhaps last, resort. Like other jays, they are omnivorous, but they are an omnivore with a specialty — pine nuts. They leave their pine forests (piñon pines, western junipers, and in California, ponderosa pines) only in winter when weather forces them to lower elevations or when the cone crop fails.

Pinyon jays are proportioned so much like crows that they are sometimes called blue crows. They fly, flock, hop, and walk like crows too. Young birds are grayer than the sky-blue adults and lack the fine blue streaking on the throat.

In most winters, pinyon jays will remain in the same area where they have cached their stores of pine seeds. Each jay may cache tens of thousands of seeds, enough to provide most of their diet for the entire winter. When there is a bumper seed crop, the birds will begin nesting in late winter, when the ground is still blanketed with snow, and raise their nestlings on cached seeds.

When pinyon jays do show up at a feeder, they can come in blackbird-like numbers. Flocks of 50 or more are seen in rural areas. Fifty pinyon jays can make off with a lot of sunflower seeds. They will also make quick work of any suet or puddings they can get to. Winter flocks are aggregations of family groups that gather for protection. Numerous sentinels watch for danger while the rest of the flock feeds.

GRAY JAYS are adapted for severe winters. They don't migrate; pairs live year-round in a home territory of spruce forest that remains frozen hard for months on end. Their thick, gray plumage protects them from the elements; cached bits of food provide their principal sustenance.

Gray jays store food by impregnating and coating small chunks of it with sticky saliva and caching them in the needles, bark, or lichens on trees. The birds are opportunists that take everything from carrion to berries, bugs, and mushrooms. Few seeds are eaten, as their small bills, particularly small for a jay, are not well adapted to cracking seed shells.

There are a number of different races of the gray jay that vary primarily in the amount of white on the head and gray on the nape. In some, the gray nape extends around the eyes; in others, the eye is set in white.

A pair of gray jays is seldom far apart from each other. FeederWatchers report seeing the birds in pairs half the time. Most other times, they are reported singly or in trios. The third bird is likely the dominant juvenile, which often overwinters with the adult pair after driving away the other young birds. Those juveniles expelled sometimes attach with adults that nested unsuccessfully. Others manage to survive with the help of feeders, but many juveniles perish. Bread and baked goods are favorite foods at feeders, along with puddings, suet, and meat scraps. Gray jays are regular feeder visitors and especially bold.

Like the pinyon jay, **CLARK'S NUTCRACKER** is an omnivore that specializes in pine seeds. The two species sometimes forage in flocks together where ranges overlap, and they share other similarities. Both are tied to their caches of pine nuts throughout the year, and when the pine seed crop fails, Clark's nutcracker wanders the lowlands much like the pinyon jay, although in smaller flocks on average.

Clark's nutcracker has a plumage pattern (gray body, black wings and tail with white markings) shared by the mockingbird (p. 94) and the shrikes (p. 116). All three are easily distinguished by shape, bill size, and the differences in the white patches in the wings and tail. Note the nutcracker's heavy bill and short tail

Because they eat carrion, bugs, and berries as well as seeds, Clark's nutcrackers might sample anything at a feeding station, from sunflower seeds to table scraps. They are tame birds that readily accept handouts, but in a typical winter, they find their way to only 5 or 10 percent of FeederWatchers yards in the Northern Rockies Region. Flocks are regularly reported, but more than half of visits are by single birds or pairs.

PINYON JAY

| | | – | | – | 47 |

GRAY JAY

13	19	–	–
35	36		
37	–		

CLARK'S NUTCRACKER

| 33 | – | – | 63 |

PINYON JAY

CLARK'S NUTCRACKER

GRAY JAY

The **RED-HEADED WOODPECKER** is the only eastern woodpecker with a wholly red head. They were much more common before starlings proliferated and usurped their nest cavities. At present, only in the Southeast and Mid-Central regions do as many as 10 percent of FeederWatchers report them.

Open areas with scattered trees, including suburbs, are the red-headed woodpecker's common habitat. They seldom drill for insects and are not dependent on trees for foraging. Instead, they often feed in shrubs or on the ground, taking insects, berries, fruits, and nuts. They typically visit feeding stations alone and are likely to explore seed as well as suet feeders.

The **ACORN WOODPECKER** has a complex but very distinctive head pattern, as illustrated. Females have a smaller red crown patch with a complete black border. The clown-like look is coupled with a comical "laughing" call that might have been Hollywood's inspiration for the Woody Woodpecker call.

The acorn woodpecker is primarily a resident of oak woodlands, pure or mixed. They harvest acorns and store them in "granary trees," which are often studded with thousands of acorns half-buried in bark. Although acorns are their winter staple, insects are this woodpecker's preferred food, and they will take suet at a feeder. They also commonly drill holes and feed on sap, like a sapsucker.

Family groups of up to a dozen acorn woodpeckers protect a granary tree from acorn thieves. They are a very social woodpecker but often forage separately and frequently are seen singly at feeders, as well as in pairs and groups. In California, about 20 percent of FeederWatchers report acorn woodpeckers, and many count them as regulars. Almost the same number see Nuttall's woodpecker, making it and the acorn woodpecker more common at California feeders than downy or hairy woodpeckers.

The **NUTTALL'S** and **LADDER-BACKED WOODPECKERS** are the size of downy woodpeckers (p. 77) but have black-and-white barring on their backs. Adult males have red markings on their crowns; females don't. Ranges of the two closely related species barely overlap in southern California. Where ranges overlap, look for the broader black cheek and neck patches of Nuttall's.

Nuttall's woodpecker often feeds in oaks, but not on acorns. It gleans insect matter from bark and takes some berries. The ladder-backed has a similar diet but likes drier landscapes and is the common small woodpecker in desert regions from Texas to southeast California. It does not require trees and often feeds on the ground. Just over 5 percent of southwestern FeederWatchers report visits by a ladder-backed woodpecker. Nuttall's is reported by 17 percent of California FeederWatchers.

NUTTALL'S   LADDER-BACKED

RED-HEADED WOODPECKER

| – | – | 37 | 41 | 55 |
| – | – | – | | 45 |

ACORN WOODPECKER

| | – | 32 | – |

NUTTALL'S WOODPECKER

36

LADDER-BACKED WOODPECKER

| – | 61 |
| – | |

ROBIN-SIZED GROUND-DWELLERS

HERMIT THRUSH

–	46	25	–
	–	–	56
–	–	–	43

EASTERN MEADOWLARK

		–	
45	–	52	
	–		
	–		

CURVE-BILLED THRASHER

	28
–	

CALIFORNIA THRASHER

50

There are seven ground-dwellers larger than the typical sparrow that come to feeders infrequently or in few regions, including representatives from four distinct families. The hermit thrush and the eastern meadowlark are widespread. The three towhees and two thrashers have much smaller and mostly separate ranges.

HERMIT THRUSHES are the only spot-breasted thrush that overwinters in the United States. Like robins (also a thrush), they manage to survive in cold climates by switching from a diet of insects to one that includes many berries. They are birds of lowland forests and thickets and are unlikely to appear at feeders that don't border such areas.

Its elongated bill distinguishes the hermit thrush from other spot-breasted ground birds, such as the fox sparrow (p. 100). In spring, there are several migrant thrushes with breast spots that may be confused with the hermit. Only the hermit shows a contrast between the back color (which varies regionally) and the rusty red tail. The tail is also habitually pumped — slowly lowered and quickly raised.

Hermit thrushes are most frequently reported in California. The number of FeederWatchers reporting them varies considerably from year to year, paralleling the more conspicuous fluctuations in varied thrushes (p. 111). In even-numbered years throughout the 1990s, 15 to 20 percent of Feeder-Watchers reported them. In odd-numbered years, 25 to 30 percent or more had them at their feeders. Visits are typically infrequent, and hermit thrushes almost never come more than one at a time. Water is the major attraction, although everything, including seeds, might be investigated. A regular visitor might well return each winter.

For **EASTERN MEADOWLARKS,** feeders are typically a last resort, to be exploited when snow covers the grains and weed seeds that are their winter staples. Although widespread, they are ranked (barely) only in the Mid-Central and South Central regions, and many of these birds may, in fact, be **WESTERN MEADOWLARKS.** The winter range of the western meadowlark includes almost all of both regions, and the two meadowlarks cannot always be separated.

The well-known yellow breast and contrasting dark V of both eastern and western meadowlarks is much subdued but still apparent in winter. The striped head, short tail, and long, dagger-sharp beak are always good marks. The best mark for separating the two species is the narrow tract of feathers next to the lower mandible. It is yellow in western meadowlarks but not in eastern birds. Western and eastern meadowlarks also have different calls and songs, but they are not often heard in winter.

Meadowlarks are not larks but blackbirds. Like other blackbirds, they flock in winter and are seen commonly in agricultural fields, marshes, and feed-lots. Small groups typically show up at feeders to investigate the black-oilers, cracked corn, or other ground-spread seeds. Water may also attract them. Come nightfall, they find a patch of thick grass and roost on the ground.

Both the **CURVE-BILLED THRASHER** and the **CALIFORNIA THRASHER** forage and behave much like their eastern relative, the brown thrasher (p. 107). All maintain winter territories and typically visit feeders alone or in pairs. They may take anything from seeds to suet, puddings, mealworms, and water.

The California thrasher is the only large bird in its range with a curved bill. There are other thrashers in the curve-billed's range that resemble it, but none have its combination of strongly curved bill, heavily spotted breast, and white tail corners. It frequently gives a loud, whistled, *whit-wheet* call.

Curve-billed thrashers inhabit the Sonoran Desert and South Texas brushlands. They are regular visitors to feeders in or near their territories and often dominate their part of a yard. A favorite roosting spot is in the dense spines of cholla cactus. Pairs sometimes build a platform on a branch and roost together. California thrashers are much rarer at feeders than curve-bills, partially because winter is the nesting season, timed to coincide with the annual rains. When nesting, they eat insects almost exclusively rather than feeder offerings. Their core habitat is dense chaparral.

CALIFORNIA TOWHEES have very nearly the same brown plumage pattern as the California thrasher — dark above, paler below, with rusty undertail coverts. The heavy conical bill of the towhee is enough to distinguish it from the thrasher. They love the same chaparral and brush that California thrashers inhabit, but they also love yards. They visit the feeders of more than two-thirds of California FeederWatchers and are regulars at most of them, eating the same small mixed seeds that smaller sparrows (towhees are sparrows) eat. They seldom scratch the ground like the spotted or eastern towhees (p. 96) and are generally bolder birds.

A pair of California towhees occupies the same territory year-round. Pair bonds and territorial bonds are relaxed somewhat in winter, but Feeder-Watchers report pairs of birds much more often than loners or groups. "Muffler birds" some Californians call them for their habit of hiding under parked cars in suburbia as if they were brush piles.

Once lumped with the California towhee as a single species, the **CANYON TOWHEE** lives in a wide variety of dry, brushy habitats in the Southwest. The two birds, which were known as the brown towhee when they were conspecific, do not share range. They behave similarly at feeders, although the canyon

towhee is not always as bold. Fifteen to 20 percent of southwestern FeederWatchers report them.

Some FeederWatchers in Arizona and bordering areas may see **ABERT'S TOWHEES** as often or more than canyon towhees. The two behave much alike. In the wild, Abert's (A-burts) towhee prefers moister areas than the canyon towhee, but both are equally willing to establish a territory in a suburban area.

Ranges of Abert's and canyon towhees overlap. Abert's is unmarked except for cinnamon undertail coverts and some black around the bill. The canyon towhee has a necklace of dark spots on its breast with a larger central spot. It also shows a rusty cap, pale belly, and cinnamon undertail coverts.

CALIFORNIA TOWHEE
– 7

CANYON TOWHEE
31
–

ABERT'S TOWHEE
– 66

WARBLERS AND PHOEBES

When the insect population in North America crashes with the onset of cold weather, most small bug-eaters migrate south of the United States. A few warblers and phoebes are able to adopt strategies that allow them to remain. The yellow-rumped warbler's (p. 104) ability to switch to a diet almost entirely of berries keeps so many of them in North America that they are ranked in the Feeder-Watcher's top 50.

The warblers that overwinter in the United States manage in different ways, but all are notable for the flexibility in how they forage. Each hunts everywhere from the ground to the treetops and often joins with mixed flocks of other bug-eaters, such as chickadees, kinglets, and nuthatches, that wander through the winter woods. Phoebes, for the most part, don't interrupt their flycatching habits in winter but retreat to portions of the continent where flying bugs are still available.

If they take any feeder foods at all, the warblers and phoebes are likely to take suet and puddings. Many times it is water that attracts them, or they come because of the concentration of other feeder birds or to check out the area for insects. Few ever become backyard regulars.

PINE WARBLERS consume pine nuts to supplement the insect matter they glean — in their methodical, creeping manner — from bark and clusters of pine needles. No other warbler eats a significant amount of seeds. Nevertheless, at feeders their favorite foods are suet and puddings.

Nearly the entire pine warbler population winters in pine forests in the southern United States. The bird is recorded by more than a quarter of Feeder-Watchers in the Southeast Region. Some are permanent residents; others, migrants. Pine warblers visit feeders in small numbers, usually one or two at a time. They are more conspicuous at feeders where individuals are attempting to winter farther north than usual.

In early winter, pine warblers are drab. Even the brightest mature males are fairly dull yellow below, and young females can lack even a hint of yellow on their breasts. The white wing bars and tail spots are helpful marks. Note the blurry side streaks and the subtle face pattern.

In other seasons, a pine warbler easily can be confused with several different warblers and vireos, none of which regularly overwinter in the U.S. It is occasionally overlooked as just another drab, winter-plumaged American goldfinch (p. 79). The pine warbler can be distinguished from the goldfinch and any of the seedeaters by its thin, elongated bill.

In southern states and along the Pacific Coast where warm winters permit some insect activity, **ORANGE-CROWNED WARBLERS** are sometimes reported. There is a concentration in the trees and shrubs of California's Imperial Valley, but statewide, only 4.3 percent of FeederWatchers report them. More than 10 percent of South Central Region FeederWatchers report orange-crowned warblers because of a winter concentration in Louisiana near the mouth of the Mississippi River.

On the Pacific Coast, the yellow wash on the orange-crowned warbler's underparts can be brighter than shown. Elsewhere, sometimes the only obvious yellow is on the undertail coverts, a key mark. The orange-crowned lacks the wing bars of the pine warbler. Note the pale eyebrow.

PINE WARBLER

	–	36
–	–	31

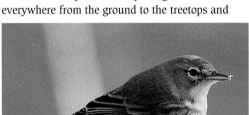

ORANGE-CROWNED WARBLER

	–	–
	47	
	–	

TOWNSEND'S WARBLER

–	47

TOWNSEND'S WARBLERS winter in a band along the Pacific Coast that is kept above freezing by winds off the ocean. There they are able to maintain a diet of insects. They do take some berries, and FeederWatchers report them eating peanut chips and hulled sunflower seeds, but insects are their winter staple. Single birds are often seen in flocks of yellow-rumps and orange-crowns.

The largest winter concentration of Townsend's warblers is along the central coast of California, where they readily visit parks, gardens, and feeders. Statewide, 8 percent of California FeederWatchers report Townsend's warbler. Banding evidence shows that Townsend's warblers are usually faithful to their wintering sites from year to year.

Male Townsend's have a bright and distinctive yellow-and-black face pattern. Females and young birds have more shadowy face patterns and streaked underparts. Note the white wing bars.

Some of the EASTERN PHOEBE population migrates south of the U.S.-Mexican border, but most birds winter in the southern United States. They rank 52nd in the Southeast Region, the last bird ranked in the region, with a little more than 5 percent of FeederWatchers reporting them. They supplement their insect diet with berries and apparently rely entirely on berries and fruit during short cold snaps. They are loners, found in a wide variety of shrubbery and open woodland habitats, including rural areas and suburbs.

The lack of a notable plumage mark on the eastern phoebe is remedied by the bird's characteristic tail wag. The tail is regularly and rapidly lowered, then slowly raised, often with some fanning or lateral movement. The birds are gray-brown above, darkest on the head, wings, and tail. Underparts are dull white. There is no eye-ring.

In perhaps the earliest example of bird banding, John James Audubon determined that eastern phoebes regularly return each year to the same nest site. He tied a loop of silver thread to the legs of several birds in fall. The next spring, "having caught several of these birds on the nest, I had the pleasure of finding that two of them had the little ring on the leg." In the nearly 200 years since, nobody has studied whether migrating eastern phoebes are faithful to their wintering sites.

Most BLACK PHOEBES are permanent residents of woody and brushy areas. They are invariably close to water, be it a stock tank, stream, ocean, or irrigation canal. Insects are sometimes plucked from the water's surface in flight, and some individuals regularly take little fish that school too near the surface. More often black phoebes flycatch or glean insects from the ground. Wasps and bees are favorites. The birds usually perch on a fence wire

EASTERN PHOEBE

—
— 52

BLACK PHOEBE

43

or bush close enough to the ground that they can capture an insect whether it is crawling below or flying by.

Like the eastern phoebe, the black phoebe is a loner except during nesting season. The two phoebes also are alike in their attachment to a specific nest site. After fledging, young males typically disperse only a short distance to establish a territory and overwinter. Young females usually disperse farther than the males.

The bold black-and-white plumage pattern is an easy mark for the black phoebe. There is some similarity in pattern to a slate-colored junco (p. 74), but the two birds are hard to confuse. Black phoebes wag their tails much like eastern phoebes.

CHICKADEES, TITMICE, AND NUTHATCHES □

Titmice, chickadees, and nuthatches are all small, generally resident birds that, throughout the winter, manage to find some insect matter secreted in tree bark or bundled into the needles of a conifer. The bugs are an important supplement to the seeds that are the birds' staple.

As all chickadees occupy the same foraging niche, they tend to separate themselves by range or elevation. Titmice are a bit larger than the chickadees and can hammer open nuts with their stout bills, so they don't compete totally with their smaller kin and can coexist with them. At a feeder, a titmouse takes the largest seed available, typically a striped sunflower seed.

Except for the titmice, the birds on this spread are social, living in flocks throughout the winter. Sometimes the birds mingle in mixed flocks that include one another and such bug-eating birds as creepers, warblers, kinglets, bushtits, and a downy woodpecker or two. It is usually a chickadee pair at the core of a mixed flock, which can include several dozen birds moving in waves.

At feeders, chickadees, titmice, and nuthatches all take suet, puddings, and seeds, especially sunflower seeds. If only a single feeder is available, members of a flock will approach it in the order of their dominance, males first.

Nuthatches select a seed from a feeder and carry it off in its shell; they wedge it into a bark crevice and hammer it open. Chickadees and titmice also carry off one seed at a time but don't need to wedge it into a crevice to open it; they can hold it with their feet. A nuthatch can't. Its feet are made for walking — upside down.

OAK and **JUNIPER TITMICE** look much like each other but are separated by range. Older books refer to them as a single species, the plain titmouse, and Cornell data are similarly combined. The westernmost birds are named for their oak habitat preference. Interior birds prefer piñon-juniper and are named accordingly.

For both species, crests are the most obvious mark. The back color of the oak titmouse has a brownish cast to it rather than the plain gray of the juniper titmouse, but the two are best distinguished by range. The **BRIDLED TITMOUSE** in Arizona also has a crest, but it has a black bib and face markings like a chickadee. It lives in oak forests, not the piñon-juniper preferred by the juniper titmouse.

Adult titmice are paired throughout the year. Young juniper titmice may overwinter with their parents or a nearby family, but young oak titmice seldom do. FeederWatch data for the combined species show that they are recorded in groups of three or more only about 10 percent of the time.

Within their core regions, the chestnut-backed, mountain, and boreal chickadees are all common, visiting about half of the feeders present. The **CHESTNUT-BACKED CHICKADEE** was only one rank shy of making the top 50 overall. Its core range is the rain forest along the coastal Northwest, where flocks twitter along foraging in the tops of mature conifers, especially Douglas firs.

The chestnut back is a good mark for chestnut-backed chickadees everywhere, but in California, the sides can be gray rather than chestnut.

Chestnut-backed chickadees are less intimidated by towns and development than the boreal or mountain chickadees. They are expanding their range into shade trees south of San Francisco and

JUNIPER & OAK TITMICE
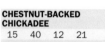
| – | 13 | 44 |
| | | – |

CHESTNUT-BACKED CHICKADEE
| 15 | 40 | 12 | 21 |

MOUNTAIN CHICKADEE
| 15 | 27 | 45 | 8 |

into second-growth Douglas fir in the interior West. Urban FeederWatchers commonly report them.

MOUNTAIN CHICKADEES, as the name implies, are high-elevation specialists, living above the black-capped chickadee wherever they share the same region. Even throughout winter, many remain in high conifer forests. Others, mostly young birds, retreat to lowlands and deciduous surroundings when the weather turns cold; the number varies from year to year. Like the other 'dees, mountain chickadees eat insect matter as well as seeds in winter. They concentrate their insect searches at the tips of branches.

FeederWatch data show that mountain chickadees are reliable guests at the birdfeeders they attend; most show up throughout the winter. The white eyebrow is distinctive but can easily go unseen if the viewing angle is bad, resulting in misidentification as a black-capped chickadee.

To see **BOREAL CHICKADEES** in winter, you have to be as hardy as they are and visit their hangouts in the northern conifer (boreal) forest. Only rarely do they irrupt south, typically with flocks of black-capped chickadees (p. 76). They share much range with black-capped chickadees — the only two 'dees that are not always separated by range or elevation — and are seen together with black-caps at feeders in winter. Black-caps are much the more frequent feeder visitor at most sites. Many FeederWatchers report boreal chickadees only sporadically, and one-third of the reports are of single birds. Usually they head for the suet and puddings before checking out the sunflower seeds.

The best marks for the boreal chickadee are its dull brown cap and back. The sides are rusty, paler than the chestnut sides of the chestnut-backed chickadee, and the face pattern is not as crisp as in other chickadees.

Boreal chickadees sometimes protect themselves at night by roosting in a cavity, but usually they roost like mountain and chestnut-backed 'dees, in dense evergreens.

PYGMY and **BROWN-HEADED NUTHATCHES** are sister species, sedentary birds with distinct and separate habitats. Pygmy nuthatches live in western pines, especially ponderosa and piñon pines. Their gray-brown cap is distinctive. Some show a pale nape spot from the back.

The brown-headed nuthatch lives in southern and Atlantic coastal forests of mature pines. It is a bit larger than a pygmy nuthatch, and its cap is a warmer brown. Both nuthatches often announce their presence with squeaks suggesting a child's rubber duck.

Pygmy nuthatches visit feeders in flocks of a half-dozen to a dozen or more typically. They are reliable guests at the relatively few feeders that attract them. Brown-headed nuthatches have different habits and are not as regular at feeders in general. When they do visit, they usually come only one or two at a time. Over the course of a winter, however, over one-third of FeederWatchers in the Southeast report one.

Pygmy nuthatches roost in flocks, typically in a tree hollow, using each other's body heat to sustain themselves through cold nights. A brown-headed nuthatch may roost in a cavity by itself or with a mate, but it usually picks a sheltered pine branch.

BOREAL CHICKADEE

5	32	–
33	41	
29	–	–

BROWN-HEADED NUTHATCH

| | | 53 |
| – | | 24 |

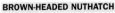

PYGMY NUTHATCH

| – | – | 52 | 29 |

FINCHES AND SPARROWS

Most FeederWatch Regions have a less common or local finch or sparrow that visits feeders.

The **BLACK-THROATED SPARROW** is a locally common bird of southwestern deserts. In winter, it is also found in fields and grassy areas away from the desert scrub. It is not common at feeders, with little more than 5 percent of FeederWatchers in their core Southwest Region reporting one. Small flocks and single birds are typically seen, usually on the ground foraging for small mixed seeds.

The black bib, broad white eyebrow, and plain back of the black-throated sparrow are an unmis-

BLACK-THROATED SPARROW
– 62
–

LARK SPARROW
53
–

HARRIS' SPARROW
– –
– 31 40

takable combination. The long black tail has narrow white edges.

The **LARK SPARROW** has broad white corners in its tail that are obvious when the bird flies. However, it is the distinctive head pattern that is the sure mark for this bird. The black dot on its plain white breast is also characteristic of the American tree sparrow (p. 88).

Large flocks of lark sparrows sometimes gather in winter. Like the black-throated sparrow, they aren't a common feeder bird, although they are numerous in the West in open areas with scattered trees and scrub. They are often seen on the fences or utility wires around pastures and ranchlands. Californians most frequently report the lark sparrow, but only about 5 percent of FeederWatchers in the region attract them. Weed seeds are their winter staple, and they take small mixed seeds at feeders.

By December, nearly all **HARRIS' SPARROWS** have completed the trip from their nesting grounds in northern Canada to their winter range in the United States. There the youngsters will get their first taste of winter on the prairies, and a good number of FeederWatchers in the Mid-Central and South Central regions will play host to them and their parents.

Harris' sparrows are regulars at many of the feeders they attend, and sometimes the same birds return year after year. FeederWatchers in the Northern Rockies and North Central regions report that the birds are also regulars at feeders during migration. Not all the migrants end up on the traditional winter range, however. Every year there are scattered reports from coast to coast of Harris' sparrows overwintering, often at feeders.

Harris' sparrow is a little larger than the related white-crowned, golden-crowned, and white-throated sparrows. It is sometimes confused with house sparrows (p. 80) but can be separated from them by its large pink bill and side streaks. There is a variable amount of black on the forehead, crown, chin, and throat of Harris' sparrows in winter, with older males showing the most.

Flocks of Harris' sparrows are transient groupings and are usually small. Often only one or two show up at a feeder. They are most likely to come to feeders adjoining wooded areas. When alarmed, they like to fly up into a tree's branches rather than into a brush pile.

Seeds and fruits are the main foods eaten by Harris' sparrows in winter. Insects are taken if available. The birds typically forage on the ground in grain and weed fields or in hedgerows and overgrown pastures. At feeders, they take striped sunflower seeds as well as the smaller mixed seeds and cracked corn that might be spread on the ground. They often find their way to water if it is provided.

There are three species of rosy-finches. The **GRAY-CROWNED ROSY-FINCH** is the most widespread and often seen. The **BLACK ROSY-FINCH** inhabits the Rocky Mountains of the northern United States, and the **BROWN-CAPPED ROSY-FINCH** lives in the Southern Rockies. In the central Rocky Mountains, all three species may be found.

Gray-crowned rosy-finches have a patch of gray on the back of the crown, extending onto the face in coastal birds. The gray crown is also present on most black rosy-finches, but their body is much darker (although not black) than that of the gray-crowned rosy-finches. Brown-capped rosy-finches lack the gray head markings.

Rosy-finches are alpine-nesting birds that retreat to lower slopes, foothills, and plateaus during winter. Many live year-round on snow or at the rocky edges of melting snowbanks and glaciers. In winter, they forage in large flocks, wandering the countryside for weed seeds. At night, up to 1,000 birds may roost together in caves, barns, or other protective enclosures. At least one flock uses cliff swallow nests in a Colorado park for roosting.

There is much variation in shade within each of the three rosy-finch species. Males of all species show pink on the wings and body. Females are duller; some are brown or blackish, with barely a hint of color. Pale underwings that contrast with the darker bodies in flight are a good mark.

Crossbills are the least seen and in some ways most interesting of the irruptive finches, which include siskins, redpolls, and evening grosbeaks. Nomadic flocks of **RED CROSSBILLS** and **WHITE-WINGED CROSSBILLS** roam the northern and western coniferous forests, stopping wherever they find a mature crop of cones. Conifer seeds are their staple, and their crossed bill tips are an adaptation for efficiently removing them from cones. Efficiency is so important that different races (which may prove to be different species) of crossbills have slightly larger or smaller bills than others to specialize in the cones of specific conifers.

The crossed bill tips of crossbills can be seen at close range, which is usually the case at feeders. Adult male white-winged crossbills are usually pinkish in winter. Their broad white wing bars are easy marks separating them from male red crossbills, which are typically a brick red but can be reddish yellow or even greenish. Females of both species are dull, olive-gray birds easily separated from each other by the presence (or absence) of white wing bars.

Because of their cone-feeding habit, crossbills are not seen by more than a few percent of FeederWatchers in any region, on average. And many of those sightings are in the home, rather than

irruptive, range. White-wings are more common at feeders in the North Atlantic and Al-Can regions than elsewhere. The red crossbill is reported most frequently in the Rockies, both the Northern Rockies Region and the Southwestern Region.

Small flocks of crossbills can settle in at a feeder for a long lunch. They take black-oil sunflower seeds from a hanging tube feeder, just as a house finch does. One FeederWatcher discovered how tame and trusting a red crossbill could be when she stepped outside to have a closer look and had one flutter down from a branch and land on her head.

GRAY-CROWNED ROSY-FINCH

ROSY-FINCHES
– 36 – – 55

WHITE-WINGED CROSSBILL

RED CROSSBILL

SOUTHWESTERN SPECIALTIES

FeederWatchers in the Southwest record some species that are seldom or rarely seen in other regions. The cactus wren, Townsend's solitaire, and the greater roadrunner are three of the most unusual and interesting. From 10 to 15 percent of southwestern FeederWatchers attract them annually.

The **CACTUS WREN** is much larger than other wrens. It has the characteristic curved bill and relatively short banded tail of wrens, but cactus wrens rarely cock their tails like other wrens. Their chunky shape and broad white eyebrow help to distinguish them from thrashers. Their song sounds like a car trying to start that just won't turn over.

Like their smaller relatives, cactus wrens are primarily bug-eaters and spend most of their foraging time sifting through ground litter for insects. But they also take significant amounts of cactus fruit and seeds in winter. At feeders, they will take various seeds and might sample almost anything offered, especially suet and puddings. They are often regulars at feeders in areas of desert scrub or cactus, especially in suburban developments.

Cactus wrens establish permanent territories and are usually reported in pairs or singly by Feeder-Watchers, although young birds sometimes overwinter with their parents. Parents and youngsters usually roost near one another on conspicuous platforms nestled among protective cactus spines, in the same manner as curve-billed thrashers (p. 123).

The most widespread of the three southwestern specialties is **TOWNSEND'S SOLITAIRE**, which is reported in small numbers at feeders in all western FeederWatch Regions. Water attracts most of them, usually individually. Their winter food is berries, with most birds feeding almost exclusively on juniper berries. Insects are also taken when available, and in summer, solitaires often flycatch conspicuously in high mountain forests.

Townsend's solitaire is a slender gray member of the thrush family. Its most conspicuous mark is the complete white eye-ring. In flight, buff patches are visible on the wings, and white edges can be seen on the tail.

Each solitaire lays claim to a patch of junipers in the fall and defends its claim throughout the winter. There is often considerable calling and fighting in establishing a claim, but by winter the defense of a territory is usually a simple patrolling of the treetops along the boundaries. Individuals often claim the same patch from winter to winter. Waxwings, bluebirds, and most other berry-eaters are harassed and driven off, in addition to competing solitaires. Robins and mockingbirds displace solitaires, however, which may be why solitaires usually defend many more berries than they can eat over a winter.

In nature, the **GREATER ROADRUNNER** doesn't spend its life outrunning coyotes, as it does in cartoons. It is a speedy predator that itself runs down small animals, including poisonous snakes. Roadrunners are often reviled and sometimes illegally shot because of their predation upon other birds and nests. When a roadrunner comes to a feeder, the other birds take off as if a hawk had arrived. Animal food, mostly insects, makes up 90 percent of a roadrunner's diet, but it also takes fruits and seeds seasonally.

Roadrunners maintain permanent home ranges. In fall, a pair divides its territory and each forages separately until pairing again in spring. They like to hunt in open land and aren't common in well-developed areas. Where they are accepted, they sometimes behave like pets, following and interacting with people.

Originally in arid and scrubby semiarid desert, roadrunners have expanded their range north and east into bordering areas of open woodlands and grasslands. Although primarily terrestrial, they fly for short distances, typically low to the ground and with considerable gliding.

Greater roadrunners are as distinctive-looking as they are special. The crest, long bill, long tail, and well-developed legs all combine to make an unmistakably shaped bird.

CACTUS WREN
– 42
–

TOWNSEND'S SOLITAIRE
– 41 – – 36
–

GREATER ROADRUNNER
– 45
–

CACTUS WREN

GREATER ROADRUNNER

TOWNSEND'S SOLITAIRE

WEIRD BIRDS

Birds with markings and features that can't be found in any field guide are reported regularly at backyard feeders — weird-looking, tailless birds or birds with odd patches of white in their plumage, for instance. Sometimes patches of body plumage can be missing.

The most common oddity is the bird with an injured or missing leg or foot. Individuals may have a marked limp or hop about on one leg. Sometimes a bird with a damaged leg will use a wing to help maintain its balance while feeding. FeederWatchers often report long relationships with such individuals, indicating that the loss of a leg or damage to it does not have to be life-threatening.

Birds with missing tail feathers are routinely reported. The absence of a tail seems to have no effect on the well-being of most birds. They fly just fine without a tail and generally manage with ease as they wait for the next set of tail feathers to grow in. But with no tail feathers, a bird loses any claim to a dignified appearance.

The common speculation is that birds lose their tail feathers when they freeze to a limb while the birds are roosting at night or because of a close escape from a cat or other predator. Unless the event is seen, it is impossible to know, but birds do not need their tail feathers yanked from their behinds in order to be tailless. They can voluntarily shed their tail feathers in a moment. The sudden release of tail feathers is thought to confuse an attacking predator.

Tail loss also can result from molt or dietary problems. Birds normally molt and replace their tail

A white-throated sparrow seems oddly balanced without its tail feathers.

feathers a pair at a time, but there are instances when some birds molt all their tail feathers simultaneously and go tailless for 10 days or two weeks while new tail feathers grow. This typically occurs in late summer or fall.

Each year FeederWatchers describe bald-headed birds that show up at feeders, usually blue jays and northern cardinals. "What's wrong?" they ask. "One of my cardinals looks like a miniature vulture." A family in Tuscaloosa, Alabama, reported a "fifth-generation black-headed male cardinal."

In my years of bird banding I have seen many healed leg injuries. They don't seem that crucial. We just clean any fresh injury, put a dab of bactine on it, and send the birds on their way. We've seen stumps and missing legs and toes, and the birds are fat and healthy.

Kathy Van Der Aue
Southern Connecticut

This California thrasher appears fatally injured, but only feathers are missing, and they will be replaced.

On a cardinal, baldness is not as handsome as it is on basketball legend Michael Jordan. The hole behind and below the cardinal's eye is its ear opening.

WEIRD BIRDS

I had a pet female jay by permit for 7 years. She always molted all her head feathers at once, and looked like a vulture 'til the new ones came in. Her molt was as regular as clockwork and otherwise normal.

Louise Grider
Rehabber from
Southern Alabama

Leucistic birds have white feathers in place of some or most of their normally colored feathers. The condition can be minimal, as in the dark-eyed junco (middle), or affect large areas, as in the American robin (top) and northern cardinal (bottom).

Rehabbers have reported instances of birds that annually molt all their head feathers simultaneously in fall and go bare-headed for a short while as the new feathers grow in. It is not common. Body feathers are usually molted and replaced in waves rather than clumps, so patches of bare skin normally aren't seen, although birds often look scruffy while molting.

Feather mites, tiny arachnids that feed on feather shafts, are a likely cause of baldness in some instances. A bird can clean mites from most of its feathers, but the head is the one spot that it cannot reach to preen.

Sick birds or ones with diet problems might also have patches of feathers missing, but otherwise, bald birds seem to undergo no unusual stress. Fortunately, they don't have to look at themselves in mirrors.

Pigment disorders of several different types affect birds. Melanism, an excess of dark pigments in the feathers, is very rare except in some hawks, which are known as "dark form" hawks. Some hawks and the eastern screech-owl also have a "red form" that is caused by an excess of reddish brown pigment. This condition, too, is very rare in songbirds.

Very pale or washed-out-looking birds (tan or fawn-colored, but not pure white) can occur if one of several pigments is missing. This is technically know as schizochromism and has been noted in house sparrows and red-winged blackbirds.

When all pigment is absent from the feathers, eyes, and skin, the condition is known as albinism. Birds that normally have white or partially white plumage are not albinos. Albinism is very rare in birds, perhaps because it tends to be debilitating. Vision is bad, and so is feather condition. A much more common condition is partial albinism, or leucism, in which pigment is absent from some of the body feathers, often in a symmetrical pattern. House finches are one of the more common birds at feeders that show odd patches of white feathers.

Leucistic birds are sometimes shunned but often appear to attract mates and live successfully. Birds can be born with the condition, or it can develop with age in successive molts, much as some people develop white hair with age or dogs develop grizzled muzzles.

Injuries or infections can result in feathers becoming white in the affected area, and there are some stories of birds turning white from shock. However, feathers are not live tissue and can't change color. A color change can occur only when new feathers replace old ones, and it would be difficult to prove a psychological cause for a bird molting into white feathers.

When looking up the name of a bird, check for a generic as well as a specific name to find additional information about the family. For example, if looking up "black-capped chickadees," also check "chickadees" for information about chickadees in general.

At the turn of the millennium, FeederWatchers reported birds from over 15,500 locations in the US and Canada. Schoolchildren, home office workers, retirees — people of every description — participated. There are no restrictions on becoming a FeederWatcher.

☐ *Yes! I want to receive a research kit and observe birds for science. Please tell me more about Project FeederWatch and how to become a FeederWatcher.*

_____
NAME

_____
STREET ADDRESS

_____
CITY, STATE   ZIP

_____
EMAIL ADDRESS (OPTIONAL)

enclose in
envelope
before
mailing

Cornell Lab of Ornithology
Project FeederWatch/WBG
159 Sapsucker Woods Rd.
Ithaca, NY 14850

Cut out or copy this card and enclose it in an envelope before mailing. Canadian residents should address the envelope to:

Bird Studies Canada
Project FeederWatch/WBG
P.O. Box 160
Port Rowan, Ontario
N0E 1M0

You may also get more information on Project FeederWatch by telephone or on the Internet.

Cornell Lab of Ornithology:
1-800-843-2473 (BIRD)
http://birds.cornell.edu

Bird Studies Canada:
1-888-448-2473 (BIRD)
http://www.bsc-eoc.org/pfw.html